COMPUTER-ASSISTED ASSESSMENT *in* HIGHER EDUCATION

The Staff and Educational Development Series
Series Editor: Sally Brown

Research, Teaching and Learning in Higher Education Edited by Peter Knight
Assessing Competence in Higher Education Edited by Anne Edwards and Peter Knight
Assessing for Learning in Higher Education Edited by Peter Knight
Resource-Based Learning Edited by Sally Brown and Brenda Smith
The Management of Independent Learning Edited by Jo Tait and Peter Knight
Enabling Student Learning: Systems and Strategies Edited by Gina Wisker and Sally Brown
Facing Up to Radical Change in Universities and Colleges Edited by Steve Armstrong and Gail Thompson
Flexible Learning in Action: Case Studies in Higher Education Edited by Rachel Hudson, Sian Maslin-Protherero and Lyn Oates
Motivating Students Edited by Sally Brown, Steve Armstrong and Gail Thompson
Benchmarking and Threshold Standards in Higher Education Edited by Helen Smith, Michael Armstrong and Sally Brown
Inspiring Students Edited by Stephan Fallows and Kemal Ahmet

SEDA is the Staff and Education Development Association. It supports and encourages developments in teaching and learning in higher education through a variety of methods: publications, conferences, networking, journals, regional meetings and research – and through various SEDA Accreditation Schemes.

SEDA
Selly Wick House
59-61 Selly Wick Road
Selly Park
Birmingham B29 7EI
Tel: 0121-415 6801
Fax: 0121-415 6802
E-mail: office@seda.demon.co.uk

COMPUTER-ASSISTED ASSESSMENT *in* HIGHER EDUCATION

Sally Brown, Phil Race and Joanna Bull

First published in 1999

Kogan Page Limited
120 Pentonville Road
London N1 9JN

British Library Cataloguing in Publication Data

A CIP record for this book is available from the British Library.

ISBN 0 7494 3035 4

Typeset by Saxon Graphics Ltd, Derby
Printed and bound by Clays Ltd, St Ives plc

This book is dedicated to Rex Stainton Rogers who was no fan of educational development but was known by his students as one of the most supportive, caring and erudite lecturers in the university system.

Contents

Notes on Contributors

M D J Barry is a Lecturer at the University of Bristol.

E Board is a student at the University of Bristol and carried out the student survey referred to in Chapter 8.

Mark Brosnan is Pathway Leader in Psychology at the University of Greenwich, UK.

Alan J Cann is currently a Lecturer in Virology at the University of Leicester. In addition to teaching undergraduate, postgraduate and medical students, he has a strong interest in developing computer-based learning materials and runs a research laboratory studying the molecular biology and pathogenesis of RNA viruses.

Dan Charman is in the Department of Geographical Sciences at the University of Plymouth, UK.

Myles Danson is the Computer Assisted Assessment Officer at Loughborough University, UK. He has been working with OMR CAA since 1996 and is now working on PC-delivered and Web-based CAA systems.

R D Dowsing has been a Senior Lecturer in Computing in the School of Information Systems at the University of East Anglia since 1979. Since 1992 his major research interests have been centred on the use of CAA for IT skills.

Jen Harvey is based at the Dublin Institute of Technology. Previously she worked for the Learning Technology Dissemination Initiative at Heriot-Watt University, Edinburgh, where she offered implementation support.

Ian Hesketh is a Technical Officer in the Faculty of Science, Technology and Design at the University of Luton. His main responsibilities are in the area of educational technology and he has contributed to the extensive use of technology in the areas of teaching, learning and assessment.

Kinshuk is Research Fellow at GMD-FIT, the German National Research Institute – Human Computer Interaction.

J Maher is a Lecturer at the University of Bristol.

Nora Mogey has recently joined the Media and Learning Technology Service at the University of Edinburgh. Previously she worked for the Learning Technology Dissemination Initiative as project coordinator.

Chris Morgan is an educational designer with the Teaching and Learning Centre at Southern Cross University, Lismore, Australia. The author advises and collaborates on the design, development and evaluation of courses for print, multimedia and Web-based delivery. High on the agenda is the design and implementation of assessments that effectively support student learning.

Meg O'Reilly is an educational designer with the Teaching and Learning Centre at Southern Cross University, Lismore, Australia. She advises and collaborates on the design, development and evaluation of courses for print, multimedia and Web-based delivery. High on her agenda is the design and implementation of assessments that effectively support student learning.

A Patel is the Director of the Computer Aided Learning Research and Software Engineering Centre at De Montfort University, UK.

Ellen L Pawley is the campus-wide Information Service Officer at the University of Leicester. As a member of the Learning Technology Group (http://www.le.ac.uk/cc/ltg/ http://www.le.ac.uk/cc/ltg/) she has helped build Web-driven learning and teaching resources across all faculties.

Malcolm Perkin qualified in Medicine at the University of Newcastle upon Tyne in 1973. After many years as a GP and in medical education as Senior Lecturer in General Practice at Barts in London, he is now working in the Institute of Public Health at the University of Cambridge. He is currently researching the use of open and distance learning in public health education.

Norma Pritchett is a Principal Teaching Fellow in the Department of Psychology at the University of Luton, where she has been involved with the introduction and development of automated assessment within the university.

Léonie J Rennie is Professor in the Science and Mathematics Education Centre at Curtin University.

Jennifer M Robinson is a Lecturer in the Department of Environmental Science at Murdoch University, Western Australia.

D Russell is the Professional Doctorate Programme Director at De Montfort University.

Alistair Sambell is Head of Division of Electrical and Electronic Engineering at the University of Northumbria, Newcastle, UK, and has a particular interest in the use of IT within teaching.

Kay Sambell is based at the University of Northumbria in Newcastle, UK. She works for the Centre for Advances in Higher Education and is involved in researching the impact of innovative assessment on student learning.

Roy Seden is Principal Lecturer in the Centre for Learning and Teaching at De Montfort University, UK. Previously he was on the staff of the university's Built Environment School, teaching structural analysis and design.

Graham Sexton is a Senior Lecturer in the School of Engineering at the University of Northumbria, Newcastle, UK, specializing in image and digital signal processing.

Leith Sly is a Lecturer in the Centre for Educational Advancement at Curtin University of Technology, Western Australia, where she manages the university's computer managed learning system.

D Spencer is a research assistant at the University of Bristol and was largely responsible for making the software system described in Chapter 8 work.

Christine Steven was until recently a Principal Teaching Fellow in the Faculty of Science, Technology and Design at the University of Luton. She is now combining teaching Computer Science part-time with research in the area of assessment techniques.

M Thelwall is a Senior Lecturer at Wolverhampton University, UK, teaching maths and computing. He runs a CAA project that produces random number based tests for diagnostic and summative assessment purposes and his research interests are in the relationship of assessment to learning.

Dave Whittington lectures at the Robert Clark Centre for Technological Education at the University of Glasgow, where he also carries out educational technology research.

J H Sims Williams is a Lecturer at the University of Bristol.

Stan Zakrzewski was Computer Adviser at the University of Luton before becoming Head of Learning Technology. He now manages and researches the implementation of learning technology, with a particular interest in modelling CAA systems.

Acknowledgements

We would like to acknowledge the help and support of Mr Dale Sharp, Computer Services Manager at the University of Luton, who provided invaluable advice about technical and technological issues and details and Susannah Patterson at the University of Northumbria who worked uncomplainingly on the production of this book.

Introduction

Interest in computer-assisted assessment is growing rapidly. It is increasingly accepted that assessment is the engine that drives a great deal of students' learning. It is also widely recognized that all processes used in assessing students' achievements need to be carried out in a highly responsible way, yet assessment is often regarded as the bane of academics' lives. With moves to widen participation in higher and further education, combined with reductions in the actual amount of resource per student to educational institutions, it is proving to be impossible to extend traditional assessment processes, practices and instruments to meet demand. In particular, it is difficult to provide students, by traditional means, with the quantity and quality of feedback that will enhance their learning, whether thinking of feedback on their evidence for continuously assessed coursework or for summative assessments such as exams.

At the same time, in most subject disciplines the use of information and communications technologies is expanding rapidly and students are learning a higher proportion of the curriculum using computer-based resources. Indeed, students' computer literacy is expanding rapidly as they make use of electronic sources and the Internet in the everyday course of their learning. The gap between how students learn and how they are assessed is widening. For students who have undertaken much of their learning with a computer keyboard, monitor screen and printer, finding themselves in a formal, silent exam room, able to communicate only by handwritten means, is a radical discontinuity in their educational experience.

This book profiles how computer-assisted assessment can help both staff and students by drawing on the experience and expertise of practitioners, in the UK and internationally, who are already using computer-assisted assessment. Collectively, their contributions in this book illustrate how computer-assisted assessment can help address the problems mentioned above by:

- reducing the load on hard-pressed lecturers and teachers by automating appropriate parts of the task of marking students' work;
- providing students with detailed formative feedback on their learning much more efficiently than is usually possible with traditional assessment;
- bringing the assessment culture experienced by students closer to the learning environments with which they are familiar and confident.

The contributions range from 'how we did it and what we learned by doing it' to 'what we need to think about to do it better'. A central theme pervading the contributions in this book is how computer-assisted assessment can enrich the learning experience of students, and help in our efforts to diversify assessment practices and processes, so that students are less likely to be disadvantaged by exposure to an unduly limited assessment culture.

We have arranged the contributions in this book into three broad sections:

1. Pragmatics and practicalities of Computer-Assisted Assessment (CAA).
2. Using CAA for formative assessment.
3. Learning from experience.

The overlap between these three categories is wide. Several of the chapters could equally have been placed in any of these sections, but as far as was possible we have tried to structure the contributions into a useful review of issues related to computer-assisted assessment today. Each chapter in its own way reflects innovation in assessment design and practice and attempts to ensure that computer-assisted assessment (like any tool in the assessment toolkit) is as fair as possible, as reliable as practicable and is valid.

SECTION ONE: PRAGMATICS AND PRACTICALITIES OF CAA

In this, the most substantial section of this book, we have collected together a wide range of contributions that offer food for thought about how best to go about planning and implementing computer-assisted assessment.

We start this book about computer-assisted assessment with a wide range of declared reasons why it won't work! In Chapter 1, Jen Harvey and Nora Mogey explore the pragmatics of integrating technology into the assessment of students' work and address a series of reasons sometimes used by staff to justify why they feel they *can't* use technology to support assessment. The authors propose a range of strategies whereby each of these situations may usefully be addressed. Among the fears of staff thinking of implementing computer-assisted assessment are concerns about security issues. In Chapter 2, by Dave Whittington, technical and security issues are explored in the context of implementing computer-assisted assessment. This chapter is the first of several in the book to look at issues related to screen and question layout and question design and goes on to give suggestions on how to approach data protection legislation and data security. The chapter ends with a discussion of the meaning of 'exam conditions' for the context of computer-assisted assessment.

Chapter 3, by Norma Pritchett, picks up the issue of effective question design in more detail. A series of illustrated guidelines is proposed for the design of multiple-choice questions. The final part of the chapter examines the kinds of cognitive skills that can be tested by multiple-choice formats and includes discussion of the element of chance unavoidably present in such tests. Chapter 4, by Alan J Cann and Ellen L Pawley, takes us into Web-based assessment format design and the use of summative and formative online tutorials. The level of complexity is moved from multiple-choice question to a tutorial-type environment, which the authors claim to be much better suited to a resource-rich open learning environment, including open access to the WWW, than multiple-choice formats.

Chapter 5, by Mark Brosnan, moves back to consideration of some of the disadvantages accompanying computer-based learning and computer-assisted assessment, in particular in the context of student computer anxiety and assessment. Biases that can affect computer-assisted assessment are discussed and some suggestions for minimizing anxiety and biases are proposed.

The remaining chapters in this section all offer advice about test design and the implementation of computer-assisted assessment. Chapter 6, by Malcolm Perkin, focuses on validating both formative and summative assessment, exploring how the need to make assessment both valid and reliable extends to computer-assisted assessment. Distinctions are drawn between task-centred and construct-centred performance assessments and suggestions are offered about how computer-assisted assessment processes can best be evaluated. Chapter 7, by M Thelwall, focuses on the design and use of randomly generated tests based on relatively large banks of questions and explores security issues and pedagogical implications of such tests. The relative suitability of randomly generated tests for procedure mastery and fact acquisition is compared. Chapter 8 ends this section of the book by further developing the discussion of random factors. This is contributed by J H Sims Williams, J Maher, D Spencer, M D J Barry and E Board and explores ways in which lecturers can set tests from a large database of questions just by making a specification of the test they require and then allowing the computer to generate a potentially large number of equivalent tests matching the specification.

SECTION TWO: USING CAA FOR FORMATIVE ASSESSMENT

This short section brings together four contributions where the principal theme is using computer-assisted assessment primarily for formative purposes. Discussion of the use of computers in formative assessment is included in many of the chapters in this book, but this section brings together four chapters where formative assessment is spotlighted. In Chapter 9, Dan Charman considers critical issues in writing and delivering formative assessment using computers and compares student performance on summative assessment before and after changing formative assessment from conventional to computer-based formats. The benefits of repeatability, immediate feedback to students and immediate marks to staff are discussed, along with a wide range of further benefits relating to using computers for formative assessment and feedback to students. Chapter 10, by Jennifer M Robinson, is about using networked computers to enhance the role of the horizontal flow in learning: that of multi-reviewer anonymous peer review. The chapter focuses on the peer review of 'complex works': substantial assignments that defy simple objective assessment and which place high demands on conventional marking processes. Chapter 11, by Christine Steven and Ian Hesketh, reviews creative development of the use of one particular piece of software, Question Mark, concentrating on its application to formative assessment and feedback. The authors claim that students can be shown to have benefited from the feedback and, at the same time, to have improved as autonomous learners. In Chapter 12, Leith

Sly and Léonie J Rennie look in particular at the use of computer managed learning and student tracking for situations where large numbers of student assessments are to be handled. Particular features of computer managed learning are explored, which can be used to promote opportunities for formative assessment, backed by case-study data in discipline areas of economics and psychology from Curtin University, Australia.

SECTION THREE: CAA: LEARNING FROM EXPERIENCE

Some common themes pervading the chapters in the final section of this book can be described in terms of 'how we did it', 'what we found', 'how it works in our particular discipline' and 'what we plan to do next'. This section brings together a series of contributions with case-study dimensions, covering a considerable range of experiences of using computer-assisted assessment in a variety of contexts and disciplines. In Chapter 13, Myles Danson gives an account of the use of optical mark reading (OMR) at Loughborough University, UK, advocating that this technology, which began in the 1950s, can become a vital tool in the implementation of modern computer-assisted assessment. The author gives comparative details of four types of stationery used for computer-assisted assessment and discusses the various formats of report in which the results of the associated assessments can be presented. In Chapter 14, R D Dowsing explores the benefits that can be realized by the computer-assisted assessment of practical IT skills. He discusses the various types of assessment that can be applied to IT skills, focusing on what lends itself to assessment in this context, and illustrates the use of a word-processing assessment system developed at the University of East Anglia. Chapter 15 is contributed by A Patel, D Russell and Kinshuk, examining the cognitive apprenticeship-based learning environments (CABLE) approach to designing tutoring systems, and their development into an intelligent tutoring system (ITS).

In Chapter 16, we return to Web-based assessment with a contribution from Meg O'Reilly and Chris Morgan, gathering experience from the UK, Australia, South Africa and the Netherlands. Their discussion illustrates convergence between on-campus, off-campus and off-shore student groups in the context of online assessment, and the growth of online learning communities resulting from changing assessment practices associated with open and flexible learning development. Chapter 17, by Roy Seden, considers the planning and delivery of automated, innovative assessment in the climate of higher education review policies in the UK and the context of the construction discipline as delivered at De Montfort University. In Chapter 18, Stan Zakrzewski proposes a generic, structured model for computer-based assessment and gives an account of the implementation in three stages of such a system based on Question Mark Designer at the University of Luton, UK.

To end this final section, we return to students' perceptions with Chapter 19, contributed by Kay Sambell, Alistair Sambell and Graham Sexton. They discuss students' reactions to computer-assisted assessment developments in engineering education at the University of Northumbria in Newcastle, UK, including a broad discussion of the role of assessment in student learning. They link a range of suggestions about good practice for computer-assisted assessment to a variety of direct extracts from student feedback that they gathered and analysed. The book concludes with a chapter from Joanna Bull looking to the future of CAA.

Overall, this book presents a compilation on computer-assisted assessment that starts with lecturers' words about 'why it can't be done' and ends with students' words about 'what happened when it was done'. Between these extremes, we believe you will find in this book a wealth of experience about computer-assisted assessment and a wide range of suggestions about good practice, which we hope will help you to implement such assessment effectively, efficiently and productively.

Phil Race, Sally Brown and Joanna Bull (1999)

SECTION ONE: Pragmatics and Practicalities of CAA

1

Pragmatic issues when integrating technology into the assessment of students

Jen Harvey and Nora Mogey

PERCEIVED PROBLEMS AND SOLUTIONS

Increased student numbers over the last few years, together with course pressures such as modularization have resulted in many academic staff having to spend an increasing amount of their time marking student assessments and collating the resultant data. Concurrently there have been changes to the technologies available to support the teaching and learning process. But to be effective, technology must be fully embedded and integrated with the wider student learning experience and the reasons for using technology must be clearly identified and understood. Taking the decision to use technology to support assessment and the subsequent first exploratory steps can often be the biggest hurdles to address.

This chapter aims to explore a range of different ways in which academics might consider integrating technology into courses and to discuss some of the issues relating to the use of technology to support assessment.

We do not propose that all assessments should be computer based, rather that using technology to support assessment can provide a number of options not always provided by paper-based methods. For example:

- large numbers of assessments can be marked quickly and accurately;

- students' responses to questions can be monitored;
- assessments can be provided within an open-access system;
- assessments can be stored and reused;
- immediate feedback on performance and advice can be provided;
- assessment items can be randomly selected to provide a different paper for each student.

Each of the following sections begins with a reason that might be given by staff as to why they feel they can't use technology to support assessment and goes on to suggest ideas as to how they might overcome such perceived problems.

MY VALIDATING BODY WON'T PERMIT IT

This is simply not true. Degree-awarding authorities and validating bodies insist on consistent and objective assessment methods, although there is perhaps some pressure to stick with a familiar and well-tested style for assessment. The presentation of a clear and convincing argument in favour of the use of technology, supported by examples of its successful and efficient use in other courses and other institutions, will rarely be rejected out of hand.

Strategies:

- **Present technology as the most appropriate assessment tool for the aims and objectives of the module**. The introduction of technology should always be motivated by how appropriate it is as a tool to support learning and teaching. If other assessment methods match more closely with the learning objectives then they should be used. But a strong case can be made for the appropriate use of technology that is able to deliver a valid test at times that allow flexibility for part-time or distant learners, which provides immediate feedback to students and can assist staff in analysing areas of weaknesses within student cohorts or course delivery methods.
- **Argue the long-term educational and efficiency gains due to the introduction of technology**. The introduction of computer-based assessment methods should always result in long-term efficiency gains, but this will not necessarily be without the investment of short-term effort. However, computer-based assessment, used thoughtfully, can enrich the learning environment for students by being used to promote reflection, which in turn can lead to longer-term deeper learning.
- **Present examples of other courses where technology is an accepted part of the assessment process**. In particular, other chapters in this book give a number of useful examples for presentation in support of this case.

NONE OF THE REST OF MY COURSE IS COMPUTER BASED

Strategies:

- **Induct your students**. If none of the rest of *your* module is computer based, perhaps some of the rest of the course is. If it isn't, it is possible to make sure that your students have some instruction on how to use a computer, prior to sending them off to work through an independent package. Some institutions provide IT beginners' courses, but if not, you could consider running a short introductory course yourself. In addition, you might want to make sure that someone is going to be there to help should students require assistance and/or suggest that students work together in small groups during their first session. It is important if you are introducing a computer-based summative assessment that none of your students are disadvantaged because they are unfamiliar with the technology involved.
- **Use computer-assisted assessment for integration**. Assessment can be used to integrate a variety of teaching and learning innovations into your course. If a particular part of a course is not going to be assessed then students are not so likely to make the effort to learn it. Equally, if the innovation being introduced is computer-supported assessment then it is vital that the material being assessed through the technology is a core part of the course rather than an option.
- **Provide a range of assessment methods**. Providing a range of different types of assessment for your students can also provide a more stimulating learning environment by introducing some variety as well as providing your students with the opportunity to develop a range of different skills. However, appropriate types of assessments should be selected for measuring the attainment of particular course objectives and not just used for the sake of it. A range of different types of computer-based assessments are now available that can be geared towards students of different abilities. For example, Modified Essay questions can lead a student through the different stages of a case study or a package can select out a set of questions designed for students who have covered only parts of a course and at the same time provide them with appropriate feedback.

I'VE ONLY GOT 20 PCS IN THE LAB, BUT I'VE 86 STUDENTS IN MY CLASS

This is only a problem if you require all your students to be in the room at the same time. If all your students do not require a separate machine at the same time then a variety of options are available.

Strategies:

- **Assess students in groups**. Why not try some kind of group-based assessment, where students work on a computer-based problem together?

You can then bring the whole class together and the solutions reached by the different groups can be discussed.

- **Carousel assignments**. Times can be set aside when one large group of students works in the lab but another group carries out a paper-based exercise in a tutorial room and a further group carries out an information retrieval exercise in the library. Thereby students could be provided with a range of different types of assessments for one course.
- **Assess students at different times**. If the assessments are set up on a file-server, each student can be asked to work through the assessments in their own time. By asking students to type in their name and matriculation number, you can monitor when and who has completed the exercise.
- **Phase access to assessments**. Another possibility might be to let one section of the class out one door of the examination room while another section of the class comes in another door. This is widely done at Luton University, for example.

I DON'T LIKE USING IT

Strategies:

- **Review your own resistance**. Think about why you don't like using learning technology. Everyone has some horror story, for example of how they were intending to use a computer package with a group of students but the network went down. Equally so, there may have been times when you had bad experiences when a group-based activity just hasn't gone to plan, but this hasn't stopped you trying out a similar but amended type of exercise on another occasion. If your bad experience was some time ago then perhaps you should give the technology another try. The software and hardware, as well as the institutional support, have moved a long way during the last five years and you might be surprised, firstly at what is available and, secondly, how much built-in support is available within computing packages.
- **Just do it!** Sometimes you simply have to do things that you just don't like. Some people never liked using overhead projectors, but in some lecture theatres it is the only realistic option. When it is the best tool for the job, personal preference shouldn't really come into it.

THINGS ARE WORKING FINE AT THE MOMENT, WHY SHOULD I CHANGE?

If things are working well then maybe you are right and there is no need to change. But maybe a different assessment strategy would be even better. How long can you be sure that the current system will maintain its effectiveness? Will the profile of the student body change and will this have implications for what assessment strategies would be appropriate?

Strategy:

- **Keep reviewing the options**. Academic staff should be in a position to choose the best possible assessment strategy from the range of options available. Without an awareness of what the options are, you cannot be in a position to make a fully informed choice.

I DON'T HAVE ENOUGH TIME TO SET IT UP

In the short term, it probably appears as if changing to using learning technologies to support assessment is likely to be a time-consuming exercise. However, there are usually ways of obtaining assistance and support, both within and outwith your institution, which can help alleviate any problems encountered during the initial stages of setting up any new computer-based assessments – remember, you do not have to be alone. The following strategies might help:

- **Look to see what is already available**. With the increase in most class sizes over the last few years, many people are moving towards assessing their students using IT and therefore there are a lot of computer-based assessments available. Some of these are commercial products, but there is also a range of World Wide Web-based assessments to which you could refer your students or which could be downloaded for your own use. These do tend to be of variable quality and should be thoroughly evaluated before integrating the questions into one of your courses. Many computer-assisted learning packages, in particular those from the Teaching and Learning Technology Programme (TLTP) [1] also integrate formative assessments. As these are usually directly linked to the subject material, they will increase the relevance for the students.
- **Address those old familiar queries!** To save time repeating the same answers to the same old questions, why not set up a question bank, or quiz, of these and ask your students to go through them (don't forget the feedback to provide students with advice about where they are going wrong). Alternatively, get your students to create a frequently-asked-question (FAQ) bank of questions for a part of their course. You could also involve other students in researching the answers. Once a bank of questions and answers has been established, these can be used again and again. You might also consider categorizing the questions under the different headings relevant to a course.
- **Set up a group to share out the work**. Some of your colleagues might be interested in setting up an assessment group and each contributing a set number of questions to a bank. This can save you the time and effort of having to do the whole thing yourself. Some academic staff have already set up cross-institutional groups, so it is worth checking with the subject centre [2] for your discipline area to find out what is already established. Entry for

these groups generally requires a set number of questions. These have to be validated questions, so you can't gain access to the bank by just submitting any old examples. Some groups have set up a planned timetable of activities by perhaps involving their staff development unit in running a session on how to go about developing effective questions or making the transition from paper-based to computer-based questions.

- **Go for quality, not quantity**. It is best to aim to develop fewer higher-quality questions rather than hundreds of questions of dubious validity. Most of the specialist assessment software now available allows you to analyse each question in turn and to identify which of your questions are good at discriminating between the top and bottom of your classes and which require a bit of rethinking.
- **Speed things up**. As your test items can be so readily analysed using a computer, it is easy to test all your test items for validity and to identify which are efficient discriminators. Although your paper-based objective questions can also be analysed, you are more likely to feel encouraged to analyse computer-based assessments because it is so much quicker and easier to do. With so many quality assessment (QA) exercises currently being carried out within departments, this is worth bearing in mind. In addition, asking your students to run through a computer-based test at different points within the course programme helps both you and them to identify any areas of weakness and encourages the revision of the basic concepts of one section prior to moving on to the next.

MY STUDENTS DON'T BELIEVE IT'S FAIR

Although students are increasingly familiar and confident with the use of computers, some will still feel concerned if computers are suddenly introduced, particularly as part of course assessment. It is important to give all students an equal opportunity and to build the confidence of students who may have less experience using computers. (See also Mark Brosnan's chapter.)

Strategies:

- **Set up practice assessment sessions or training sessions**. Arrange times when your students can learn to use the assessment system that they will be expected to use. If this is not the first year that computers have been used, try to get one or two of last year's students along to help answer any questions about how it feels to have computers involved in the assessment process.
- **Try the technology in parallel with a traditional form of assessment**. Run an assessment twice – once traditionally and once using technology. It is easy to persuade the students to agree by awarding them whichever mark is higher. Split the class into two, so half does the traditional assessment first and the rest do the computer-based assessment first. This comes up with lots of data that can be used to discuss with staff and with students the relative merits of the computer-based and the traditional assessment.

- **Let the students practise as often as they like, so that they decide when they are ready to sit the real test.** Using banks of questions for rehearsal allows students to have as much practice as they feel they need. Students who are more confident can take the test when they feel ready and then spend their time on subjects that they find need more effort. The practice questions can be kept in a separate bank, so that there is no chance of students learning by rote answers that they later use in the real test.

I PREFER TO USE MORE INNOVATIVE WAYS OF ASSESSING THE QUALITY OF MY STUDENTS' LEARNING, NOT JUST MULTIPLE-CHOICE QUESTIONS

Although there tends to be an automatic association between computer-assisted assessment and objective tests, not all objective tests are multiple choice. Computers lend themselves to the design and analysis of objective tests and, with the software now available, it is relatively easy to present your students with questions that incorporate a range of multimedia and a range of objective types. For example, students can be asked to fill in the blanks, to rank-order a series of options, click on different 'hot spot' areas of graphics or review various multimedia options. Levels of feedback and assistance can be provided depending on how many times the students have got the wrong response.

Strategies:

- **Use self- and peer-group assessment methods.** It is also possible to structure questions in such a way that the students respond using free-format text. Students can then compare their responses to those given by the lecturer and go on to self-assess their work. By setting up a marking system for this type of question, students can also see the weightings awarded for different parts of the question and how their responses related to that of the rest of their class. Another possibility might be to ask students to mark other students' work; for example, lab reports or open-ended questions could be submitted electronically and marked using a student-designed scoring grid. The setting up of such a grid could then form part of a tutorial type session in order to raise some issues relating to assessment and how students might improve their skills in, for example, essay writing. (See also Jennifer Robinson's chapter.)
- **Adopt a multimedia approach.** There are now a number of simple-to-use software packages that enable the synthesis of material, which can in turn form part of a course assessment, rather like a portfolio of work. In addition, students could be asked to design their own basic computer-assisted learning packages. This could replace final-year projects and also provide a source of material for the next year's students. The packages could then be assessed by the rest of the class. Another possibility might be to ask groups of students to set up a resource base of research work on a particular part of the course, which could be assessed

but, at the same time, it also provides the foundations for a resource library for students.

MY STUDENTS WOULDN'T GET THE SAME LEVEL OF FEEDBACK THAT I CAN PROVIDE FOR PAPER-BASED EXERCISES

One major advantage of using computer-based assessments is that the feedback can be immediate and structured according to an individual student's need. If you are writing new computer-based assessments for your students, it is important to consider the way in which you construct and word the feedback. In the extreme, a loud noise followed by the flashing word 'wrong' covering the screen is not going to encourage students to continue to work through a set of questions, whereas some advice as to where they might have gone wrong is more likely to encourage them to continue.

Strategy:

- **Use the available technology to maximize feedback**. Computers also enable material to be catalogued and stored in such a way that students can access the information when and how often it is required. They could also access questions on the subject areas with which they are having difficulty. Good and bad examples of coursework can be made available with detailed notations from the lecturer as to all the relevant good and bad points. Scoring grids are also useful in providing students with feedback on different aspects of their work and, if stored electronically, can be used to see the trends in marks across a particular class, which would not otherwise be available for students to refer to.

HOW CAN I ENSURE SECURITY?

This question is most relevant for summative assessments. For a summative assessment, traditionally a cohort of students assembles in a large hall and all sit a formal examination within a controlled environment. Using technology in the assessment process may introduce the opportunity for new and more innovative methods of assessment, perhaps more appropriate to demonstrating the knowledge, understanding or skills of the student.

Strategies:

- **Make the assessment flexible**. All assessment strategies have their limitations. However, the limitations of paper-based systems are different from the limitations of computer-based assessment systems. The methods and types of assessment that are appropriate for paper-based tests are not necessarily the same as the methods which are appropriate for computer-based strategies. Best practice in the use of technology to support assessment demands flexibility in both the design and the execution of assessment strategies. Does security *need* to be a major issue? Flexibility is also needed to take account of the changing student population. As more and more educational institutions try to meet the increasing demands for part-time and distance learning options, flexibility in assessment methods is also being demanded. For students with jobs, or families, the option to take an exam at one of a number of times is invaluable.

- **Use common sense to improve security**. Let us assume that the decision has been made to deliver an end-of-course examination using a computer. The first security question is, then, 'How can I ensure that the questions are stored securely?' Electronic files can be protected with a password, so that they are only accessible to individuals with knowledge of the password. Using a less intuitive directory name (eg 3labcl rather than 'exam' or 'assessment' or the course title) may make files look less interesting to a casual passer-by. There is, of course, no need to store files on a general network – they can be stored on a departmental machine, or a floppy disk that can in turn be locked securely in a desk, cupboard or safe. Files can also be time protected, so that they can only be accessed between set dates and times.
- **How can I ensure security in the examination room?** Here, technology surely wins hands down on more traditional assessment methods. In addition to traditional methods of supervising examination rooms, it is straightforward to introduce variables into the structure of the programme, so that students have no real incentive to try to copy from a neighbour. When questions are presented to the candidates, they are identical in terms of structure, but not in terms of the precise content. Mathematics and science subjects lend themselves to such an approach, but equally a list of text variables can be established from which passages can be created with exactly the same structure and volume of information, but where the detail of the words changes.
- **How can I ensure security after the exam?** If students are sitting the exam at different times, staff may be concerned that the stored responses may be attractive targets for hacking students. Networks can be protected, so that all accesses to the system are automatically logged. Also, results do not need to be stored on a network where they might possibly be open to tampering.

I HAVEN'T GOT ACCESS TO TECHNICAL SUPPORT

There is no point in pretending that technical support is not a most useful aspect of any attempt to integrate technology into teaching. But it doesn't need to be essential, especially if you plan in advance.

Strategies:

- **Test things out beforehand**. Whenever you plan to use learning technologies within teaching, always try them out in advance on the machines that the students will be using. Similarly, don't expect a network to work at the same speed for a single member of staff as it does when a whole class of students are using it simultaneously. If you plan to record student responses to a file, check that students have the appropriate permissions, ie try logging on with a student ID not your own.

- **Investigate whether it is possible to get some technical support for a short time**. Perhaps your department could offer a placement to a computing student specifically to assist with setting up a computerized assessment scheme, or to offer technical support more generally within the department. Perhaps a member of staff from central computer services could be allocated to your department to help set up/test/implement the assessment strategy.

IT WILL BE AN ADMINISTRATIVE NIGHTMARE

Computer-based examinations provide a comprehensive solution to many of the shortcomings of traditional assessment methods. For example, computer-delivered testing offers fully electronic and instantly accessible registration, scheduling, administration and sophisticated reporting, with comprehensive statistical feedback on candidate and test performance.

Strategies:

- **Communicate electronically**. A last-minute change in any examination details, such as a change of venue or a reminder about special equipment that might be needed, could pose a problem in many institutions. Where students have access to electronic mail, and where it is used as a principal mode of communication, e-mail offers a quick and efficient method of delivering an important message (*if* you can be confident that your students will check their incoming mail). Assignments submitted using e-mail can be automatically time and date stamped, eliminating possible disputes over the time of submission of an assignment.
- **Use automated marking**. The use of computers to automate the marking process is for many people the initial attraction to the use of technology in assessment. All objective tests and some other structured tests delivered using the computer can be quickly, efficiently and accurately marked by the computer without any further input from academic staff. Results along with constructive feedback can be reported immediately to students as well as being recorded and analysed for staff. For objective tests, where students complete pre-printed response sheets, optical mark readers (OMRs) can be used to read all the response sheets and present the collated results in the desired form. The use of OMRs is by no means a new idea, but for many it can still offer a cost-effective option. One OMR can be used to process thousands of forms in an hour and can cost from as little as a few hundred pounds.
- **Use computers for collation and reporting of results**. Computers are excellent tools for the manipulation and presentation of data. Results can be stored electronically (taking up very little office space, incidentally) and then sorted, tabulated and analysed at the press of a button. Marks can be scaled,

distributions can be investigated and trends can be explored. Should an examination board decide to adjust any mark then this can be effected by making a single change and all reports or calculations using this mark are automatically updated.

- **Try diagnostic analysis of the responses**. Careful analysis of responses can be a source of useful information. Results can be used to compare different cohorts of students and to identify any topics where students generally perform less well, perhaps indicating areas of the teaching programme that could usefully be revised.

BUT WHAT HAPPENS IF THE SYSTEM CRASHES ON THE DAY?

All computers crash from time to time and, of course, Murphy's Law ensures that the worst will sometimes happen.

Strategies:

- **Try to have one or two spare computers**, so that if it is just a problem with an individual machine then students can swap with relatively little difficulty. But think about whether the student will need to start again at the beginning of a test and whether their work so far will be retrievable – it probably depends on the configuration of the software you select.
- **Keep colleagues informed**. Tell your local technical officers that you are planning to use the computer laboratory for an important exercise, so that they don't choose that day to try to experiment with the installation of the latest version of Windows Like-You-Have-Never-Seen-It-Before (or whatever). Discuss the possibility of a network problem on the day of an assessment with your local computing staff – is there a backup fileserver that could be quickly brought into service?
- **Don't panic**. Students find assessment stressful enough anyway. If a problem does occur, tell students what action you are taking and what action they are expected to take. If the system does go down, it is probably worth waiting a little while before abandoning the assessment; it may not take long to fix. If students have lost time for the assessment as a consequence of a technical problem you could: (1) add the lost time to the end of the exam; (2) reduce the number of questions that students are to answer and scale marks up accordingly; (3) accept less detailed or incomplete responses to some questions; (4) allocate all students some marks to compensate for the extra stress.
- **Have a non-technological option (paper copies?) up your sleeve for the worst possible scenario.**

I'VE DECIDED TO GO AHEAD AND USE TECHNOLOGY; WHAT SHOULD BE THE FIRST STEPS?

Don't be too ambitious in the initial stages. Start off with a small and manageable project – set up a pilot scheme and try it out within one course, within one department. Build a thorough evaluation programme into the pilot and use that to inform and advise your later developments. Seek opinions from students, colleagues and administrative, technical or other support staff. Reflect on the feedback and revise your strategy accordingly.

We conclude with some comments from students and staff, which reinforce our suggestion that, having considered the drawbacks, you should consider using computer-assisted assessment anyway.

Some opinions from students

'The feedback was really helpful and I liked it because it was only me that saw it.'

'I got my mark straight away so I didn't need to wait ages until I knew that I had passed.'

'I liked having a variety of different types of questions – I thought it would only be multiple choice, but for some of the questions you had to type in a sentence.'

'It was better for me because I could do the test at a time that suited me.'

'It was really interesting because my group all worked together to produce our own little package.'

'It was useful to look at other students' work; I began to see where I had been going wrong.'

Some opinions from staff

'Once we got it set up – it was so easy; I had 350 students this year and wasn't looking forward to marking all those mid-semester assignments.'

'I liked the way in which we used peer-group assessment. I think that the students found this very useful – it involved them and they learned a lot more.'

'I had never thought about asking the students to write their own questions; we now have a question bank, which we can add to next year.'

'I have always hated invigilating exams – now I know the answer!'

'We have now been able to add a section to our quality assessment document that related to the quality of our first year students' coursework.'

'I was able to identify three or four students who really needed some help with one of the topics and it was great to see how well they eventually did in the end-of-year exams.'

'The computer officers were brilliant – although there weren't any major problems it was so reassuring just to have them there.'

REFERENCES AND FURTHER READING

1 Teaching and Learning Technology Programme (TLTP) phases I and II was jointly funded by the four higher education funding bodies, HEFCE, SHEFC, HEFCW and DENI, largely to develop computer-assisted learning packages

2 At the date of writing, the Computers in Teaching Initiative (CTI) Centres offer a service to higher education through a network of 24 subject-based centres. It is known that a new network of subject-support centres is to be established sometime after July 1999, building on the work of the CTI, but their exact structure is not yet known

Teaching and learning in an expanding higher education system, The MacFarlane Report (1992). Report of a working party of the Committee of Scottish University Principals

Griffiths, Frances (Dec 1994) Freedom and flexibility in the higher education examination process, *Active Learning*, 1

2

Technical and security issues

Dave Whittington

INTRODUCTION

This chapter describes the technical, technological and security-related issues of implementing computer-assisted assessment. Not all of these issues relate to all aspects of CAA. The use of optical mark readers (OMRs), for example, would not require rooms of computers to be placed under examination conditions. Nevertheless, many of these issues are clearly interrelated. Compliance with data protection legislation will probably require data security issues to be addressed. Each section of this chapter describes an issue and how it relates to CAA. Strategies for minimizing the risks associated with an issue and their relation to CAA will be discussed wherever they exist.

BUILT-IN BIAS INTRODUCED BY THE DELIVERY MECHANISM

Any assessment may be unfair if the method of delivery favours one group of students over another. This is true for all forms of assessment, not just CAA. However, with computer-delivered tests, there is a serious risk that those students most comfortable with the technology will have a distinct advantage over those who are most anxious about using computers. Steps must be taken to ensure that assessments are fair and particular care must be taken to ensure that students with special needs are not disadvantaged by the introduction of CAA.

One way to address this issue would be to offer all the candidates a choice of test-delivery media. Having some students sitting a computer-delivered test while others sit a paper-based test would create its own problems. Some mechanism would have to be put in place to record and evaluate the effects of different students using different types of test. Some of the efficiency gains of automated assessment would be lost. The overhead involved in running two types of test would be greater than any time saved by having a sub-section of students using CAA.

Another approach would be to ensure that all the candidates were sufficiently familiar with the computer-delivered test format so that no group of students had an advantage over any other group. This would involve delivering practice tests that would familiarize the students with the CAA system (as is discussed by Norma Pritchett in Chapter 3). This approach has been used in the past and has predominantly been accepted by the students involved. It has the added advantage of ensuring all students, including the most computer-anxious who might otherwise slip through the competency net, achieve a basic level of computer literacy.

It is also important that sitting a computerized assessment in a non-IT-based subject should require nothing more than very basic computer skills, such as maze navigation and 'clicking procedures'. Great care should be taken when designing the test to ensure that what is being assessed is not a student's ability to operate the assessment system but the subject matter of the test itself, unless, of course, it is computer skills being assessed.

QUESTION DESIGN: THE HUMAN-COMPUTER INTERFACE (HCI)

This is not to be confused with the design of the question (that is, content, the stem, distracters and so on – see Chapter 3). This section deals with the look and feel of the questions. When a computer delivers a test, it is important that the operation of the computer does not interfere with the material being assessed.

Clearly the appropriateness of the display is related to question type and, depending on the CAA system in use and how the use of it is organized, the assessment designer will have varying degrees of control over the visual design. It is important to resist the temptation to use as many features as the system makes available. If templates are made available, it may be best just to use them rather than create new designs and layouts with which the students will be unfamiliar.

Information should be clear and easy to read, while avoiding mixing too many different font styles and colour combinations on the same screen. Care must be taken not to overload the screen with too much text. Good design of computer-based systems requires careful thought and is not just a matter of making a paper-based test readable on a computer screen. Where *appropriate*, test designers should make use of graphics, video and sound in their questions. Navigational controls should remain consistent throughout the test.

It may be advisable to have a house style that ensures consistency of look and feel through all of an institution's online tests. The use of a house style ensures that students need not learn how to operate new assessment software repetitively. This is especially important within modular multidisciplinary courses.

Students should be able to review their answers at any time during a timed test just as they would in a paper-based test. It should also be possible to make corrections to any answers given at any time. The tests should be robust: pressing the wrong key at the wrong time should not break the test. It should always be possible to undo anything right up until exiting from the test. The way feedback is presented in formative tests should remain consistent throughout the assessment.

Response time from the system should be such that it does not interfere with the student's ability to complete the test. Particular care should be taken when students are taking time-limited tests so that the students are not kept waiting by the system.

Finally, it is crucial to fully test or pilot the delivery mechanism before it is presented to the students. Letting students use early versions of software might help iron out bugs but it will not instil confidence in the students or help to validate the new delivery method. The application of sound HCI principles is vital for the smooth running of computer-delivered tests.

QUESTION BANKS

Question banks are used to store large numbers of questions, usually from one subject area. For any particular test, questions can be selected from the bank at random. Questions in a bank are often organized by level of difficulty so that a single bank can be used to generate tests of different but controlled difficulty.

Generating different sets of questions of the same difficulty is a common approach used to deter cheating. This ensures that no two adjacent students are likely to gain any advantage by viewing the other's computer screen.

Randomizing factors within otherwise identical questions is another way of creating a large number of questions of the same difficulty. Using questions involving the application of standard formulae to a set of numerical values is an obvious methodology of many computer-generated and assessed variations.

Students may sometimes be tested repeatedly from the same question bank. In cases such as this, it is important that the bank is large. A sufficient number of questions must exist so those students cannot gain an advantage by recognizing questions as they get repeated.

If the question bank contains some measure of the difficulty of each question then this must be checked and updated regularly. The performance of the students should be continuously monitored and the level of difficulty of individual questions updated as and when necessary.

ROBUSTNESS AND NETWORK RELIABILITY

Some systems, depending on their implementation, are intrinsically more robust than others. A well-maintained system will always be more reliable than one that has been poorly planned and starved of physical and human resources. Without adequate support staff, possessing appropriate skills, a system's reliability will be less than it could be.

The World Wide Web is becoming an increasingly attractive delivery mechanism for assessments. A system that allows students easy but controlled access to tests that need only be installed on a single server has obvious advantages. A Web-based system may, depending on design and implementation, also have a more familiar look and feel, as many students make increased use of the Web in their day-to-day studies. More sophisticated Web-based systems include reporting mechanisms. Reports would typically include details of students' performance along with where and when they took the test.

The reliability of Web-based systems is, however, suspect. Software vendors are under enormous pressure to release ever-more sophisticated versions of their systems. Often the software is released in incomplete and not fully tested versions. Compound this with the existence of different browser versions that each support and different features of Web technology and reliability become a serious problem. Making use of the very latest features may be very attractive but is unlikely to create robust and reliable tests. Try to stick with widely implemented, tried and tested features whenever possible.

Strategies for implementing a robust CAA infrastructure

- Find out if and when you might be affected by scheduled maintenance periods. Most problems occur when someone makes changes to the system, so avoid any scheduled maintenance periods like the plague.
- Keep everything as local as possible; if you can make use of local file servers and/or Web servers then you'll only be relying on a small proportion of the network. The delivery of tests from further afield may, depending on the infrastructure, rely on more than just your local network.
- Leave the critical areas to members of staff who know what they are doing, particularly setting up and maintaining file servers and Web servers.
- Think about the things that could go wrong. Assess how likely the problem might be and how likely it is to occur. Develop strategies for dealing with problems before they arise and be sure everyone involved is aware of the action that needs to be taken to minimize the impact of any problem.

DATA PROTECTION LEGISLATION

The basic principles of data protection legislation are straightforward. Data users (sometimes referred to as data controllers) must register with a central authority. They must clearly state what data they are keeping, who it relates to, what the purpose is and which third parties, if any, they will pass it on to. Data subjects, the people whose details are being stored, have the right to know what data is stored and have any mistakes either erased or modified.

How these principles are implemented in actual legislation will vary in time and from jurisdiction to jurisdiction. Typically, legislation will endeavour to:

- define which organizations or individuals must register as data users and which are exempt;
- detail the registration process;
- list the responsibilities of a data user;

- explain the process by which data subjects can view and propose modification to their own records.

Using CAA may not necessarily change the way you or your organization use data but it would be prudent to ensure that you (or your organization) are registered to collect and use data for assessment purposes. It must also be stressed that it is the responsibility of the data user to ensure security of the data.

Remember that data subjects (the students you are assessing) will have rights to view any data stored about them, and procedures will need to be set up to support this. There may be provision for charging a fee for this service but it won't be very much.

Most data protection guidelines include the following:

- make sure any personal information is obtained and processed fairly and lawfully;
- ensure the information is used for a registered purpose;
- make sure the information is not disclosed to anybody or any organization that hasn't a right to the information;
- the quantity of information stored should be adequate and relevant for the purpose but not excessive;
- the information should be accurate and up to date;
- personal information should not be stored any longer than is necessary for the registered purpose;
- personal information should be granted proper security.

It is important to remember that most data archives are created purely for backup purposes and would only ever need to be accessed in the event of a fault. Archived assessment data is kept for different reasons and it therefore needs to be both more accessible and more secure at the same time. Given the students' rights to view data held about them and any examination result appeals procedures, the data regarding a student's assessment results needs to be more accessible than would normally be the case with archived data. On the other hand, data protection legislation compels data users to surround personal data with appropriate ring-fencing procedures.

DATA SECURITY

Before the assessment using CAA takes place, the questions should be afforded the same level of security as that given to traditional assessments. Particular care needs to be taken when the questions are being made available over a network. Examinations should not be loaded on to the server until the last minute, unless security can be guaranteed. Once again, a well-maintained and properly staffed system will provide the best security. Whoever administers the network and the server will have to keep up to date with the latest security problems associated with the system and ensure that any necessary changes to the system are made to keep it secure.

There are many security issues during the test. Some of these are covered in the section on exam conditions and include strategies for dealing with plagiarism. Thought must also be given to the protection of any answers given in the event of computer failure during an exam. As much of the students' work as possible needs to be backed up to a server or floppy as the exam progresses.

After the test, when computers are used to store student marks, security of the information will be subject to data protection legislation (see the earlier section). Encryption of both the questions before a test and the answers after the test will add another level of security.

WHAT DOES 'EXAM CONDITIONS' MEAN FOR CAA?

All the computers must be audited to ensure that only what is supposed to be available is available in terms of student communications. Particular care would have to be taken with networked computers and computers connected to the Internet will be particularly difficult to make secure. Disabling e-mail is not enough. Internet relay chat (IRC), newsgroups and Web-based e-mail such as hotmail.com are all realistic avenues for help. Security can only be guaranteed if the network of student machines and the server containing the questions is isolated from the rest of the Internet. This is not always an easy thing to achieve but it should be possible with the help of local systems support staff.

Computers should be positioned carefully to ensure comfort. Things to consider that might not normally be an issue in a traditional exam include glare from windows, noise from the computers and privacy. Screens should be clean and there should be sufficient space for the keyboard, mouse and any other equipment or documentation required to take the test. When a test includes audio, headphones should be provided. Sufficient space should be provided between workstations to allow for privacy and comfort. Extra privacy can be provided by screening off workstations or by alternating students taking different assessments.

Health and safety legislation within the European Union demands, if tests last for six hours, that all workstations are equipped with tilt and swivel screens and adjustable chairs that are positioned in such a way as to reduce to a minimum the glare from windows and artificial light sources. Care must be taken when setting up a room for a computer-delivered exam that any health and safety requirements are carefully adhered to.

Computers are not as reliable or as readily replaceable as pen and paper. This fairly obvious fact needs to be taken into consideration when planning summative CAA. You would expect to have in a normal exam room close to 100 per cent occupancy. In a computer-based exam, it is always a good idea, if possible, to have some spare machines, along with some spare mice, keyboards and monitors. Technical support should also be on hand throughout the duration of the exam.

If the timing of the exam is automated, care must be taken to ensure sufficient flexibility is built in to cope with students with prior determined special needs who may be entitled to take longer over the exam.

Emergency backup procedures should be agreed before the examination and it is vital that the invigilators are properly briefed in the operational aspects of these procedures. Backup plans might include the provision of paper versions of the test that could be distributed in the event of a major system failure.

STUDENT AUTHENTICATION

Traditionally, students are authenticated by the visual inspection of identification cards and the matching of signatures and faces to photographs. In a computerized exam, a similar inspection can take place initially but care must be taken to ensure that the answers produced by the student can be verified as belonging to the student. Students may print their name on a disk containing their work but what is more likely is that they will have to have 'logged on' to the computer before taking the test.

When access to the computers is controlled with a username and password, invigilators and technical support should have access to this information in case any students have forgotten their details. This will be most important if the students concerned haven't made regular use of their username and password.

Once student access is controlled by username and password, it should be possible to link with student record systems. Student registration details could be used to only allow access to exams for courses on which they are registered. It should also be possible for exam marks to be added to the student records electronically, saving some administrative time.

3

Effective question design

Norma Pritchett

BACKGROUND

In higher education, much assessment has been traditionally based on an essay format. The essay has been thought of as being particularly good at assessing knowledge of intellectual skills associated with graduateness, such as subject knowledge and understanding, criticism and analysis, skills of argument and exposition, fluency and expression. Clearly a free response form of assessment, such as the essay, allows students to demonstrate their expertise over a range of skills, but it may not possess very great precision in identifying exactly which skills are being assessed and to what level. Certainly some studies have shown that there can be very wide variation in the grades awarded to the same set of essays by a group of experienced lecturers. This seems to imply that there is some misunderstanding about what is being tested and/or a failure to recognize the nature of the skills being demonstrated. Moreover, it suggests a highly interpretative element in essay assessment.

The use of objective testing, predominantly in the form of multiple-choice questionnaires (MCQs), is one answer to some of the problems identified above. But MCQs often attract the criticism that such forms of assessment test only low-level knowledge and that there can be a large element of chance involved in passing the examination. However, if properly designed, it is possible to produce an MCQ instrument that can be sensitive, can identify and test a range of skills and can also reduce the possibility of chance success (Gronlund, 1982). The availability of automated MCQ assessment packages makes that task somewhat easier and allows fast and detailed feedback. It requires a certain level of skill and some careful thought to produce good objective tests but the guidelines given below should help in designing effective, objective questions.

There are some general principles to observe when designing any form of assessment:

- If learning outcomes are identified for the course then the test should address those learning outcomes.

- The test should try to assess across the whole course, not just parts of it.
- In an assessment, the attention devoted to a particular topic should be a reflection of its importance in the course.
- Assessment should be integrated into the design of a course, not treated as an afterthought.

There are a number of specific dos and don'ts for designing objective tests. The rules given below are designed to reduce any possible confusion and ambiguity in the test material and to produce a valid and reliable test instrument. Some are self-evident but others are less obvious. If you are using an objective test, you might find it helpful to show the questions you have constructed to a colleague. It is surprising how items that seem to be transparent and unambiguous when you devise them can become much less so when someone casts a critical eye on them.

GUIDELINES FOR CONSTRUCTING MULTIPLE-CHOICE QUESTIONS

A multiple-choice question should present a task that is relevant, clear and, ideally, capable of being answered correctly only by those who have achieved the necessary learning. Multiple-choice questions will consist of a question stem that states the problem and a set of choices comprising a correct answer and distracter items. The following guidelines should be applied:

1. **Construct each item to test an important learning outcome.** Avoid testing for trivial details, unrelated bits of information and material that is irrelevant to desired outcomes. Try not to increase test difficulty by resorting to more obscure and unimportant details.
2. **The stem of the item should contain only one question.** The task set out in the question should be so clear that it could be answered without looking at the answer choices.
3. **Use simple and clear expression.** The problem stated should be precise and free of unnecessarily complex wording and sentence structure. Badly expressed question stems may introduce enough ambiguity to confuse a knowledgeable student and prevent them from answering a question that they might otherwise have been able to do. Try to make questions brief and clear so that they are easy to read and understand.
4. **Put as much of the wording as possible in the stem of the question.** Avoid repeating the same material over again in the choices – this increases reading time. A neatly expressed question should remove the need for this.
5. **There should be only one correct answer.** When the correct answer form of multiple choice is used make sure there is only one unquestionably correct answer. Check that any of the distracters could not be claimed as possible correct answers.

6. **Give the stem of the question in positive form and avoid negatives.** A positively phrased question tends to measure more important learning outcomes than a negatively phrased one. If there are occasions when a negative expression must be used then it should be highlighted by the use of capitals or underlining, eg Which of the following is NOT found in limestone regions?

7. **Make sure that all the answer choices are grammatically consistent with the stem of the question and that they are all parallel in form.** Inconsistencies can give a clue as to which is the correct answer. A general guide that can avoid inconsistency is not to use 'a' or 'an' at the end of the stem, so that respondents are not prompted inadvertently towards (or away from) options beginning with a vowel.

   Sometimes students can derive the correct answer from unintended clues in the wording of statement and distracters, such as:

   - Similarity of wording in the stem and in the correct answer.
   - Stating the correct answer in textbook language or stereotyped phraseology – may cause the student to select it because it looks better.
   - Stating the correct answer in more detail than the other choices may provide a clue. Also including modifiers (may, usually, sometimes) may cause an item to be chosen.
   - Including absolutes in the distracters. This enables students to reject them since such terms are commonly associated with false statements (always, never, all).
   - Including two all-inclusive statements. This allows students to reject the other alternatives since one of the two must be correct.
   - Including two responses with the same meaning. This allows the student to reject both since clearly they cannot both be correct.

   Sometimes it is advantageous to break the above rules in order to lead the uninformed away from the real answer but this tactic should be used sparingly.

8. **Avoid verbal clues, which may enable students to select the correct answer or eliminate an incorrect alternative.**

9. **Make all the responses in a question approximately the same length**. If one response item is longer than the others, this can give a clue that it is the correct answer.

10. **Avoid the use of 'all of the above' and 'none of the above'.** These will often enable the student to answer correctly on the basis of partial information: if the student detects that two of the answers are correct, it is possible to deduce that the correct answer is 'all of the above' and if he or she detects one incorrect answer, it is possible to reject it on the basis of partial information. The 'none of the above' is open to the same sort of problem but

carries an additional disadvantage that while a student may recognize a wrong answer there is no guarantee that they know what is correct.

11. **Vary the position of the right answer in a random way.** This is frequently taken care of automatically with automated testing.
12. **Locate questions on the same topic together.**
13. **Make sure that each item is independent of other items in the test.** Other items should not give clues to subsequent items nor should correct answers in one item depend on correctly answering a previous one.
14. **The layout of the question should be clear.** List alternatives on separate lines and use letters before them rather than numbers. If the stem is an incomplete statement then the choices should begin with lower case letters and end with a question mark.

The above are guidelines and not cast-iron rules. From time to time you may wish to modify the above procedures to obtain a particular effect.

All assessment instruments need to relate to the course curriculum and the proposed learning outcomes. The use of objective testing requires that relationship to become more open and explicit. In an essay-assessed course, there is an assumption that the students will demonstrate, in a relatively open-ended way, the knowledge and understanding they may have drawn from a variety of sources. In an MCQ-assessed course it may be necessary to indicate more precisely the material to be tested. For example, it may be appropriate to advise students that the questions will be based only upon lecture content, or seminar topics, key texts, selected readings or key topics.

There are a number of misconceptions about what MCQs can and cannot do. It is frequently suggested that they can only test straightforward factual recall and it is probably true to say that many MCQs will tend to fall into that category. This represents the basic level of testing and, although there is value in assessing low-level factual knowledge, it is a limited form of assessment. It fails to exploit the potential power of the objective test to provide a detailed and searching test of achievement.

WHAT ARE WE TESTING?

The task in higher education is not merely to instil in our students certain levels of subject knowledge. We hope, also, to encourage them to develop a range of intellectual abilities that will enable them to use that subject knowledge well. If we can identify and differentiate those higher-order cognitive skills then we can begin to test for them and thereby gauge the intellectual development of our students.

Bloom *et al* (1956) developed a taxonomy of educational objectives that identified within its cognitive domain a hierarchy of knowledge and intellectual abilities. Although subsequently the taxonomy has been criticized for being simplistic, it nevertheless presents a very useful and simple framework for us to use in identifying learning outcomes. I have given below a brief and summarized version of the taxonomy before going on to illustrate how it is possible to direct questions towards the assessment of particular cognitive skills. It is important to note that it is a hierarchy through which students might be expected to progress and that each higher-order skill will embrace those that are below it in the hierarchy:

1. **Knowledge**: the lowest level of the hierarchy refers to the simple ability to recall previously learned material. It can be thought to include simple factual knowledge of theories, terms, conventions, classifications and categories, principles and methodologies. Although it is the lowest level of learning in the hierarchy, it is still important to assess.
2. **Comprehension**: this involves understanding the meaning of learned material sufficiently to be able to translate or convert it from one form to another, to interpret material and to extrapolate from the data.
3. **Application**: this involves applying what is learned in one context into another situation.
4. **Analysis**: this involves being able to identify the component parts of material, their relationships and the principles underlying their organization.
5. **Synthesis**: this involves drawing together material from different sources to produce a unique item such as a plan or a theory.
6. **Evaluation**: this involves the ability to estimate the appropriateness of a certain item according to particular criteria.

OBJECTIVE TESTS OF HIGHER INTELLECTUAL ABILITIES

Most objective tests will contain questions that attempt to differentiate students' ability by supplying questions that reflect a range of difficulty. The use of the hierarchy above gives some framework for representing that difficulty. A good test will allow the weaker student, as well as the more able, to demonstrate what they know. Therefore, most tests will contain a number of items that assess factual knowledge. Because these will probably be the most common forms of questions, I have given below a series of examples of how such questions might be formulated:

1. **Knowledge of terminology:** What word means the same as. . . ?
2. **Knowledge of specific facts:** What is the most important difference between. . . ?
3. **Knowledge of trends and sequences:** Which one of the following sequences shows the correct order of. . . ?
4. **Knowledge of class and category:** What are the major classifications of. . . ?
5. **Knowledge of methodology:** Which method is the most useful for. . . ?
6. **Knowledge of theories and structure:** What evidence best supports the theory of. . . ?

The above are in a fairly general form and for specific subjects the language will change to better represent the nature of the discipline. Some types of formulation will be more useful than others in particular subject areas. Sometimes it is helpful to use an incomplete statement as the stem or initial part of the question in order to clarify what is required, eg Baddeley proposed a. . . memory model.

Objective tests are not limited merely to the assessment of the factual knowledge a student has managed to retain. It is possible to test a wider range of learning outcomes such as comprehension, application, analysis and evaluation. It should be noted that some aspects of the higher-level skills are more difficult to assess using forced choice tests and they may benefit from the addition of some novel stimulus material around which the higher-level questions are based. Essentially, such tests will assess what meaning a student has attached to his or her factual learning. However, the construction of such tests demands a greater degree of skill and care. Most importantly, it requires a very clear idea of the learning outcomes to be tested.

The following question stems illustrate how a question may be framed to test a particular intellectual skill:

Comprehension (includes translation, interpretation and extrapolation)

- Which one of the following is closest in meaning to the term. . . ?
- The statement '. . . ' means that. . .
- If we present expert and novice chess players with a set of random board positions there will be little difference in their recall of them. Which of the reasons listed below best explains this?
- From the options listed below, indicate what is most likely to happen to reaction times if, in a discrimination task, the amount of contextual similarity is increased. . ..

The examples above assume that the appropriate answers have not been taught or discussed in class, in which case they would become merely knowledge recall items.

Application
This involves being able to apply what is learned about one set of circumstances to another set of conditions.

- Indicate under which of the following circumstances a problem solver will be able to utilise prior experience. . .

Analysis (analysis of parts, relationships and organizing principles)
The analysis of parts/elements includes such things as recognizing unstated assumptions, distinguishing fact from opinion and distinguishing conclusions from the supporting facts.

The analysis of relationships includes such things as identifying cause and effect relationships, relationships between ideas and distinguishing relevant and irrelevant arguments.

The analysis of organizing principles involves such abilities as recognizing a writer's point of view, theoretical perspective or purpose.

Some examples follow:

- Gick and Holyoak write that problem solvers require a hint in order to utilize prior experience. Which one of the following assumptions is being made by the authors?
- Read the following two statements and select the answer which best expresses their relationship.
- Which one of the following best expresses the perspective of the author?

This type of question can assess some aspects of analysis but may be better with a larger piece of stimulus material; for example, the description of an experiment on which a more extensive set of questions may be based.

Synthesis

This is the most difficult learning level to test by using forced choice responses. It involves the production of some novel response based on material drawn from several sources. The unique and novel response is perhaps most easily expressed through free response methods and, while it is possible to assess this learning level using MCQs, it may be easier to use other methods. It is probably easier to objectively assess this level in some disciplines rather than in others. As with the other complex skill levels it may be best to provide a piece of stimulus material around which questions may be based.

Evaluation

Evaluation skills can be tested in a limited form by objective testing but some aspects may be better tested in a less constrained format. However, if evaluation skills are tested by MCQs then, over a series of questions, it is possible to test various aspects of the skill. As with analytical skills, exposure to a longer piece of work on which the questions are based may be a more revealing test.

Evaluation may be based on the internal content of the stimulus piece or it may be based on external evaluative criteria. In either case, evaluative skill will involve the student in identifying explicit criteria to use for evaluation

THE ELEMENT OF CHANCE IN MULTIPLE-CHOICE TESTS

Multiple-choice tests are often criticized on the basis that chance can play a large part in the successful completion of the examination. In practice, the element of chance can be quantified and controlled. In a simple two-choice question requiring a Yes/No or True /False response, there is a one in two (or 50 per cent) chance of arriving at the correct answer by chance. In an MCQ with four possible answer choices, there is a one in four (or 25 per cent) chance of reaching the correct answer by guessing. If we increase the number of choices to five then we further reduce the possibility of chance providing the correct answer to one in five (or 20 per cent). One could theoretically reduce the chance element further by simply adding further question choices, but it may not be practicable to do so. It is not generally advisable to have more than six answer choices. In practice, it is often difficult to find five or more suitable distracter items that are equally possible answers. When faced with the difficult task of finding many distracter items, there is always the temptation to fall back on choices that are either poorly phrased, clearly incorrect, jokey or provide clues to the correct answer. It is also possible that a large set of possible answers may be overly confusing to candidates because they can not really differentiate the possible answers. It needs to be remembered that generally increasing the number of choices will also increase the required reading time and decision time across the exam. If reducing the role of chance is important, there are other methods that may be adopted.

One strategy that may be employed is to discourage guessing by penalizing wrong answers: the correct answer may gain a point but an incorrect choice will cause the deduction of a point. Clearly candidates need to be advised of this possibility before the start of the examination, since the strength of the approach relies on its deterrent effect. One needs to consider very carefully before adopting this method, since it could be considered somewhat harsh and intimidatory. It may inhibit not only the wild guess but also those correct responses that are based on a nearly certain knowledge. If the object of the exercise is to obtain some estimate of what students actually know then the application of penalty points may obscure that perception.

An alternative method is to construct questions that have more than one correct answer and require the candidate to select several answers from a range of possible choices. Under these circumstances, it may be advantageous to have some increase in the number of distracter items. In this type of question it is a particular pattern of response that is rewarded and it is even possible to develop the approach further by constructing questions that require a graded or weighted response. Such questions might, for example, ask candidates to 'select the three most important reasons' or 'place the following factors in order of importance'.

Undoubtedly, the automatization of marking and the consequent reduction in workload is a really attractive feature of this form of assessment. There is a further, possibly underused, facility that qualitatively differentiates the automated system from other manually marked assessments. Most automated assessment packages will give a range of fast and detailed feedback that is not available without considerable effort when using manually marked examinations. It is very easy to obtain a statistical analysis of the results that can inform you about the results of individual students, the performance of the group as a whole, the effectiveness of the whole examination and of individual questions. This sort of feedback can indicate which areas of a test are effective and which need to be redesigned.

Producing a multiple-choice test that is both reliable and valid is a task that requires some care and skill. To produce one that can also differentiate between various levels of intellectual ability is even more demanding but, with practice, it is possible. It can also give a level of sophisticated and informative feedback that is advantageous to both lecturer and student.

REFERENCES

Bloom, B S *et al* (1956) *Taxonomy of Educational Objectives: Cognitive domain*, David McKay Co Inc, New York

Gronlund, N F (1982) *Constructing Achievement Tests*, Prentice Hall Inc, Englewood Cliffs, New Jersey

4

Automated online tutorials: new formats for assessment on the WWW

Alan J Cann and Ellen L Pawley

INTRODUCTION: WWW-BASED ASSESSMENT FORMATS

Over the last few years, we have written a series of online, interactive tutorials at the University of Leicester. A diverse range of presentation styles has deliberately been created, partly as a programme of pedagogical research and partly as a pragmatic response to practical considerations: every year more students and less money! Some of these tutorials are not used as part of formal teaching, but rather as open learning material in what is intended to be a resource-rich environment, incorporating open access to the World Wide Web (WWW). Others are intended for summative assessment purposes and were primarily written to take advantage of automation. This chapter describes the rationale for the use of the WWW for delivery of these materials, the range of presentational styles employed and the practical details of implementation.

In the five years since the WWW became widely available, a considerable proportion of development resources have been devoted to the investigation of computer-assisted assessment (CAA). Unfortunately (in our opinion), the vast majority of effort has concentrated on multiple-choice questions (MCQs). The reasons for this are straightforward: the relative ease with which MCQs can be converted to computer-based formats and the resulting efficiency gain in calculating and recording student marks. Much of the rest of this book refers to computer-based implementation of MCQs, so we will not go into the matter in detail here. We are not opposed to the MCQ format *per se*; indeed, we have been involved with the development of software for online MCQs ourselves [1, 2]. In certain disciplines, notably medicine, MCQs have long been accepted as a standard assessment tool, considerably predating computer-assisted learning (CAL). In other subject areas, notably the humanities, MCQs are seen as an inadequate form of assessment that represents the 'dumbing down' of the educational system. Our own view is effectively midway between these extremes, namely that carefully designed and used with restraint as part of a varied overall assessment plan, MCQs can be a valuable part of computer-assisted assessment.

FORMATIVE ONLINE TUTORIALS

The potential of the WWW for assessment amounts to much more than can be achieved with MCQs alone. For this reason, some four years ago we began to develop the format we refer to as *tutorials*. These consist of a network of linked hypertext documents, where the links serve to guide students through the information to be assimilated [3, 4]. Initially, the tutorials were intended for student-centred formative assessment: sneaking in information via the backdoor. Two distinct formats were intentionally developed:

- *Didactic* – essentially a linked series of MCQs where progression through the tutorial depends on correct choice of hypertext links (eg the complement tutorial [3]).
- *Entertaining* – a consciously lighter pedagogical approach, incorporating a prominent narrative style, humour and extensive use of visual material (eg 'A dose of the pox. . . ' and 'The Panama Puzzle' [3]). This style proved to be enormously popular and has been cited as 'an excellent illustration of an interactive-computer-based lesson [in problem-based learning]' [5]. This style of tutorial was extended further in an attempt to test if WWW-based material could be used to promote student reflection by the inclusion of elements such as role play/fictional accounts, humour and open questions [3, 6]. This latter tutorial has also been the subject of a detailed evaluation of user responses to this format [7].

SUMMATIVE ONLINE TUTORIALS

Subsequently, a series of tutorials were written specifically for the purposes of summative assessment. The intention was deliberately to use the potential efficiency gains of summative computer-based assessment without resorting to the perceived limits of traditional MCQ. These developments were initiated because of the following perceived advantages of Web-based assessment:

- Low cost: the HTML format of the tutorials did not require any additional software for authoring or use; cf. commercial packages such as Question Mark or Authorware.
- Student data entry: reduces errors and academic/clerical time required for transcription of data, in addition to improving students' transferable IT skills.
- Data security: answers are automatically time and date-stamped and stored on a secure disk not accessible to students (outside the server tree). Regular backups are required to ensure long-term data integrity, but this can also easily be automated.
- Efficiency gain: resulting from reduction of staff time required for marking and providing student feedback. The *multiplier effect* comes into play

strongly with increasing student numbers. There is a fixed overhead for each tutorial, irrespective of whether it is utilized by 5 or 5,000 students.

The tutorials themselves can be seen online [8]. Briefly, students enter and submit their answers via online forms. The form data is processed by a CGI (common gateway interface) script running on the server that parses and stores the data and generates a reply for the user. Each submission received is stored in the form of a single line in a tab-delimited text file. This is stored in a secure area not accessible to students (outside the server tree) and is automatically time and date-stamped. In response, each student receives a time and date-stamped receipt for their submission. The data is passed to a Microsoft Excel spreadsheet, which marks the questions and generates an annotated report using the spreadsheet formulae to 'mark' the answers (number within acceptable range, word matched, etc). The report generated is extracted from the spreadsheet and personalized comments are e-mailed back to students via a simple Unix shell script [8]. This system is highly efficient in terms of resource usage, requires no specialized software and, most importantly, encourages student motivation by providing interaction with the tutor, ie all students receive a personalized report on their performance without additional staff input.

The great problem for all forms of computer-based assessment, irrespective of format, is data authenticity. The problems arise from a number of sources:

- User identification. Although it is straightforward to use simple identification methods such as password access to WWW documents and personal smartcards are promised in the near future, none of the available technical solutions make it possible to ensure the identity of a user at a remote client.
- Collaboration. Even if a remote user can be positively identified, this does not guard against score improvement by collaboration. It could be suggested that if students use this route to improve test scores, they have gained a valuable transferable skill. Unfortunately, collaboration makes it impossible to accurately gauge individual student abilities and therefore to provide an appropriate response.

The only practicable solution to these problems currently available is to block book a computer laboratory and to carry out summative assessment under examination conditions. In addition, we use Server Side Includes (SSI) to control time/location availability of the tutorial documents [9]. We also use this powerful technique as a general courseware management tool; for example, online lecture notes are delivered the day after the lecture at Leicester but are constantly available over the WWW elsewhere. Since we only use the summative tutorials as a small part (10 per cent) of the overall assessment, the tutorials are conducted as workshops in which we encourage group working. This has further benefits in terms of student responses to the tutorial material (see section on outcomes below).

EVEN FURTHER FROM MCQS

Although the summative tutorials described above have had very positive learning outcomes, we wished to be able to use the more innovative and popular format of the formative tutorials for assessment purposes. This requires tracking of user progress though the series of tutorial documents. Although it is possible to do this by analysis of server logs or constructing each page of the tutorial as a WWW form with the link to the next page via the submit button, which writes to a dedicated logfile via a server CGI/Perl script [7], these methods are laborious and require considerable staff time.

The solution chosen was to use browser 'cookies' (persistent client side information) [10]. A cookie is a small piece of information sent by a Web server to a Web browser so the server can later read it back from that browser. This allows the server to register, maintain and retrieve context-sensitive information from the browser for identification purposes or to track accumulative events between client requests to hypertext transport protocol (HTTP), eg passwords, user IDs or personal preferences [11]. Each cookie is dynamically generated by a script that is prompted by a browser event. A script is usually written in a programming language, close to natural language and more intelligible than hexadecimal machine code. This may be a CGI script or, as in our case, JavaScript. JavaScript (like Java) is an object-oriented language. Put simply, JavaScript can manipulate certain elements of a hypertext mark-up language (HTML) page, depending on the document object model of the client browser, giving a level of interactivity (and appearance of intelligence) not possible with static HTML code, eg remembering people's names, the time/date, performing calculations, etc, and hence write HTML in an interactive fashion ('on the fly'). JavaScript's security model is designed to prevent access to client machines and browsers, for example any attempts to read, write or print a file, but there are specialist technologies that extend JavaScript's capabilities in this area, for instance Netscape Communicator's *signed objects* [12]. However, JavaScript will write to the browser page cache and the browser cookie file, where client side information is stored.

Our JavaScript-powered 'smart' summative tutorial [13] uses JavaScript to:

- track the path a user takes through the tutorial documents;
- calculate a score (running total) depending on correct or wrong choices and on the marking scheme set;
- write a non-persistent cookie (which expires at the end of the 'session', ie when the user quits the browser) to the client, which records the score and reports it onscreen to the user.

Unfortunately, JavaScript is not yet a truly cross-platform or cross-browser language, limited partly by differences in the document object models used by the various browsers [14]. At the present time, the script works with the following:

- Netscape 3 or 4 (any computer);
- Microsoft Internet Explorer (MSIE) 4 for Windows (any version).

However, it does not work with:

- Netscape 1 (which is not JavaScript-enabled);
- Netscape 2 (which has bugs in the JavaScript implementation);
- MSIE 3 (which incorporates Jscript not JavaScript);
- MSIE 4 for Macintosh (which has a bug in the JavaScript implementation).

All of the files described below are available for download [15]. Because of the problems listed above, the first stage is to screen browsers to ensure they are compatible with the script. This is done by the file 'start.html'. This refers unsuitable browsers to the file 'warn.html'. The file 'template.html' is edited to create the tutorial pages. There are two basic types of page that can make up the tutorial: text-based questions (equivalent to MCQs) and image-based questions (including imagemaps).

However, any WWW-compatible format can be incorporated into the tutorial by editing the template.html file. The template document contains no <BODY> tag. This is deliberate: the <BODY> tag is written by the script itself. If you know a little about JavaScript, it is fairly easy to work out how the script works from the comment lines ('//'). Otherwise, it is a simple matter to edit defined lines of the template file to create a tutorial [15]. 'JavaScript URLs' are used so that the hypertext links call a JavaScript function, which then updates the score: <A HREF="javascript: onClick="runningTotal(a);">An answer</A> [11]. The letter in brackets ('a' in this example) refers to an instance of the object type 'Answer', whose value has been set by the script: a=new Answer('true'); etc.

The following two modifications both add to the functionality of the tutorial. Instead of including the script in every page, it is preferable to call the script as a JavaScript header file. To set this up, two more files are required: 'tutorial.js' and 'template2.html' [15]. This has two advantages. First, assuming client browser caching is on, the client only needs to call the script from the server once, so the tutorial runs faster, with less load on the server. Second, although the script-marking array was deliberately written in a cryptic fashion to deter users from cracking the marking code via the page source code, by serving a separate JavaScript header file, this is even more difficult, since the marking array is no longer contained in the page source.

For the purposes of this tutorial, the JavaScript code rewrites the score on each page, depending on the value of the cookie. This avoids the need for forced reloading of pages.

The second modification allows users to submit their scores from the last page of the tutorial via a WWW-based form. To take advantage of this feature, a CGI script appropriate to the server must be used to process form data, since

JavaScript has no file management capabilities. A working example can be seen online at the URL below [13].

OUTCOMES

Although there was a considerable overhead in setting up each of the tutorial formats initially, editing templates to produce new tutorials of the same style is relatively simple. The initial staff input into the project has been amply repaid by the resulting efficiency gain. From the summative tutorials [8], approximately 3,000 student answers have been recorded, marked and personalized responses given over the last three years at a cost of less than six hours' staff time. Approximately 150 student answers have been recorded using the JavaScript 'smart' tutorial over a four-month period with no additional input, allowing staff time to be directed to academic follow-up rather than routine activity.

However, efficiency gains are only a small part of the benefit of this approach; altered student responses to 'difficult' material are much more important. Although not intentional, early on we discovered that the WWW-based format had a pronounced effect on student reaction to the content of the summative tutorials. All of the tutorial formats described in this chapter have been developed for students of Biological Sciences at Leicester University. Many of these students do not have an advanced-level Maths qualification and many were attracted to Biology because of its perceived non-mathematical nature (cf. physics or chemistry). The content of the summative tutorials is biologically relevant arithmetic and algebraic problems, material that normally causes considerable anxiety to this student population. However, the subject matter of the tutorials is not revealed to students in advance, who simply turn up to the computer laboratory at the allotted time and download the tutorial pages from the link on the course timetable. The tutorials are run as a workshop exercise and collaboration is encouraged. The interaction between students and the familiar WWW format are powerful distractors, which greatly reduce the stress that is otherwise experienced when encountering this subject matter. Student responses to these tutorials, as measured by course questionnaires, are highly positive.

CONCLUSIONS

MCQs are a crude measure of student ability. While they offer a potential efficiency gain in saving staff time, they are limiting in terms of pedagogical outcome. The online tutorial formats described in this chapter are much better suited to a resource-rich open learning environment incorporating open access to the WWW. Summative tutorial formats offer much the same efficiency gain as MCQs but have the additional benefit of a highly positive student reaction to the format, encouraging group working and a more accurate reflection of the true academic potential of all students. Never mind the width, feel the quality!

REFERENCES

1 http://www-micro.msb.le.ac.uk/mcqs/mcq.html
2 The Computer Assisted Teaching and Learning (CASTLE) Project (http://www.le.ac.uk/cc/ltg/castle/)
3 http://www-micro.msb.le.ac.uk/tutorials/tutorials.html
4 Cann, A J (1997) Working with the Web: a case study at the University of Leicester, *Life Sciences Educational Computing*, **8** (2), pp 20–22 (http://www.liv.ac.uk/ctibiol/lsec/July97.pdf)
5 Martorella, P H (1999) Concept learning and higher-level thinking, in *Classroom Teaching Skills*, ed James M Cooper, pp175–176, 6th edn, Houghton Mifflin, Boston
6 Cann, A J and Seale, J K (1997) How now mad cow: educating the reflective practitioner, *Computers in Biology Education* (CUBE) (http://www.liv.ac.uk/ctibiol/vCUBE97/html/alan_cann.html
7 Cann, A J (1999) Approaches to the evaluation of online learning materials, *Innovations in Education and Training International*, **36**, pp 44–50
8 http://www-micro.msb.le.ac.uk/demo/tut2.html
9 http://www-micro.msb.le.ac.uk/demo/ssi.html
10 http://home.netscape.com/newsref/std/cookie_spec.html
11 http://home.netscape.com/eng/mozilla/3.0/handbook/javascript/advtopic.htm
12 http://developer.netscape.com/viewsource/goodman_sscripts.html
13 http://www-micro.msb.le.ac.uk/tutorials/balti/start.html
14 http://developer.netscape.com/viewsource/goodman_stds.htm
15 http://www-micro.msb.le.ac.uk/demo/diy.html

5

Computer anxiety in students: should computer-based assessment be used at all?

Mark Brosnan

> As the number of students entering higher education increases along with the requirement for greater cost efficiency, the potential benefits from computer-based learning and computer-based assessment are great.
>
> Whittington and Sclater, 1998

INTRODUCTION

While embracing the potential benefits of computer-based assessments within higher education, Whittington and Sclater also acknowledge that the primary motivation for the increasing role of computers within education largely revolves around managing the assessment of an increasing number of students with decreasing financial provisions. Using computers within the assessment process can take many forms such as requiring students to word process their written work, using objective test examinations assessed with optical mark readers and assessments entered directly via a computer terminal. As the primary motivation for the use of computers within education has been financial, the increase in the use of computers within the assessment process has developed largely unchecked. The aim of this chapter is to highlight that individuals' levels of computer anxiety impact upon assessments that involve computers. Computer-based assessment will be shown to disadvantage specific groups of students. This is implicit in a more guarded evaluation of the benefits of computers within education by Lens (1994), who states: 'In the absence of computer anxiety, computer-assisted learning can enhance several types of intrinsic student motivation because it allows for highly individualized learning.'

This chapter will highlight that, while 'in the absence of computer anxiety' the benefits of 'computer-based learning and computer-based assessment are great', in the *presence* of computer anxiety the *disadvantages* of computer-based learning and computer-based assessment are great.

COMPUTER ANXIETY

Despite initial perceptions that anxiety about computers would be a transitory phenomenon mainly affecting older individuals, research has identified that in fact computer anxiety is becoming increasingly prevalent (Brosnan, 1998a). Computer anxiety is defined as: 'an irrational anticipation of fear evoked by the thought of using (or actually using) computers, the effects of which result in avoiding, or minimizing, computer usage' (Brosnan, 1998a,p 17).

Computer anxiety can manifest itself from a feeling of mild discomfort through to palpitations and panic attacks when using a computer. There has been a great deal of research into the causes and correlates of computer anxiety, prompting Modafsky and Kwon (1994) to assert that 'computer anxiety is a real phenomenon' and, with the increasing role of computers within education, that 'lessening the resistance to computer technology is more important than ever before'.

Children at primary school (aged 5 to 11) through to university students have been found to register as computer-anxious (Brosnan, 1998b, c). Indeed, a large proportion of the computer anxiety research has focused upon students in higher education, with estimates that as many as 50 per cent of students are computer-anxious (Rosen and Maguire, 1990). Additionally, this phenomenon has been found to be universal, with computer-anxious students being identified in the US, Europe, Japan and China (Weil and Rosen, 1995).

One of the most consistent findings within these samples is that females register as more computer-anxious than males (see Brosnan and Davidson, 1994; Maurer, 1994; Whitely, 1997 for reviews) and this undoubtedly underlines the continuing decline in the proportions of females taking Computer Science undergraduate programmes. A recent review of higher education applications highlighted that while many females chose to study a language (73 per cent) or social science (63 per cent), only 16 per cent of applicants for undergraduate Computer Science courses were female (Brosnan, 1998d).

The discomfort that computers create in students can therefore not be underestimated. Even those who might appear to be using computers effectively may be uncomfortable. Indeed, those who gain technology experience and use the technology, still prefer not to use it. In a study of 444 first-year students at an American university, 61 per cent of high-experience users reported strongly avoiding computers (Larson and Smith, 1994).

COMPUTER ANXIETY AND ASSESSMENT

It has long been thought that anxiety has a detrimental impact upon performance generally (Friend, 1982) and when learning to use computers specifically (Bloom and Hautaluoma, 1990; Modafsky and Kwon, 1994). Anxious individuals devote cognitive capacity to off-task efforts such as worrying about their performance. Thus, with a limited capacity working memory system, anxious individuals will take longer on tasks and will make more errors (Rosen and Maguire, 1990). Specifically, computer anxiety can lead to 'simplification of conceptual reasoning, heightened polarization and extremity of judgement and pre-emption of attention, working memory and processing resources' (Tseng *et al*, 1998). Individuals high in computer anxiety will therefore under-perform in computer-based versions of assessment.

STANDARDIZATION OF COMPUTER-BASED ASSESSMENT

Partly arising from these concerns, psychologists in particular have been interested in the impact of the medium upon the assessment. Given the prevalence of computer anxiety in higher education, 'individuals who are uncomfortable with computer use may show negative reactions to a computerized test, but no such reactions to a conventional one' (Tseng *et al* 1998).

The American Psychological Association's (1986) *Guidelines for Computer-based tests and interpretations* calls for equivalence to be established between the computerized and original versions of the assessments. This necessitates comparisons of means, distributions, ranking of scores and correlations with other variables. Tseng *et al* (1998) argue that for equivalence to be truly established, individual characteristics should not differentially affect a person's responses to a particular administration mode of an assessment.

Thus, equating computer-based assessments with pencil and paper tests must be explored for fair and useful assessment (Wise, 1997). As one might expect, computer anxiety only becomes a relevant variable when the assessment is computer-based and not when the assessment is pen-and-pencil based (Tseng *et al*, 1997; 1998). The salience of computer anxiety in computer-based assessment is highlighted in the finding that negative feelings towards the computer can increase during the assessment itself (Gaudron, 1998).

Most of the research explicitly comparing computer-based versions with a pencil-and-paper-based version of an assessment has taken place within the field of clinical psychology. As with education, computer-based assessments of clinical disorders (such as depression and phobias) have been developed primarily in response to the demands placed upon highly trained professionals. While some research suggests that computer-based assessment offers a reliable, inexpensive, accessible and time-efficient means of psychological assessment (Kobak *et al*, 1996), other research reports that computer-based assessments offer unacceptably low levels of reliability (Brugha *et al*, 1996). Ross *et al* (1994) conclude that, with a small number of exceptions, computer-based psychological assessments showed poor agreement with (human) clinician-based assessments. Despite this, research into computerizing existing pencil and paper assessments has continued, largely as a result of the potential cost-effectiveness of the computerized system. Yokley *et al* (1990) estimate that computerized clinical assessments can represent as little as 20 per cent of the cost of a human clinician's assessment. This has lead First (1994) to propose two fundamental principles that should underlie all computer-based assessment: (1) a human must remain as a necessary component of the assessment process to ensure validity and (2) this human must be one who completely understands the strengths and limitations of the computer-assisted assessment procedure.

Within the educational field, embracing these principles may take a fair amount of investment from the educator. The enormity of this task is reflected in the title of Race and McDowell's (1996) text, *500 computing tips for teachers and lecturers*, especially as many educators are themselves computer-anxious (Rosen and Weil, 1995). Many educational practitioners avoid undertaking educational research into computer-based assessment, as their own prior experience with technology, statistics and research design have produced insecurity and anxiety in the practitioner (Dereshiwsky, 1992).

Off-the-shelf test banks of multiple-choice questions for student exams are available to educators. Indeed, these are often supplied free to the educator if a related text is placed upon the course's reading list (particularly in the US). This widespread practice, designed to sell the textbook, reflects the reality of the situation. The justification for using computer-based assessment often revolves around easing the load of the academic. Providing the computer-based assessment simply extends this principle, while simultaneously violating First's two principles of computer-based assessment (see above). This is particularly salient as the format of the assessment, whether multiple-choice or open-ended questions, determines the score achieved by the student (Schuwirth *et al*, 1996). Understanding exactly what impact the format of the assessment has upon what is being assessed is an essential part of First's second principle. A move towards computer-assisted assessment, with optical mark readers for example, can result in increased use of the multiple-choice format.

BIASES IN COMPUTER-BASED ASSESSMENT

In addition to technology shaping the format of the assessment, the use of computers in assessment can have a detrimental impact upon the performance of computer-anxious individuals. That is to say, those who are computer-anxious will under-achieve within higher education, not because of their academic ability but because of the computer-based medium of the assessment selected by the institution. A case in point is the requirement by many higher education institutions for students to word-process their course work. For those who are not computer-anxious, the medium through which the essay is presented (handwritten or word-processed) does not impact upon the quality of the work. Computer-anxious students, however, are apt to perform better when their essay is composed with pen and paper (Wolfe, 1995). Tseng *et al* (1998) also directly compared computer-based and pen-and-paper-based versions of a visual search task and a sentence verification task. The authors were investigating the impact of computer anxiety upon being able to find a specified letter in a whole array of letters and the decision time to determine if a sentence was true or not. While computer anxiety did not correlate with performance upon the pencil-and-paper versions, there were significant correlations for the computer-based version. Those who were computer-anxious were slower to detect both the target letter in the visual array and whether the sentence was true or not. The more anxious individuals were, the slower they were to perform the tasks. Additionally, prior computer experience has been shown to be a significant factor in computer-based test performance. Students confident with computers were able to complete the assessments faster (Gaudron, 1998).

Computer-confident students with prior experience therefore do better in computer-based assessments. From the computer anxiety research, we would predict that the increase in computer involvement within the assessment process will have a detrimental impact upon female students' performance compared to their male peers. This does not reflect female students' academic abilities, but the higher levels of computer anxiety found within female students. Even if equivalence is demonstrated for computer-based learning and assessment within a (male-dominated) Computer Science programme, it cannot be assumed that this equivalence will extend beyond this academic domain.

WHAT CAN BE DONE?

Hopefully, this chapter has highlighted the significance of considering computer-anxious individuals when developing computer-based assessments. One strategy would be to make computer usage optional and to allow those who were computer-anxious to avoid technology. Indeed, there are calls for 'techno-luddites' to formally reject all technologies that are imposed upon us (Sale, 1996).

However, computer-based learning and assessment are seen as increasingly necessary with the expanding number of undergraduate students. Many higher education institutions also include IT skills as some of the transferable skills that they hope to impart to produce a well-rounded graduate. Indeed, it is now a requirement at some American universities that new students own their own computer when they start at the university.

Computer courses *per se*, however, are ineffective for those who are computer-anxious and even increase levels of computer anxiety (Carlson and Wright, 1993). Individually tailored computer anxiety reduction programmes often help to reduce computer anxiety. Details of how to achieve this are presented in *Technophobia: the psychological impact of information technology* (Brosnan, 1998a). This embraces many psychological principles to reduce computer anxiety generally, rather than teach a specific software package. For example, highly computer-anxious individuals learn significantly better from computer-aided learning that embraces a collaborative element to the learning (Keeler and Anson, 1995). In some cases, it may be possible to build a collaborative element into assessment, too. As computer-anxious individuals are likely to self-select away from any computer-related experience, compulsory use of technology can overcome this only if the computer-related experience is structured and tailored to the needs of the computer-anxious individual (Arch and Cummins, 1989).

It is the responsibility of the educators to evaluate the impact that the computer-based medium of their educational provision has upon student learning and achievement. Only then can the impact of computers be shown to be unbiased. Obviously, this has to be done with great care to ensure that computer-anxious individuals are included within the evaluation of computer-based assessment. Asking for volunteers to undertake a computer-based version of the assessment will undoubtedly bias the sample to computer confident individuals for whom the medium has little impact upon their performance. Many researchers do not include details of who did not want to take part in their evaluation. Spinhoven *et al* (1993) represent an exception, reporting that less than half (46 per cent) of those asked agreed to undertake a computerized version of their assessment.

SUMMARY

Many students are computer-anxious, as are many of their educators. When this is the case, performance upon computer-based assessment will be impaired and females in particular are likely to be disadvantaged. Provision of structured anxiety reduction programmes is recommended. Full equivalence between computer-based and pencil-and-paper-based versions of assessment should be demonstrated. This necessitates the evaluation of the impact of computer-based assessment upon computer-anxious individuals.

REFERENCES

American Psychological Association (1986) *Guidelines for computer-based tests and interpretations*, APA, Washington, DC

Arch, E and Cummins, D (1989) Structured and unstructured exposure to computers: sex differences in attitude and use among college students, *Sex Roles,* 20, pp 245–54

Bloom, A J and Hautaluoma, J E (1990) Anxiety management training as a strategy for enhancing computer user performance, *Computers in Human Behaviour.* **6** (4), 23–46

Brosnan, M (1998a) *Technophobia: the psychological impact of information technology.* Routledge (Europe)

Brosnan, M (1998b) The role of psychological gender in the computer-related attitudes and attainments of primary school children (aged 6–11), *Computers and Education,* **30** (3/4), pp 203–08

Brosnan, M (1998c) The impact of psychological gender, gender-related perceptions, significant others and the introducer of technology upon computer anxiety in students, *Journal of Educational Computing Research,* **18** (1), pp 63–78

Brosnan, M (1998d) The implications for academic attainment of perceived gender-appropriateness upon spatial task performance, *British Journal of Educational Psychology,* **68**, pp 203–15

Brosnan, M and Davidson, M (1994) Computerphobia: is it a particularly female phenomenon? *The Psychologist,* **7** (2), pp 73–78

Brugha, T, Kaul, A, Dignon, A and Teather, D (1996) Present state examination by microcomputers: objectives and experience of preliminary steps, *International Journal of Methods in Psychiatric Research,* **6** (3), pp 143–51

Carlson, R and Wright, D (1993) Computer anxiety and communication apprehension: relationship and introductory college course effects, *Journal of Educational Computing Research,* **9** (3), pp 329–38

Dereshiwsky, M (1992) Making hi-tech my tech. Helpful hints for educational practitioners on planning and conducting educational research with the help of technical specialists (ED354215)

First, M (1994) Computer assessment of DSM-III-R diagnoses. *Psychiatric Annals*, **24** (1), pp 25–29

Friend, K E (1982) Stress and performance: effects of subjective work load and time urgency, *Personal Psychology*, **35**, pp 623–33

Gaudron, J (1998) The effects of computer anxiety and past computer experience on computerized test performance, *Travail Humain*, **61** (3), pp 263–80

Keeler, C and Anson, R (1995) An assessment of co-operative learning used for basic computer skills instruction in the college classroom, *Journal of Educational Computing Research*, **12** (4), pp 379–93

Kobak, K, Greist, J, Jefferson, J and Katzelnick, D (1996) Computer-administered clinical rating scales: a review, *Psychopharmacology*, **127** (4), pp 291–301

Larson, J and Smith, M (1994) An assessment of the computer literacy and the computer attitudes of incoming first year students at the University of Wisconsin-Eau Claire. Paper presented at the National Convention of the Association for Education and Communications, Nashville, TN

Lens, W (1994) Personal computers in the learning environment and student motivation. *Scandinavian Journal of Educational Research*, **38** (3/4), pp 219–30

Maurer, M M (1994) Computer anxiety correlates and what they tell us: a literature review, *Computers in Human Behaviour*, **10** (3), pp 369–76

Modafsky, N I and Kwon, I W (1994) Attributes affecting computer-aided decision-making – a literature survey, *Computers in Human Behaviour*, **10** (3), pp 299–323

Race, P and McDowell, S (1996) *500 computing tips for teachers and lecturers*, Kogan Page, London

Rosen, L and Maguire, P (1990) Myths and realities of computerphobia: a meta-analysis, *Anxiety Research*, 3, pp 175–91

Rosen, L and Weil, M (1995) Computer availability, computer experience and technophobia among public school teachers, *Computers in Human Behaviour*, **11** (1), pp 9–31

Ross, H, Swinson, R, Larkin, E and Doumani, S (1994) Diagnosing comorbidity in substance abusers: computer assessment and clinical validation, *Journal of Nervous and Mental Diseases*, **182** (10), pp 556–63

Sale, K (1996) *Rebels against the future: lessons for the computer age*, Quartet Books Ltd

Schuwirth, L, van-der-Vleuten, C, Stoffers, H and Peperkamp, A (1996) Computerized long-menu questions as an alternative to open-ended questions in computerized assessment, *Medical Education*, **30** (1), pp 50–55

Spinhoven, P, Labbe, M and Rombourts, R (1993) Feasibility of computerized psychological testing with psychiatric outpatients, *Journal of Clinical Psychology*, **49** (3), pp 440–47

Tseng, H-M, Macleod, H and Wright, P (1997) Computer anxiety and measurement of mood change, *Computers in Human Behavior*, **13** (3), pp 305–16

Tseng, H-M, Tiplady, B, Macleod, H and Wright, P (1998) Computer anxiety: a comparison of pen-based personal digital assistants, conventional computer and paper assessment of mood and performance, *British Journal of Psychology*, **89**, pp 599–610

Weil, M and Rosen, L (1995) The psychological impact of technology from a global perspective: a study of technological sophistication and technophobia in university students from 23 countries, *Computers in Human Behaviour*, **11** (1), pp 95–133

Whitely, B (1997) Gender differences in computer-related attitudes and behaviour: a meta-analysis, *Computers in Human Behaviour*, **13** (1), pp 1–22

Whittington, C and Sclater, N (1998) Building and testing a virtual university, *Computers and Education*, **30** (1/2), pp 41–47

Wise, S (1997) Overview of practical issues in a CAT program. Paper presented at the Annual Meeting of the National Council on Measurement in Education, Chicago, Il

Wolfe, E (1995) The influence of computers upon student performance on a direct writing assessment. Paper presented at the Annual Meeting of the American Educational Research Association, San Francisco, CA

Yokley, J, Coleman, D and Yates, B (1990) Cost effectiveness of three child mental health assessment methods: computer assisted assessment is effective and inexpensive, *Journal of Mental Health Administration*, **17** (1), pp 99–107

6

Validating formative and summative assessment

Malcolm Perkin

INTRODUCTION

Assessment is to check out students: how much do they know, what can they do, did they improve, where does the class go from here? The process of evaluation, on the other hand, is to check out teaching. In the context of evaluating computer-based assessments it is trying to answer two simple questions. Was an assessment accurate? And was it helpful? Unfortunately, the answers are not always as simple as the questions! Assessments can be evaluated in different ways and at different levels. In the early days of computer-aided learning, the evaluations tended to be of 'knowledge gained'. Now, there is a move towards more complete and more complex assessments, with attempts to measure how new knowledge is utilized or applied, the related topic of problem-solving skills acquired by a student and longer-term learning outcome ('retention and use') measures. The last measures are really behavioural measures; it is inferred that deep leaning occurred in the students who continue to use new knowledge and skills. In principle, it should also be possible to measure the extent to which new knowledge becomes integrated with other (pre-existing) behaviour.

ASSESSMENT AND THE JOHARI WINDOW

The timing of an assessment is crucial – assessments of individual students taken a little earlier or a little later in their course of study will produce widely different results and so, when it comes to evaluation of the assessment process, great care must be taken to standardize the conditions under which the assessments were done. The Johari window is a well-known model of the learning process that makes it easier to visualize a given assessment as a snapshot of the complex process of learning, taken at a particular moment. Luft and Ingham published their account of the Johari window in 1955, which they described at the time as 'a graphic model of interpersonal relations' (Figure 6.1).

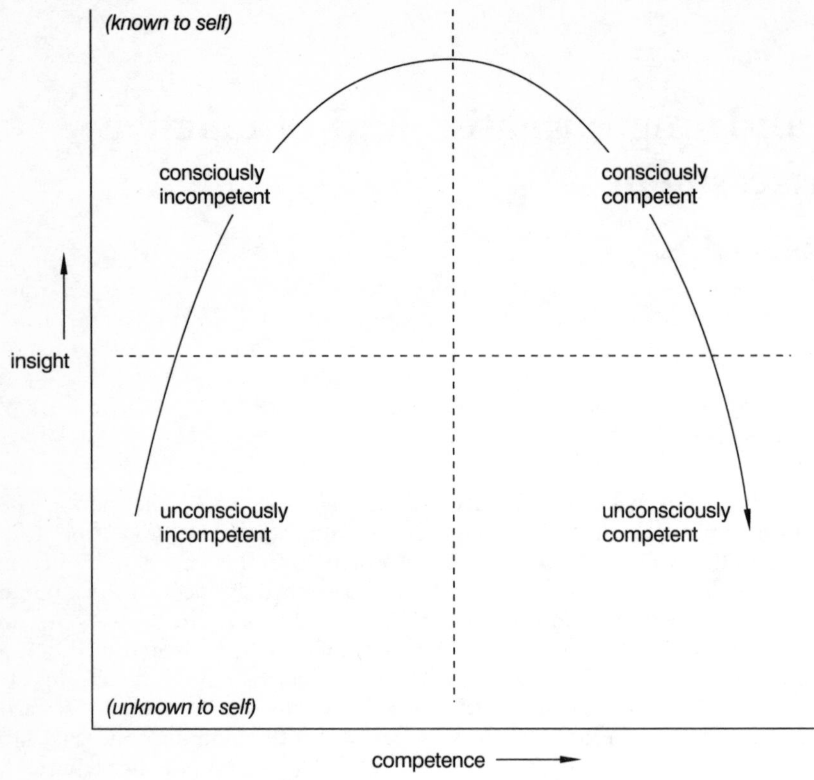

Figure 6.1 *The Johari window* (© Luft and Ingham 1955)

Since then, over a period of about forty years, the nature of the learning process has gradually become more clearly understood and, in particular, there has been an increasing realization that most learning (even in children) takes place in the androgogic mode, that most individuals learn when they see the need and have the opportunity and that education should encourage the student to manipulate his or her new knowledge so as to integrate it with what was there before.

As a result, the Johari window has opened up. What started out as a tool for describing interpersonal relationships has subtly changed. Now, its chief use is as a model of the processes of adult learning. It provides a valuable and vivid image of the situation where a student, by becoming aware that he or she has a knowledge gap to fill, acquires motivation to learn. I suggest that it is the *language* of the Johari window that appeals to us because it describes this psychological scene so clearly: the learner becomes aware, suddenly, of what he or she does not know and, with the realization that 'I am incompetent', remedial action will follow.

Beittel (1984), among others, examined the relationship between experience and the acquisition of competence in educational settings. A student approaches a new subject for the first time without a clear idea of its extent or ramifications, that is, without understanding the *knowledge space* of the topic (a state of unconscious incompetence). As the course of study progresses, he or she realizes the extent of his or her ignorance (consciously incompetent) and then, through further listening, reading and interaction starts to grasp the new knowledge (the beginning of unconscious competence). At this point, there is a need to test new knowledge and understanding, to use feedback, to define what is and isn't understood. The student may cycle between these different states many times while learning a subject, with a different Johari profile each time. That is to say, the student will have a unique, personal mix (of unconscious and conscious competence and incompetence) in different aspects of the subject being studied before eventually reaching an adequate level of understanding and becoming consciously competent.

The *raison d'être* for individual formative assessments at the start of a course of study is to take a snapshot of these transient individual patterns of knowledge and ignorance. This is not news; good teachers have assessed their students' strengths and weaknesses throughout history. Teachers use informal performance assessments all the time. In the absence of formal assessment tools, they do so intuitively. By making formative assessment *formal*, it is possible to reduce bias and error and the argument for doing formal formative assessments by computer is that it reduces bias and error further – as well as simplifying the administration (Bennett, 1993, Bloom, Hastings and Madaus, 1964; Clough, Davis and Sumner, 1984). Students' learning needs have traditionally been assessed in a subjective, error-prone way and, perhaps in some quarters, there has been a reluctance to assess the extent of the problem or acknowledge a need to address it. Recently, however, the topic of educational standards and the problem of error have been addressed explicitly. For example, Wilson (1998) described how people are categorized in educational settings and highlighted the dangers of hidden misclassification.

VALIDITY AND RELIABILITY

With or without computers, it is often difficult to rate an educational assessment. Firstly, there is the question of selectivity. Assessments must always be selective in what they attempt to gauge inasmuch as they can only measure a few of the complex processes going on inside the student. Reducing complicated individuals to simple statistics is, however, a necessary feature of assessment, not only to allow comparison between students but also for the practical reason that otherwise assessment would not get done (resources being limited). Secondly, assessments are essentially subjective. Like all human constructs, they tend to be biased by a range of unpredictable factors such as the interaction between individuals, past experience, the vagaries of individual perception and differing degrees of familiarity with the subject. This is still true, although perhaps to a lesser extent, where knowledge is supposedly scientific and objective. Thirdly, what is being measured changes over time, sometimes quite rapidly. Finally, not all the measured changes are due to what is being actively or consciously learned: extraneous influences can play a much bigger part than anyone realizes.

Which of these problems can computer-aided assessments help to solve? I suggest that computer-based methods have the potential to become both more reliable and more valid than traditional assessments... under the right circumstances. They can be used to complement the unreliable human perspective by providing an unbiased, tailored evaluation of each student's learning needs. They can also supplement the necessarily limited range of local assessment resources by being distributed in electronic format countrywide or worldwide, with the same tests being widely used and hence becoming better and better validated over time (an iterative process involving many investigators, subjects and settings).

Standing in the way, however, is the large, complex and so far largely unsolved problem of evaluation: how to demonstrate that the results of computer-based assessments are indeed valid and reliable. Different means of assessment, each with their own scales, tend to be used during a course of study. Consequently, it is difficult to decide about the overall validity and reliability of the system, which depends on the *quality* of its individual components as well as the administrative procedures associated with the system. Rafilson (1991) discussed the extent to which evidence of validity obtained in one setting can be generalized to another without further study of validity in the new situation, as follows:

> The extent to which predictive or concurrent evidence of validity can be used as criterion-related evidence in new situations is, in large measure, a function of accumulated research. In the past, judgments about the generalization or transportability of validity were often based on nonquantitative reviews of the literature. Today, quantitative techniques have been more frequently employed to study the generalization of validity. Both approaches have been used to support inferences about the degree to which the validity of a given predictor variable can generalize from one situation or setting to another similar set of circumstances. If validity generalization evidence is limited, then local criterion-related evidence of validity may be necessary to justify the use of a test. If, on the other hand, validity generalization evidence is extensive, then situation-specific evidence of validity may not be required.
>
> Rafilson, 1991

Reliability is defined in terms of the consistency of scores across evaluators or over time. An assessment is considered reliable when the same results occur regardless of when the assessment occurs or who does the scoring. There should be compelling evidence to show that results are consistent across raters and across scoring occasions.

PERFORMANCE ASSESSMENT

Performance assessment consists of assessment task(s) and their associated scoring methods (of which there can be more than one). Following Messick (1994), performance assessments can be divided into two broad categories:

- task-centred performance assessments (to evaluate *specific* skills and competencies);
- construct-centred performance assessments (to access and sample from a *domain* of skills and competencies).

Task-centred performance assessments tend to consist of tests where there is little student control and scoring is tailored to measure performance on specific assessment tasks. On the other hand, *construct-centred* performance assessments consist of tasks that may allow a fair amount of student control; they often utilize a generic scoring rubric (or some other, non-specific criteria) for judging student performance.

Task-centred performance assessments are easier to use and to score (because the scoring rubrics are specific), but they may not necessarily convey to students the principles behind the tasks. The reverse is true for construct-centred assessments. Construct-centred performance assessments are often harder to administer but, because they relate to general skills and competencies within the domain, they are better at helping students and teachers to recognize what is of importance within the material to be learned.

An authentic performance assessment measures the ability to apply knowledge to real problems and provides an opportunity for the learner to be actively involved. Baker, O'Neil and Linn (1993) have described the following characteristics of an ideal performance assessment:

- the learner performs open-ended tasks;
- higher-order skills are tested;
- the learner must use context-sensitive strategies;
- complex problems requiring several types of performance are used;
- students may be assessed either as individuals or in groups;
- the assessment may allow a significant degree of student choice.

Evaluating an assessment means addressing these questions (after Stiggins, 1994):

- Exactly which concept, skill, or knowledge is being assessed?
- What should the students know?

- At what level should the students be performing?
- What type of knowledge is being assessed: reasoning, memory or process?

In most cases, students should see the scoring rubrics and other information about the criteria used for assessment (secrecy should be minimal) and perhaps make an attempt at peer review, since self-assessment and self-adjustment are essential steps on the route to improved performance. However, some types of learning (chiefly hands-on activities) may be more readily assessed by means other than performance-based assessments (Wiggins, 1998). In an assessment, individuals must have to apply their knowledge and skills in context, not merely to perform an activity on cue.

One of the potential advantages of computer-based learning, in this context, is that the *process* of learning can be made more visible. Regardless of the context and the teaching methods used, the active involvement and participation of the learner is crucial. In the traditional classroom setting, the teacher's assessment of who is involved and who isn't is subjective. Extrovert students often appear to be more active learners. In a computer-based class, however, the interface between student and coursework is rather different and the computer can log the learner's activity (by recording his or her path through the material, the time taken, the number of key stokes and mouse clicks and so on). These are good data: collected in equal quantities for all students in the class, unbiased by any personal characteristics and directly proportional to the student's level of involvement.

EVALUATING THE UTILITY OF COMPUTER-BASED ASSESSMENT

From the teacher's point of view, the most meaningful way to test the utility of computer-based assessment may be to compare it with what existed before. For research purposes, however, it may be necessary to invest more resources in developing a robust methodology, for example by triangulating the results of a particular formative or summative assessment exercise with other routes of evaluation.

At the same time, a student's ability to use the package should be considered, since apparent differences in learning outcome can arise from variations in the ability of individuals to use the programme as intended. There are several ways in which this can be done, including directly observing the subjects using the package (checking off their actions against a predetermined list), encouraging students to verbalize their thoughts as they work with the package and using qualitative methods such as focus groups where both teachers and students can be asked what they can suggest to improve the assessment, what was most and least valuable about it and, in their opinion, did it meet its objectives? The relevance of a particular package to the group of students can be assessed both within the class (by asking if the subject matter seemed too easy or too difficult and by asking if it told them what they wanted to know) and also externally by analysing the content of a module and comparing with the course syllabus.

It should be reasonably easy to use a programme to plan lessons and set individual student goals and its use should not isolate the student or make mentoring tasks harder to perform. The acid test is that an instructor would not want to teach by an alternative method.

Students should perceive that doing the computer-based assessments is better than the alternatives and should report that courses planned on the basis of computerized formative assessment are successful. Actually performing the assessment should be pleasant, allowing students to come away feeling good and willing to repeat the process when the occasion demands.

Practical considerations such as having adequate documentation and instructions are important, as is the pace of the assessment, the total duration of the activity and the physical environment (including health and safety aspects of the workstation). Effective use of computer-based media also requires that text and hypertext, graphics and animation, pictures, sound and video are appropriately used. In cases where several media are used, their integration should be seamless. Ease of navigation within the package can also be assessed, although in practice navigation difficulties usually present themselves as failure to complete the allocated tasks.

One of the features of a well-designed assessment package is the programme's ability to adapt and evaluation should address this specifically. In other words, a good package will be able to accommodate a wider range of aptitudes and prior knowledge among the students and target the assessment process accordingly. One example of this is adaptive interrogation: all students taking the assessment are asked an identical set of questions in the first round, but subsequently the questions are selected (tailored to the individual) by making use of earlier responses. The student should find these later questions are probing weaknesses and identifying areas of performance risk.

CONCLUSION

There are rich veins of unanswered questions and much research is still needed. Rigorous research methodology is being developed with, among other things, an emphasis on measuring and correcting for factors that potentially confound the association between computer-based assessment and other measures of outcome. For example, the extent to which computer-based assessments may be biased by a learner's IT skill or lack of it. At the same time, a sea change is occurring in most educational establishments. The rate at which new technology is used is increasing and may now increase until computer-based assessment is routine on nearly every course. Then, the task of evaluating assessments should get easier because, with increasing experience, everyone concerned (students, teachers and researchers) will become confident that they know what computer-based assessments really mean: when to trust the results and when not. Once that point is reached, computer-based methods can confidently be used alone in the right circumstances, that is to say, once people believe that what they measure is valid and reliable. The niche for the computer-based assessment of tomorrow is being shaped by the evolving evaluation techniques of today.

REFERENCES

Baker, E L, O'Neil, H F and Linn, R L (1993) Policy and validity prospects for performance-based assessment, *American Psychologist*, **48** (12), pp 1210–1218

Beittel, K (1984) Great swamp fires I have known: competence and the hermeneutics of qualitative experiencing, in *Competence: Inquiries into its meaning and acquisition in educational settings*, ed E Short, pp 105–122, University Press of America, Lanham, MD

Benett, Y (1993) The validity and reliability of assessments and self-assessments of work-based learning, *Assessment and Evaluation in Higher Education*, **18** (2), pp 83–93

Bloom, B, Hastings, J and Madaus, G (1964) *Handbook on formative and summative evaluation of student learning*, McGraw Hill, New York

Clough, E E, Davis, P and Sumner, R (1984) *Assessing pupils: a study of policy and practice*, NFER-Nelson, Windsor

Luft, J and Ingham, H (1955) *The Johari Window: a graphic model for interpersonal relations*, University of California Western Training Lab

Messick, S (1994) The interplay of evidence and consequences in the validation of performance assessments, *Educational Researcher*; **23** (2), pp 13–23

Rafilson, F (1991) *The Case for Validity Generalization*, ERIC Clearinghouse on Tests, Measurement, and Evaluation, Washington, DC

Stiggins, R J (1994) *Student-centered classroom assessment*, Macmillan Publishing Company, New York

Wiggins, G (1998) Teaching to the (authentic) test, *Educational Leadership*, September, pp 41–47

Wilson, N (1998) Educational standards and the problem of error, *Education Policy Analysis Archives*, **6** (10), http://olam.ed.asu.edu/epaa/v6n10/

7

Open-access randomly generated tests: assessment to drive learning

M Thelwall

INTRODUCTION

There are a number of initiatives in education and industry that use computer-based summative assessment tests generated by random factors. Various test creation methods are employed, from bespoke software to spreadsheets and commercial test authoring packages. Both networks of personal computers and the Web are used to deliver the assessment. In some cases, tests are also made available to students beforehand for formative assessment and to serve as a learning resource. A discussion of this will be the main focus of this chapter. We shall start by surveying the types of random-factor-based tests in use and examining the methods used to create them. The educational implications of allowing tests to be released to students in advance and how they can be used to motivate students to study and drive their learning will also be discussed. The focus of the discussion will be on the types of learning outcomes assessed.

TYPES OF RANDOMLY GENERATED TESTS

Random-factor-based tests have been used by many assessors in various ways and for different purposes. One common reason to use different assessments is to combat plagiarism by having a selection of papers or by giving every student a different one. This is useful for coursework assessments taken outside a supervised examination environment and is widely practised on an *ad hoc* basis. One project does this systematically, using Excel to produce personalized printouts for assessments with student ID numbers as the random-factor generators. The same program also prints out a tutor's mark sheet for each test (Simonite *et al*, 1998).

Another innovative way of using individualized tests is practised in some physics classes in the USA. In a number of universities, students are given a weekly set of individualized problems by a computer program and have a week in which to input the correct answers (Thoennessen and Harrison, 1996). The computer marks their answers immediately and allows them as many attempts at each question as they like. Multiple-choice questions are not appropriate in this context and so numerical-answer questions are used instead. This approach requires a larger set of questions than a single test but has the pedagogical advantage of encouraging the students to study the subject more evenly throughout the semester, rather than concentrating on a single test. This methodology is appropriate for subjects requiring many numerical calculations, or for subjects that can be assessed by questions demanding numerical answers, for example maths, statistics, some sciences and technologies and basic computer programming. It is possible to imagine a modification of this approach for multiple-choice questions, where the student would only get one chance at answering but could have the whole week in which to research and ponder the issue. This would require a large question bank to give all students a different set of questions.

Random factors can also be used in a traditional time-constrained computerized assessment test. This has been achieved in maths, statistics, engineering technology, computer programming and information technology (Hunt, 1998; Kapur and Stillman, 1997; Lloyd *et al*, 1996; Thelwall, 1998, Wolverhampton University Computer Assisted Assessment Project, http://cba.scit.wlv.ac.uk). The advantages of having different tests delivered in a computerized assessment are in increased flexibility of test delivery and increased security against cheating. A randomized test could be staggered over a period of days or longer, for example, without compromising test security.

Once a randomly generated test has been written, it may be desirable to allow students to have open access to it for practice and revision. This approach is not only used inside the education sector but also by others such as the US Federal Aviation Authority as well as for some national driving licence tests, including possibly the UK test in the year 2000. The FAA publishes a large multiple-choice question bank for a number of its examinations, such as the parachute rigger test, from which the actual test for any individual is guaranteed to be selected.

METHODS OF GENERATING RANDOM TESTS

There are two main methods of generating random tests: culling from large question banks and constructing from questions already containing random factors. Assessment software normally allows the test owner to build up a personal question bank from which random tests can be generated manually if not automatically. The simplest, but probably most time-consuming method of putting this together is for the lecturer himself or herself to construct each individual question. Many lecturers already have large question banks accumulated over a number of years and can produce a test by selecting a subset or several subsets if the test is going to be taken in more than one time slot. Software such as Question Mark Designer and Question Mark Perception explicitly support this operation (Question Mark Computing Ltd, http://www.qmark.com). Increasingly, however, instructors' versions of student texts come with large electronic question banks that can speed up this process.

A common sense solution to the problem of needing access to a large question bank seems to be for academics in the same discipline to pool resources and produce combined subject question banks. This has been attempted in a number of disciplines, for example, in medicine, by MedWeb (MedWeb Computer Assisted Assessment, http://medweb.bham.ac.uk/http/caa). There are, however, a number of practical problems with producing pooled question banks. Firstly, there has to be an agreed format for storing the questions. Ideally, it would be convenient for the retrieval of the questions for delivery through a variety of different assessment software. Standards-based approaches to this have been proposed by Question Mark Computing and others, based upon the standard generalized mark-up language (SGML). SGML was used to write HTML, the language of Web pages, and is an obvious choice for standardizing the encoding of assessment questions. If a standard was adopted then assessment engines could be expected to support it, solving the question-storage format problem.

A more fundamental problem is that of agreeing standards to classify the questions themselves. There are two main issues here: classifying the subject material of the questions and classifying their difficulty. Even in relatively static subjects such as mathematics there is great diversity: no two universities seem to have identical content in their introductory maths modules, for example. There seems little hope of producing question banks to cover anything as large as a module without resorting to classification and subdivision, but any classification would have to be reached on the basis of widely recognized standards in order to be meaningful. Classifying question difficulty is probably more difficult than a subject-based classification. Lecturers will differ within institutions and certainly between institutions as to the relative difficulties of questions and their relevance to assessing particular groups of students. Furthermore, some lecturers may prefer different styles of questions to others, possibly as a result of using the same subject material to assess different learning outcomes. A practical solution to this problem, suggested by David Davies in the context of MedWeb, is for lecturers to point the students at the question bank, telling them that their examination will be chosen from it, but for the lecturers themselves to select only those questions considered appropriate. This approach would be suitable if the lecturers believed that their students would still benefit from exposure to the questions not considered appropriate for the examination.

Subjects with a quantitative element can produce huge virtual question banks by including random factors in the questions themselves. A simple example, used in various numeracy diagnostic tests, is to have a question testing the ability to add up two double-digit numbers, which would randomly generate the numbers to be added. Here, there are thousands of different possible questions. A test built from randomly generated *questions* would not need collaboration to build up a test that ran with large enough virtual question banks. Randomly generated questions would not be appropriate for all subjects, but have been written for computer programming, engineering technology, maths, physics and statistics (Hunt, 1998; Lloyd *et al*, 1996; Thelwall, 1998; Thoennessen and Harrison, 1996). The Transmath computer-aided learning (CAL) program for example, although not a formative assessment tool, contains hundreds of randomly generated questions covering a broad range of basic university maths skills (Kelly *et al*, 1996; Transmath, http://caliban.leeds.ac.uk).

SECURITY ISSUES

There are normally three security issues for any formative assessment test: ensuring that students do not see the paper beforehand; ensuring that they do not copy during the test and ensuring that the marks are not tampered with after the test. Combating plagiarism is the main reason for using random factors, as in the physics exercises previously discussed for example, and is recognized as a potential problem in non-random tests where computer screens are in close proximity to each other (Zakrzewski and Bull, 1998). Plagiarism is not normally a problem in a summative test situation but can be with coursework assessments, particularly those with a single correct answer, such as maths problems. Delivering individualized assessments does not make it impossible for students to cheat, but makes it more difficult and reduces the temptation.

Ensuring that students do not have access to a test before it is delivered is an important concern of most types of computer-assisted assessments (CAAs). The problem of ensuring that either the test is password protected or installed or made available just in time for the test is often a non-trivial one. It requires careful planning and effective technical support to avoid mistakes, particularly if many such assessments are being undertaken (Stephens *et al*, 1998).

An open-access randomized test does not have to be hidden; it can be available all year round. Apart from the time savings this causes at the implementation stage, there are a number of other advantages. Firstly, random-based tests can be staggered, reducing the resourcing implications of having to find the computers to assess all the students at one sitting or during one day. This means that a test for a large class could be taken in groups of 20, for example, throughout a week, perhaps in the normal timetabled computer workshop sessions. Secondly, the same test can be used on courses running at different times of the year – and for resits. The open-access randomized test is therefore inherently scalable: there are no problems with assessing large student bodies or even classes in many different institutions with the same test. For similar reasons, the randomized test can be more robust in some aspects. A network failure at a crucial time does not mean the need to write a new test; the students can take the same one again the next week. It is also more flexible: students missing the test for good reasons can sit it at the earliest available opportunity. Distance learners can also sit the test at home if it includes security information to prevent cloning of the test output.

The extra time taken to author randomly generated tests has advantages in saving time in the areas of security and scalability. These savings will be bigger for larger classes and in more stable subjects where the same test can be used for a number of years.

PEDAGOGICAL IMPLICATIONS OF OPEN-ACCESS RANDOM TESTS

Different question types, methodologies and pedagogical considerations are appropriate for different assessments. We shall therefore discuss the pedagogical implications of open-access random tests under three categories organized according to the type of learning outcome implicitly or explicitly being assessed. For a discussion of learning outcomes see Allan (1996). Random-factor-based tests that are not open access have the same pedagogical implications as all computer-based assessments, but this will not be discussed here.

Procedure mastery

A common use for random factor tests is in disciplines where the intended student-learning outcomes include the ability to execute a procedure or algorithm. This is frequently the case in mathematics, statistics and operational research as well as in aspects of science and technology and is a component of numeracy. In order to demonstrate mastery of a procedure, the student must normally carry it out with a variety of data, possibly of different types, and in a variety of different settings. Providing that the assessor does not wish to assess the student in their use of the procedure in a novel context, a randomly generated assessment involving sufficient use of random factors for data and context would not have its summative assessment value compromised by being open access. An example of this is the 'hypothesis test for a mean' question on the Wolverhampton statistics test. This tests the ability of the student to perform the numerical calculations required for a hypothesis test and delivers thousands of different data sets for these calculations. There are also eight different settings for the data.

There are immediate pedagogical benefits from making this type of test open access. The first is that the students will be motivated to practise the test simply because it is the assessment tool. The feedback that the test will give is therefore directly relevant to their grades and will be taken seriously. For procedure mastery, repeated practice is often an important part of the learning process and student motivation to practise the test will therefore aid their learning. In fact, this practice can also increase motivation as students almost always see their marks increasing with repeated practice and gain confidence accordingly. For example, in all the random tests at Wolverhampton that assess this type of learning outcome, the students practise at least two to three times on average. The procedures vary from numerical calculations for statistics to algebraic manipulations for maths. Studies from data logs also show that practice improves performance, at least of the test, in all except a very few cases (Thelwall, 1998). The open-access test may seem at first sight like a rather impoverished Skinnerian programmed learning tool, but this would be an inaccurate characterization. The difference is that the assessment is not isolated from the learning: students access other resources, such as notes, tutors, books and peers in order to improve their scores. The feedback enables them to identify areas for study and therefore empowers them to spend time attaining manageable targets.

There are possible pitfalls with this approach, however. Many students concentrate on practising an open test at the expense of their other studies and this can skew their learning style, for example away from a deeper theoretical understanding or proper contextualization of a procedure. There is also a risk that insufficient randomness in questions can produce a narrower breadth of mastery than is desirable. Solutions to the first problem can come from two possible angles: either adding extra questions or having additional assessments to assess wider issues in the subject. In the statistics test, containing the question mentioned above, both approaches are used. Multiple-choice questions at the end of the test cover wider outcomes and other module assessments cover the more specific learning outcomes.

In summary, an open-access randomly generated assessment test can be used by students for formative assessment before being used for summative assessment. It can enhance motivation and allow useful practice for students, but must be carefully written to provide sufficiently varied questions. It must also be balanced with other assessments or with the inclusion of non-procedural questions in order to promote effective subject learning.

Fact acquisition

In some subjects, such as languages, history, law and medicine, knowledge of a large number of facts can be an important component of subject skills. In medicine, for example, doctors need to have an encyclopaedic knowledge of the association of symptoms and illnesses. This is tested, for example, in the Part 1 exam for the important postgraduate qualification of Member of the Royal College of Physicians (MRCP), which is a multiple-choice/multiple-response test that is norm-referenced to allow only 30 per cent of doctors to pass each sitting. In all subjects, knowledge of at least some basic facts is a desirable outcome and is assessed at least indirectly, but this is often not stated as an objective. In terms of assessments, facts are normally expected to be assessed in the context of demonstrating other skills. In a computer-based assessment, questions are often relatively small and numerous and a section testing factual knowledge could easily be mixed in with the rest of a test. A by-product of this would be making explicit to students this knowledge requirement in a way that is often overlooked. Assessors may, however, take the view that in their subject it is not desirable to test facts in isolation from other skills such as the ability to construct a critical argument supported by evidence.

In a situation where students are assessed on their knowledge of facts, the security of an assessment is not compromised by allowing it to be open access provided that the question base is large enough or is exhaustive. A pedagogical advantage of making open access a factual knowledge assessment, or one with a factual knowledge component, springs from examinees' motivation to master the test questions and therefore learn the facts. Publishing a question bank will also make it clear exactly what is being assessed, especially if the coverage of the question bank is exhaustive. Students' use of the question bank for practice will give them valuable feedback on their progress, which would be particularly relevant to an exam with a very wide coverage of facts such as the MRCP Part 1. In fact, although the (continually changing) question bank for this particular exam is not open access, many published books of tests and solutions fill the vacuum.

Other learning outcomes

The vast majority of intended learning outcomes in higher education are neither of the fact acquisition nor the procedure mastery type. Many are not behaviourist and most would not require repeated practice for effective learning. Essay questions are a common means of assessment but in most cases at least part of what they assess could be meaningfully assessed by other types of question more amenable to computer marking. Multiple-choice questions in particular are enjoying a resurgence in recent times. Although they cannot test everything that an essay can, for example originality and the development of an argument, they do enable an examiner to test many outcomes more directly, reliably and objectively (Kniveton, 1996). Kniveton suggests that '*some* essay tests could be replaced by multiple-choice tests within an assessment programme'.

Two dangers in allowing students access to a large bank of questions in this context are the likelihood of compromising the validity of the assessment if the question bank is not large enough and the possibility that some students may be directed away from more profitable avenues of study. Test practice gives valuable formative feedback to students about the current state of their performance and would work best if it encouraged them to examine their incorrect answers in conjunction with other subject resources. Poorly designed question banks could encourage an encyclopaedic approach to study at the expense of deeper understanding, as could one that was too small. A well-designed question bank would avoid these pitfalls and produce a scalable source of valuable formative assessment. An open-access test of this type is a motivator and driver of student learning and therefore extra care should be taken to ensure the relevance of its questions. However, in some subjects, such as maths, the numerous small questions needed for a question bank may have to be produced by deconstructing larger natural units of knowledge in some way. This may lead to an assessment that is not as 'authentic' as could be desired and would therefore be most suited to being a stepping stone to a later, more complex and realistic assessment. The natural place for this type of test would thus be in the middle, rather than at the end of a unit of study.

SUMMARY

Randomly generated computer-based assessment tests are more difficult to construct than standard computerised tests because of the need for a larger bank of questions, but they have security, flexibility and scalability benefits that give them distinct advantages where their construction is practicable.

Open-access random tests give personalized feedback to students about their degree of mastery of the assessed learning outcomes, as well as making clear exactly what those outcomes are. They are particularly pertinent in areas where practice of a procedure is an important component of learning. This is often the case in subjects with a quantitative element. They can also be useful when fact acquisition needs to be assessed, an important component of a minority of disciplines but present in some form in all others. CAAs may also be used to test a great variety of skills outside the previous two categories and an open-access test of this kind would provide formative assessment in the standard way: by trialling students' knowledge and by giving feedback concerning the extent of their progress. Tests can, of course, be written for combinations of different types of outcome as well, simultaneously providing different kinds of feedback. The advantage of open-access random tests over CAL packages that would teach as well as giving feedback is that student motivation to use them is intrinsic to their use for summative assessment. As with other types of CAA, these tests perform their summative assessment role best in combination with other assessment methods. When used in conjunction with other resources for formative assessment or practice, they can motivate and drive learning, providing a useful addition to the learning environment.

REFERENCES

Allan, J (1996) Learning outcomes in higher education, *Studies in Higher Education*, **21** (1), pp 93–108

Hunt, N (1998) Computer-aided assessment in statistics: the CAMPUS project, *Alt-J*, **6** (2), pp 58–67

Kapur, S and Stillman, G (1997) Teaching and learning using the WWW: a case study, *Innovations in Education and Training International*, **34** (1), pp 316–322

Kelly, A, Maunder, S and Cheng, S (1996) Does practise make perfect? Using TRANSMATH to assess mathematics coursework, *Active Learning*, **4**, pp 30–36

Kniveton, B H (1996) A correlational analysis of multiple-choice and essay assessment measures, *Research in Education*, **56**, pp 73–84

Lloyd, D, Martin, J G and McKaffery, K (1996) The Introduction of computer-based testing on an engineering course, *Assessment and Evaluation in Higher Education*, **21** (1), pp 83–90

Simonite, V, Ells, P and Turner, W (1998) Using IT to generate individualized coursework questions and solutions for an introductory course in statistics and probability, *CTI Maths & Stats*, **9** (1), pp 16–18

Stephens, D, Bull, J and Wade, W (1998) Computer-assisted assessment: suggested guidelines for an institutional strategy, *Assessment and Evaluation in Higher Education*, **23** (3), pp 283–294

Thelwall, M (1998) A unique style of computer-assisted assessment, *Alt-J*, **6** (2), pp 49–57

Thoennessen, M and Harrison, M J (1996) Computer-assisted assignments in a large physics class, *Computers & Education*, **27** (2), pp 141–147

Zakrzewski, S and Bull, J (1998) The mass implementation and evaluation of computer-based assessments, *Assessment and Evaluation in Higher Education*, **23** (2), pp 141–152

8

Automatic test generation from a database

J H Sims Williams, J Maher, D Spencer, M D J Barry and E Board

INTRODUCTION

This chapter describes an ongoing experiment in allowing lecturers to set tests from a large database of questions just by making a specification of the test and then allowing the computer to automatically generate a potentially large number of tests that match the specification.

The motivation for this experiment arose in 1992 when the author was asked to mark some first-year exam scripts on mathematics. It was obvious that the students did not have a basic understanding of quite large parts of the first-year mathematics course. This was an end-of-year exam so they had either to be failed or allowed to carry on regardless of their misunderstanding. Neither of these outcomes is desirable. This led to the idea that students should have a set of tests that they were required to take during the year. If a student was found not to have mastered the topic then he or she would be required to re-take tests until the subject had been mastered.

This idea required a lot of tests on the same topic. Additionally, the manpower costs were out of the question unless the tests could be administered automatically and marked automatically. To fully satisfy the goal of reaching mastery by repeated testing required a computer system that would allow lecturers to set multiple versions of a test on the subject of interest. Conceptually, no two students would ever get the same test but all the tests would be of similar difficulty and take about the same length of time to complete. In this way it was hoped that we could allow students to repeatedly take a test, in their own time, until they had mastered all the topics.

Since most universities now teach quite large classes and do not have proportionately as many computers, it is usually impossible to get all the students attending a particular course to take a test on a computer simultaneously. If, however, every test that each student took was different then they wouldn't need to take the tests simultaneously, thus solving another problem.

A FIRST IMPLEMENTATION

In 1994, a research assistant at Bristol built a delivery system that allowed tests, generated in an Oracle database, to be taken on PCs attached to the computer network. The questions were coded in SGML (Standard Generalised Mark-up Language), so that a reasonable range of mathematical symbols could be used and these were stored in a single large field of the Questions record in the database. Each question had a unique number and some metadata describing the question as follows:

> {Question_id, Main-topic, sub-topic1, sub-topic2, time-to-do, difficulty}
> for example:
> {376, differentiation, products, simple-algebraic-functions, 120, 1}
> from which one can read that question number 376 is a question on the differentiation of products of simple algebraic functions. That the question takes about 120 seconds to do and has a difficulty of 1 on the scale (1 is easy, 5 is hard).

Tests were set by specifying the 'Main-topic' (differentiation in this example) and then questions were randomly picked out of the database so that the average difficulty was, say, 3 and the sum of the 'time-to-do' of the questions was about 30 minutes.

This system worked well and delivered tests on demand so that students did not get the same test. All the data of the students' use of the system was recorded so that we could provide feedback to students. The feedback told them which questions they got right and listed the sub-topic1 and sub-topic2 for each question so that they could go and look up these sub-topics before trying the test again.

The tests were, however, unsatisfactory for the following reasons:

1. The time-to-do data had been guessed and sometimes the question writer had got this estimate quite seriously wrong. This error led to tests that were too long or too short.
2. Similarly, the question setter's estimates of difficulty were often wrong, leading to tests that were not of the same difficulty.
3. More importantly, by randomly choosing questions on such a broad topic as differentiation or integration, it was possible for several of the questions chosen to be on a very similar sub-topic, eg the use of the product rule for differentiation. This had the effect that the test is not properly balanced between the sub-topics that should have been assessed.
4. The number of questions available in the database was only a few hundred and so, although the tests were randomly generated, the same questions were turning up sufficiently frequently for students to have a good chance that they had seen the question before by just watching other students do the test.
5. Quite a significant number of the questions in the database had errors. By providing a very responsive system of responding to queries from students, it

proved possible to maintain student confidence while improving the database questions. This did, however, point up the not-inconsiderable difficulty, and hence cost, of maintaining a large database of high-quality questions.

In 1996, the university received a grant of £50,000 from the Higher Education Funding Council of England and Wales to develop the system from being a purely mathematics test server to be able to handle chemistry questions as well. New staff were appointed to provide the chemistry input and to carry forward the project. An assessment of the problems of the existing system led to a re-examination of the goals that we had originally set.

Three main problems had arisen:

1. The test setter, which just randomly selected questions corresponding to the chosen main topic, did not produce well enough structured tests.
2. The number of different tests that the system generated was not large enough to make students feel that they would have a different test from their friends or neighbours.
3. The system only allowed the questions to be made up of a sequence of symbols. Using SGML coding we could use some special mathematical symbols but diagrams and graphs were not possible, let alone the symbols and diagrams required by chemistry.

The following programme was set up to address these problems:

1. A new test-setting algorithm was required that would allow the examiners to specify in some detail exactly what sort of question they would have for each of the questions in his test. The nature of the specification will be described later.
2. The problem of not being able to generate enough different tests was primarily one of not having enough questions from which to choose. This is a serious problem as the amount of effort that has been put into question generation and classification suggests that the average cost of a question is about £20. To make students feel that the test they take is unlikely to be the same as a friend's test, we need the probability that the two tests are the same to be less than 0.05 and preferably close to 0.01. Aiming for the higher figure of 0.05 means that we must be able to automatically generate at least 20 entirely different tests. If a test is made up of 10 questions on different combinations of topics and sub-topics (hereafter called a Topic-ID) then we need to have significantly more than 20 questions on each Topic-ID used in the test. This means that each test set must draw on at least 250 questions and if we are to set four tests a year then a database of 1000 questions is a starting point. (The constraints on the difficulty and length of the test, mean the number of questions supplied to the algorithm must be more than the number actually used.) This must be worth £20,000 in effort. The magnitude to this investment in a database means that these sorts of database need to be nationally not just university based.

3. We were now proposing to test chemistry and potentially many other subjects instead of just mathematics and so needed an ability to provide well-illustrated questions as well as a variety of types of objective questions. Fortunately, the development of Web technology made this relatively simple. By deciding to use a standard Web-browser as our delivery mechanism we could benefit from all the developments in plug-ins for the Web that have transformed the range of displays that can be presented. The original system required the users to download some code that was specific to PCs to drive the test system on their own machines. This also ran the display. By choosing to run a system from inside a Web-browser, we were able to create a JAVA code version of the client test system. This means that students or indeed lecturers using the system do not need to have any code on their machines but the JAVA code they need is loaded over the Web.

A NATIONAL DATABASE OF QUESTIONS

While it is clear that there would be benefits from having a national database of questions, this idea is not new and history is littered with failed collections of questions. The typical scenario is that some institution sponsors the idea and noble people round the country contribute their own small collection of questions. The database is established and people then draw down questions to suit their own requirements. Everyone is then reasonably happy but the project dies as there is nothing to support the continued updating and provision of information on the database's content. We have inherited a large collection of questions from the Royal Society of Chemistry and a smaller collection of mathematics questions. These sorts of collections are not immediately usable but often provide a good basis to develop modernized questions. We would be grateful for any other collections in whatever state.

The world has changed in some ways since the days in which these former databases were collected. We can now provide online access to our database from the desk of any lecturer who is connected to the Web, so that improvements and corrections can be available almost instantaneously to anyone round the world. The technology has changed, but human beings have not. There are still generous people who will give of their work to support a new database, but just to make a one-off collection would repeat the previous scenario.

The author proposes the following three modes by which the database might become viable:

1. The country, indeed the world, contains many people who have small collections of objective questions that they may be willing to donate. Funding can probably be found to convert these questions into a suitable format for the database and to add the metadata needed to make the questions into a homogeneous resource.

2. If the testing system is made available to lecturers running their own course units in their own institution then they will almost certainly find that the set of questions does not satisfy their needs completely but that they would like to make their own questions. Each course unit can have its own private space in the database where it can build up a set of questions for its own use. When the lecturers have tested these questions on their own students and validated the metrics of time-to-do and facility for their units then they will be encouraged to make these questions available to the wider community. Since this will be an almost pain-free process it should not require much encouragement to make the questions available, thus increasing and updating the general stock.
3. The model above assumes that lecturers will want to use this database of questions in the way in which it is provided. It may well be that this is too constraining an environment or that the quality of service cannot match up with their requirements. Nevertheless, these people may like to make use of some of the question material in the database. This latter group cannot be given the questions but must be required to contribute to the maintenance and improvement of the database either in cash or by contributing new questions that they use on their own systems in exchange.

The interchange of questions between systems is not at a very advanced state although QuestionMark are proposing a format they call QML. Our system uses an approximation to the QML format at present. There are international attempts by Instructional Management Systems Project (http://www.imsproject.org.uk/) to generate a standard, which would make questions interchangeable between different testing systems that subscribe to the standard.

In the preceding sections, the history of this project has been discussed and the ideas that motivate the creation of a new system described. Now a fuller discussion will be given of how these ideas have been translated into reality. Not quite all of this is fully working at the time of writing but most of the system will be available in due course.

A SECOND IMPLEMENTATION – AUTOMATIC TEST GENERATOR

The original test generator was very simple. A main topic was chosen for the test. A query on the database found all the questions with that main-topic. Questions were then randomly selected and swapped in and out until a set of questions that had roughly the same total time-to-do and the same average difficulty had been found. This set of questions was then presented to the current student. The process was repeated with a new set of randomly chosen questions for the next student and so on.

The results of this approach were not satisfactory and a new, more structured approach has been implemented. The test is planned on a question-by-question basis (see Figure 8.1).

Example Test Design
Test Name: test1 — Course Unit: EMAT1011
Setter: Jon Sims Williams — Dates available: 3/5/99–15/5/99

Question No.	*Main-topic*	*Sub-topic1*	*Sub-topic2*
1	functions	drawing of graph of function	
2	functions	domain and/or range	simple algebraic functions
3	differentiation	practical application	speed
4	differentiation	function of function rule	trigonometric functions

length of test: 11:34 +/- 2 minutes
Facility of test 60 % +/- 5%

Figure 8.1 *A simple specification of a mathematics test*

This test specification is for a four-question test. Tests as short as this are unlikely to provide reliable results. However, it illustrates the ideas. Each question is defined in terms of three levels of data (Main-topic, sub-topic1, sub-topic2) which are represented by a Topic-ID. When the user specifies a question like this, the system will go and look up all the questions in the database corresponding to this Topic-ID and return a list of additional topics or sub-topics that this complete set of questions would require. For example, Q779 is a question on functions in which the student needs to be able to draw a hyperbolic function. This question satisfies the specification for question 1, but its sub-topic2 is hyperbolic functions. The system adds hyperbolic functions to its list of other sub-topics for question 1; the user can then define which of these should be excluded.

The system provides the user with the 'length of the test'. This is the sum of the average length of questions for the specified Topic-IDs. When tests are generated, they are only accepted if the sum of the 'time-to-dos' lies in the range 11.34 ±2 minutes. Similarly, all the tests must have an average facility of 60 ±5%. These values can be changed by the lecturer so that, if an easier test is wanted, a facility of 80 per cent can be specified or, alternatively, the lecturer may not mind what the length of the test is, provided it is less than half an hour and more than 10 minutes. It would then be specified that the length of the test would be 20 ±10 minutes. Since this length of test is considerably greater than that given as the mean for the set of questions specified, the number of tests generated might be very small and the lecturer would be better advised to add more questions to the specification.

THE CLASSIFICATION SYSTEM FOR MATHEMATICS

There seems to be no standard classification of the mathematics used by engineers and scientists that is suitable for classifying questions. We are proposing a system of question classification as follows:

One or possibly two main topics

The main topics are the focus of the question, ie what the question was intended to test. The main topic is, however, too broad a classification for setting tests so, normally, it will be specialized by one or two sub-topics, called Sub_Topic1 and Sub_Topic2 in the test-design interface. These two sub-topics are primarily intended to be used for specifying the sort of question required. Sub-topic1 should be chosen to be the more significant criterion for choosing the question as part of the test. In addition to sub-topics 1 and 2, there is a list of other sub-topics that are used to show the other pieces of knowledge or expertise that are required to do the question. In the test-setting software these are available for exclusions. So you can say, 'I want a question on main-topic1 particularly concerned with sub-topic1 and sub-topic2 but excluding the following sub-topics.' In the test generator, when you specify your question, a list of the other sub-topics is displayed, so that you can choose which to exclude.

Other types of sub-topic

The simplest sub-topic defines the types of function involved, for example:

- simple algebraic functions;
- trigonometric functions;
- exponential/log functions;
- inverse/hyperbolic functions.

It is assumed that if there are simple algebraic functions, then there are not trigonometric functions or any of the other function types further down the list, but the converse does not apply. A similar set of sub-topics defines the set of shapes with which the student may need to be familiar, eg cone, right circular cylinder, etc.

When setting a question, the lecturer may want a question to motivate students or to test their ability to generate or use simple models. To provide this flexibility we have defined the following sub-topics:

- Simple model construction: a simple model must be generated to complete the question.
- Model application: a model is provided as part of the question and must be used. This does not imply that knowledge of the application area is required.
- Practical application: a practical application of the main topic to some application area. The application area should also be specified as a sub-topic so that practical application is used to say, 'I want a practical application' and the sub-topic could be used to exclude particular applications. Practical application *does* imply that knowledge of the application area *is* required as *no* model is provided.

Simple model construction, model application and practical application would usually be used deliberately as part of the design of a test, ie 'We want to include a practical application question in our test.' Thus, when a question is classified, these will be inserted as sub-topic1. The difference between simple model construction and practical application is that the model in the model construction is assumed to be part of general knowledge rather than a special application area. Thus, a question that requires one to find the number of times that a cylindrical roller rotates as it rolls the length of a path requires a simple model to be constructed, but is hardly an application of a set of special knowledge about rollers.

There are other sub-topics that are bits of extraneous information or technique that are necessary for the question but are not normally associated with the main topic. Thus, if the question requires, say, unit-conversion from feet to metres, the necessary data would normally be provided but not all test setters would want their students to have to do the conversion. 'Unit conversion – the question requires a change of units.'

Another distinction is between questions that require a numerical rather than an algebraic answer: 'Evaluation to a numerical value.'

Other classifications

In addition to the classifications {Main-topic, sub-topic1, sub-topic2 and other-sub-topics}, there are the following descriptions of questions:

Style

For motivational purposes, the tester may wish to have at least one of the questions in his test with a special emphasis on the main subject that his students are studying, eg mechanical engineering. There is also the opposite problem. A question that has been written in a style suitable for pure maths students may make it unsuitable for another group of students. The style of a question is thus a marker, taking the value of the particular group of students (if any) at which the question is aimed.

Theoretical

This indicator is given a value in the range 0–9, so that test setters can have the opportunity to ask for a more theoretical question (5–9) or a less theoretical question (0–4).

Extent to which Bloom's educational objectives are evident

Bloom classifies educational objectives according to the complexity of the activity students are involved in:

- Knowledge: states that the question simply checks if the student knows something factual.
- Comprehension: usually refers to a question in which data is given and the question checks if the student understands what it means.
- Application: the use of previously learned information in new and concrete situations to solve problems that have single or best answers.
- Analysis: the breaking down of informational materials into their component parts, examining (and trying to understand the organizational structure of)

such information to develop divergent conclusions by identifying motives or causes, making inferences and/or finding evidence to support generalizations.

- Synthesis: creatively or divergently applying prior knowledge and skills to produce a new or original whole.
- Evaluation: judging the value of material based on personal values/opinions, resulting in an end-product, with a given purpose, without real right or wrong answers.

Feedback requirements

All questions in the database are required to have feedback that will tell the students (for each wrong answer that they can select) either why the answer they gave is obviously wrong or, more often, to give the students some ideas that may help them to solve the problem. As a matter of policy, the main topic of a question must be explicitly part of the question or the feedback or both. For example, Question 51, as shown in Figure 8.2.

Determine the point of intersection (if there is one) of the lines

$$\frac{(x-1)}{3} = \frac{(y-3)}{2} = z+2 \text{ and}$$

$$x = \frac{(7-y)}{3} = \frac{(z+7)}{2}$$

Figure 8.2 *Question 51*

The main topic for this question is vector algebra, but the question can be treated as just the solution of four simultaneous equations. To make it a valid vector algebra question, it must have a vector solution and this must be reflected in the feedback.

This scheme of classification has been proposed so that we can start building up a database with the range of choices available in the future. At present, the number of mathematics questions (about 1100) in the database is not large enough to allow much choice of question when 20 equivalent tests are required. However, if we are not ambitious now, the full potential of the database will not be realized.

A SECOND IMPLEMENTATION – A STUDENT'S VIEW

The student's view of the test system is much the same as any other Web-delivered test system. Students start up the test system from a Web page using an 'applet'. They are then asked to log in. This identifies the units for which they are enrolled and allows them to choose any of the tests that are currently available to them. They select a test, which is then downloaded into their computer. They can peruse all the questions in this test and answer them in any order. They are encouraged to commit answers to questions when they have finished and then receive feedback to tell them if the answers are correct. If the answers are wrong, they receive messages to explain why they are wrong or some advice on how they might have approached the question differently. We encourage our students to work in a workbook so they have a record of their work and lecturers can ask to see their working to help them. At the end of the test, they get the feedback from all the questions so they can rework the questions.

Although the original conception was that students would be required to do tests until they had gained mastery of each topic tested, we have been unable to implement this idea due to a shortage of questions. The students are, however, allowed to take each test up to three times and we record the best mark that they get. This is popular with students and has the effect of giving them more exposure to the subjects as well as providing them with some teaching (from the questions they get wrong). The use of workbooks is important here as otherwise students tend to do the tests on scraps of paper and then cannot go back and rework their tests.

A questionnaire was recently given to students to try to gauge the student view of the use of the open testing environment used. Each question is followed by a bar chart, which shows the range of responses given based on the scale 1–9 (see Figure 8.3).

The results from the questionnaire clearly show that there is more work to be done to improve the questions and our measures of difficulty. This is the first year in which we have been testing 300 students and so in future we will be getting much more reliable data on our questions. The perceived level of cheating is still too high; we have found that some students have exploited weaknesses in our handling of the exit procedure and have removed this weakness. We are investigating the cause of this perception. The reason for the penalty in question 21 is that, in multiple-choice questions, the limited set of possible answers makes guessing relatively easy and so we have a penalty to discourage guessing.

A SECOND IMPLEMENTATION – A LECTURER'S VIEW

A lecturer gains access to the system in exactly the same way as a student and, when logging on, is recognized by the system as a lecturer and allowed privileges to look at students' marks, to register new students, to set new tests and so on.

As with every exam, it is important to ask what the system is measuring. Since this is an objective assessment system, it primarily measures the competence of the student at answering objective questions. The design of each question has a significant impact on what the question is measuring. Students take four progress tests during the year and some groups have done this on paper and some using the objective testing system as described above. Table 8.1 records the correlation between the score that the students in each group obtained on their progress tests (all four) and their final exam.

1. How do you rate the ease of use of the system?

Easy Difficult

2. I would prefer the progress tests to be:

Written Computer marked

3. My reasons are:

a. I find doing maths at a computer difficult

Yes No

b. I like to be able to have more than one try at the test

Yes No

4. I can sometimes give very quick answers to questions because:

a. I have seen the questions before

Yes No

b. I can guess the answer without working it out

Yes No

c. Someone will tell me the right answer

Yes No

5. An immediate response is something I:

Like Dislike

6. The timing bar helps me

Yes No

7. The time allocated for the progress tests is:

Too little Too much

8. As a whole, the questions asked in the progress test are:

Too easy Too hard

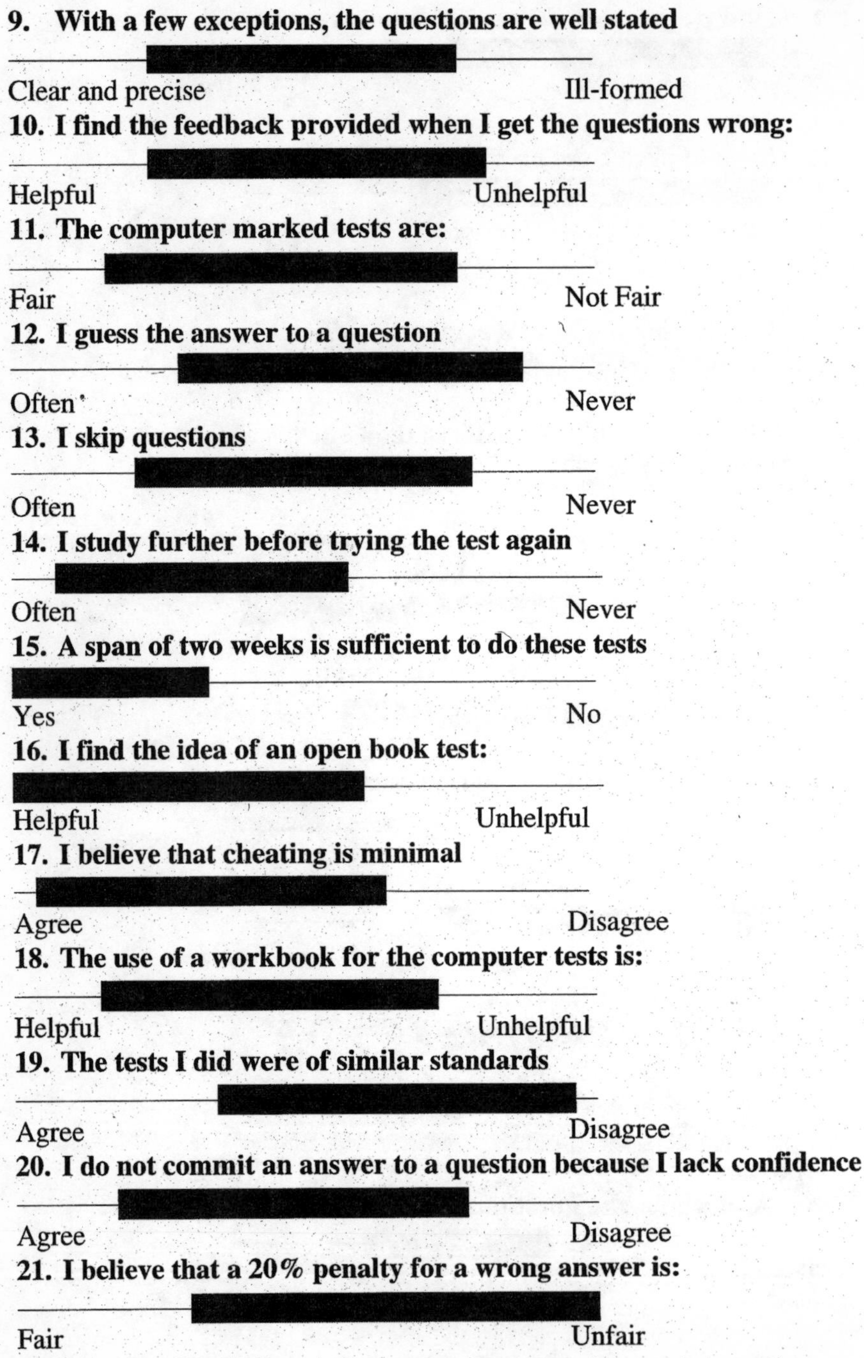

9. With a few exceptions, the questions are well stated

Clear and precise Ill-formed

10. I find the feedback provided when I get the questions wrong:

Helpful Unhelpful

11. The computer marked tests are:

Fair Not Fair

12. I guess the answer to a question

Often Never

13. I skip questions

Often Never

14. I study further before trying the test again

Often Never

15. A span of two weeks is sufficient to do these tests

Yes No

16. I find the idea of an open book test:

Helpful Unhelpful

17. I believe that cheating is minimal

Agree Disagree

18. The use of a workbook for the computer tests is:

Helpful Unhelpful

19. The tests I did were of similar standards

Agree Disagree

20. I do not commit an answer to a question because I lack confidence

Agree Disagree

21. I believe that a 20% penalty for a wrong answer is:

Fair Unfair

Figure 8.3 *The results of the test and learn (Tal) computer assessment questionnaire*

Table 8.1 *Correlations between progress test and end-of-year exams*

Student Group	*1997*	*Both written*	*1998*	*Both written*
1	0.75	yes	0.98	yes
2	0.83	yes	0.80	yes
3	0.76	yes	0.78	yes
4	0.87	yes	0.87	yes
5	0.83	yes	0.68	no
6	0.55	no	0.49	no

Group 6, which took objective progress tests in both 1997 and 1998, is clearly different for reasons that are not yet clear. Group 5, however, took written progress tests in 1997 and objective progress tests in 1998 and the results suggest that the objective tests are significantly less correlated with exams than the paper-based progress tests. The questions used in paper-based and objective tests are quite different, so the only reason for expecting a high correlation is that one would hope that a student who understands mathematics would perform well in both types of test and vice versa. These student groups correspond to different engineering departments. The departments have different average A-level entry levels and different motivations towards the mathematics course that they share.

CURRENT USAGE

At present, the system is used routinely for setting mathematics tests for over 300 engineering students in five different departments. It is also used for several small groups on one-off tests where the lecturer sets one test and the class takes the test simultaneously. Tests have been set for software engineering (C++), advanced maths with Maple, chemical formulae and diagnostic mathematics for chemists.

THE PROBLEMS AND CHALLENGES FOR THE FUTURE

The overwhelmingly largest problem is to persuade academic colleagues in other universities that, although this system was not created by them and for them explicitly, it may be worth trying. We are heartened by our previous experience. This system was built in the Department of Engineering Mathematics and yet most of our colleagues did not believe that it was worth changing the way they did things. If students were sick or otherwise did not take the progress test that was required then staff grudgingly suggested that perhaps we could set a test for the odd student (since it was so easy). Now they willingly sit back and allow the testing system to set the tests, do the marking and the automatic generation of mark sheets. Both the universities of Brunel and Coventry have given us questions. When these are added to a database of questions that was built 'Bristol style', we will be able to offer a more eclectic style of test and hope other universities may join in this endeavour.

The only database that can be used, at present, for the generation of multiple instances of tests on the same topics is designed for first-year mathematics. Tests have been set from this database to suit mathematics, engineering and chemistry students. We have now coded a set of 156 questions on vector calculus, a second-year mathematics subject, as a result of student demand, and the development of the Royal Society of Chemistry questions is proceeding.

At Bristol, we use the system mainly in an open-book, open-environment style. We restrict the hours of access to between 0830 and 1740, so that students have to do the test in a public computer laboratory where they may be observed. We are aware that, even under these conditions, it is possible for one student to impersonate another. Students have found other ways of cheating the system but we have been able to close all the loopholes except the use of a surrogate. In due course it will be possible to use an intelligent camera eye to check if the right person is taking the test.

A recent quality audit of mathematics at Bristol (http://www.niss.ac.uk/ education/ hefce/qar/uni_of_bristol.html) praised the Tal system and, although there is a long way forward to the goal of a national database of test questions, it appears that the opportunities and pressures of today mean that its time is nearly come. Readers are invited to explore our Web site: http://www.tal.bris.ac.uk/

REFERENCES

http://faculty.washington.edu/krumme/guides/bloom.html

SECTION TWO: Using CAA for Formative Assessment

9

Issues and impacts of using computer-based assessments (CBAs) for formative assessment

Dan Charman

INTRODUCTION

Computer-based assessments (CBAs) are now in widespread use in higher education. This is linked with a general diversification of assessment procedures which reflects the widening remit of higher education in producing graduates with a range of specific and transferable skills from entrants with a broad spectrum of abilities. However, it is also a response to increased pressures on teaching staff, shown by increased student-staff ratios and a decreasing unit of resource. The development of student-centred learning has been widely promoted with the intention of shifting prime responsibility for learning to students, while the role of teaching staff turns more to provision of opportunity for this learning. CBAs can play a key role in this process and have often been implemented as a way of reducing the time spent on assessments by staff without any impact on the student experience. However, many people have since recognized that CBAs may play an even more valuable role in formative assessment and that their pedagogic advantages may be more important than their strictly economic benefits. In this chapter I will review pedagogic aspects of the design and implementation of CBAs and consider the critical issues in writing and delivering formative assessments. Finally, evaluation of the impact of the introduction of CBAs should not be forgotten and I will conclude with some results from an evaluation of student performance in summative assessments before and after a change in delivery from conventional to computer-based assessment.

PRACTICAL AND ECONOMIC BENEFITS OF CBAS

In the face of increasing student numbers, Gibbs (1992) suggests:

- reducing the assessment loading for students;
- evaluation of the function of each piece of assessment;
- diversification of the assessment portfolio.

The introduction of CBAs is part of the third response and the prime motivation is generally to make the assessment process more efficient (see, for example, Stephens, 1994). The main considerations in constructing economically beneficial assessments can be listed as follows:

- **The timescale**. Time savings are maximized over the longer term. The 'upfront' costs may not be defrayed in the first one to two years of operation but benefits will accrue over a longer period.
- **Additional resources for development**. Development costs can be very high for CBA. Time spent by an individual teacher can be saved by employing someone to assist with putting the questions on the system and providing graphics and so on while the academic concentrates on actually writing the text for materials.
- **Changing course delivery and use of teaching assistants**. Introduction of CBA may be part of a restructuring of the module delivery. It may be cost-effective to employ teaching assistants (typically postgraduate students) to help in the administration of CBA and other assessments.
- **Wider departmental/institutional benefits**. Development of materials for an individual module may not save time but if a broader departmental or even institutional strategy exists for CBA then the balance of the equation may alter. The case of the University of Luton is a good example of this (Zakrzewski and Bull, 1998).
- **Existing assessments in the subject area**. The number of projects in different aspects of educational technology has grown enormously in the last five years. There are thus many existing assessments that are of direct use. This is obviously a major potential time saver.
- **Question banks**. National or even international question banks are currently available or under consideration for some subject areas. Clearly this makes sense in subjects where there is a large amount of subject material in common and bespoke assessments could then be constructed by question selection.

However, while time savings may undoubtedly be the result in some circumstances, if it were the only motivation it seems likely that many existing CBAs would not have been initiated and many others would be abandoned at an early stage of development when the real cost became apparent. The fact that there are so many CBAs in existence and being actively used throughout higher education is a testament to the fact there are also other less immediately tangible benefits from their introduction. The next section reviews these pedagogic advantages.

FORMATIVE ASSESSMENT AND CBA

When time savings are the main motivation for initial interest in CBA, the fundamental questions of why and what we wish to assess sometimes do not receive as much attention as they should (Parshall, 1995). In general, we take relatively little time out to re-evaluate what function we want assessment to perform, a consideration that really should come first! There is plenty of good advice available on these considerations: see, for example, Brown and Knight (1994), Brown *et al* (1996, 1997) and Knight (1995), which should ideally be followed in any new assessment.

CBA, in common with paper-based objective testing, has many advantages in a summative assessment process. Student responses can be regarded dispassionately and marked consistently and, assuming suitable questions can be designed, all the functions of summative assessment (discrimination between students, gauging student progression, motivation of students and quality assurance) can be fulfilled with CBA. However, it can also deliver the functions of formative assessment (ie that assessment which is part of the learning process), which can be summarized as:

- to give students feedback;
- to guide student effort;
- to diagnose problems in learning;
- to help staff direct their teaching effort;
- to encourage students;
- to give students experience of assessment methods.

Specific advantages of CBA as a formative assessment tool will vary between subject and type of assessment. Some of the benefits relating to the provision of feedback have only recently been fully recognized with the widespread use of easy-to-use software such as Question Mark. Others, in particular those relating to the use of multimedia and interactivity, will continue to be significantly improved with technological advances. The main pedagogic advantages are briefly reviewed below. Further discussion of particular experiences is available in the literature (Charman and Elmes, 1998b and references therein).

Repeatability

CBAs can be run many times over by the same student. While this is unlikely to be important in summative assessment, it may be extremely useful in formative assessments. Re-running CBAs will entail little or no extra input from staff but is virtually never possible in conventional assessments. There are several possibilities in making use of this facility. Firstly, an assessment could be entirely open access, used only for student learning as and when they want to use it. In this case there may be no reporting of marks to the lecturer. Secondly, an assessment can be retaken until a threshold mark is achieved. Thirdly, students may receive their first marks as a measure of their performances but may resit the assessment at will in order to improve learning subsequently in preparation for a later summative test. One of the important aspects of re-running assessments is to provide enough questions in the question banks from which a particular assessment is drawn so that students do not always receive the same selection.

Immediate feedback to students

A key advantage of CBAs over any other form of assessment is the immediacy of response. Often feedback is delivered after each question or, alternatively, at the end of the test. This has several consequences. Firstly, students like to get immediate feedback; it keeps the activity and the result closely connected. This contrasts with typical feedback on essays and reports which always occurs much later than the writing itself and is thus divorced from it and seen perhaps as a separate activity by students (who inevitably focus primarily on the mark obtained). Secondly, it provides a rapid guide to student effort: lessons learned can be immediately put into action. Finally, it encourages students and keeps them focused on their work and gives them a clear indication of their progress and their next targets.

Immediate marks to staff

The immediacy of the process has important advantages for staff, too. Results are normally available immediately after the student has logged off and they can usually be accessed remotely. Problems in learning can be diagnosed immediately and staff can observe these and adapt teaching strategies to address them, if necessary adapting lecture materials and time in a following session.

Reliability and equitability

Objective testing is generally seen as fair by students; they know that their marks will be unaffected by expectations of staff, personality, race, gender or any other factor. This means that they trust the system and are perhaps more prepared to accept the feedback that they receive and to act on it. With large numbers of assessments to mark, staff judgement may fluctuate and powers of discrimination can fade over a long marking period, but computers don't suffer such effects!

Diversity of assessment

Diversity of assessment practices is often encouraged as it allows suitable assessment of a greater range of skills and contributes further to equitability, as different students perform better on different types of assessment. There are some students who find adaptation to CBAs difficult but there are others who are far better at them than they are at other types of assessment.

Content versus presentation

Most of us are influenced to a degree by the standard of presentation of work, even if it is the content that is the central focus of the assessment. In CBAs, there is usually no effect of presentation or style on judgement of quality.

Timeliness

Timeliness in assessment is one of the key values mentioned by Brown *et al* (1996). Clearly it is important to get the timing of assessment correct. Short, frequent (and therefore less stressful) assessments that are embedded in the learning process may achieve better student learning, especially in subjects where knowledge has to be gained incrementally. CBAs offer this potential, since it is often easy to break up what would otherwise be a very large assessment into small blocks and to use the software to make them available at the time when they are needed in the curriculum. This potential for increased frequency of assessment also helps the lecturer to identify problems at an early stage rather than getting to the end of a module to find that a large percentage of students have failed!

Flexibility of access

Increased distance learning, student commitment to part-time employment and mature students with families all benefit from a flexible time and place of assessment. Assessments based on the World Wide Web operated via the Internet offer enormous flexibility and allow equal opportunity to students who would otherwise be disadvantaged.

Student interest and motivation

CBAs have a lot of potential for providing more stimulating and interactive assessment processes to engage students more effectively in formative assessment, which they may otherwise treat rather casually if it has no summative marks attached to it. This has already happened to an extent and the use of colour, graphics, animation, sound and video is possible in assessments if not commonplace at the moment. Currently this aspect is restricted technologically and by the skill-level of most lecturers. However, it will undoubtedly change in the future.

Student-centred skills and learning

Very many CBAs operate on an open-access basis. This encourages students to take responsibility for their own learning – they have to manage their time to prepare for and sit the assessment, often as part of a broader self-paced learning package. This engenders good attitudes to learning and helps in establishing a broader range of transferable skills. Open-access assessments may also encourage group work and discussion.

FORMATIVE FEEDBACK

The crux of successful formative CBAs is the provision of online feedback to students. In its simplest form, this is, of course, telling them whether they are correct or not. While this may be adequate in some circumstances, it is much more effective to explain why a response is incorrect and to provide the correct answer for them to ponder. Even for correct responses, it is best to give an explanation since they may have been arrived at by incorrect reasoning or guesswork. Recommendations on writing feedback for CBAs are given by Charman and Elmes (1998a):

- Make it clear whether the response is correct or incorrect.
- Keep it as positive as possible. Even if an answer is not correct, give credit for being nearly right and don't give the impression that the response given was a completely idiotic one. On the other hand, you don't need to be excessively effusive for correct answers unless they are the really difficult questions.
- Give feedback on correct responses, too. Some answers may have been arrived at by the wrong reasoning or even by chance. Even if the reasoning and answer were both correct, feedback can reinforce this.
- Make sure there is adequate time for reading of feedback. Formative assessments should not be strictly time limited if you are expecting students to make good use of feedback.
- Consider using graphics in feedback to make them more interesting.
- Explain why a wrong answer is not correct. Give the correct answer and explain how to derive it. If the response was only slightly wrong, try to suggest where the student could have gone wrong.
- Avoid over-jovial responses but do keep it reasonably simple and friendly.
- Use feedback to adjust the possible responses. You may need to change the question once you come to write the feedback!
- Consider the timing of feedback – will it be given after each question or at the end of the assessment? This may affect the detail and form of feedback. Instant feedback on each question can be very effective but you need to bear in mind the time it takes for students to read and digest this.
- Give pointers to further learning opportunities and information such as page references in textbooks, course materials and journal literature.

IMPACT OF FORMATIVE CBAS ON STUDENT LEARNING

There have been a large number of articles published on the introduction of CBAs into existing modules and most of these include an evaluation of the change (eg Lloyd and Holden, 1994; Parrington *et al*,1994; Proctor and

Donoghue, 1994; Beevers *et al*, 1995; Sensi *et al*, 1995; Donkers, 1996; Mansen and Haak, 1996; Martin *et al*, 1996; Thoennessen and Harrison, 1996; Charman and Elmes, 1998b). However, most of these evaluations concern the attitude and preferences of the students as well as the staff experience but do not evaluate the impact of the formative assessment on student learning. The only real way to assess this quantitatively is to compare performances in summative assessments before and after the introduction of a CBA. This causes problems because summative assessment often also changes along with the inclusion of CBAs. One exception to this, concerning a micropalaeontology module at Liverpool (Boyle *et al*, 1997; Paul and Boyle, 1998) shows that variability in student performance was related more to the subject being taught than to the method of delivery. A further example from a statistics module for geography students (Charman and Elmes, 1998c, 1998d) shows that examination performance at the end of the module was improved after the introduction of CBA to deliver formative assessments. A comparison of the module results with the entry level ability of the year cohorts shows that the improvement in results of the group who used CBA goes against what would be expected from the average ability of the group (Table 9.1). Further data of this kind need to be collected to clearly establish the impact of the introduction of CBAs and other innovations in teaching on student learning and performance in summative examinations. Without these data, arguments over the relative merits of different approaches will be hindered by subjective and anecdotal experience.

Table 9.1 *Comparison of examination performance in groups of students before (1996) and after (1997) the introduction of CBAs for formative assessment together with summary statistics on entry qualifications of the two groups (see also Charman and Elmes (1998d)).*

Year	*1996*		*1997*	
Examination marks %				
Mean	54.1		56.8	
Standard deviation	12.3		12.9	
Minimum	28.5		26.7	
Maximum	85.0		90.0	
Entry qualifications				
(A-level points)	Mean	n	Mean	n
Geography (Single honours)	17.3	148	16.4	144
Geography (Combined honours)	18.1	42	15.7	39
Earth Science	11.9	46	10.4	49
Non A-level entry	-	19	-	18
Mean/Total	16.4	255	15.0	250

CONCLUSION

It is clear that there is mounting evidence for the pedagogic advantages of CBA in providing feedback on student work in higher education. In addition, new studies are beginning to provide hard evidence for improved performance in summative assessment as a result of the use of CBAs. While economies of scale and time savings will always be important in the adoption and development of CBAs, the pedagogic advantages to be gained also provide a strong motivation.

REFERENCES

Beevers, C E, McGuire, G R, Stirling, G and Wild, D G (1995) Mathematical ability assessed by computer, *Computers and Education*, **25**, pp 123–132

Boyle, A P, Bryon, D N and Paul, C R C (1997) Computer-based learning and assessment: a palaeontological case study with outcomes and implications, *Computers and Geosciences*, **23**, pp 573–580

Brown, G, Bull, J and Pendlebury, M (1997) *Assessing student learning in higher education*, Routledge, London

Brown, S and Knight, P (1994) *Assessing learners in higher education*, Kogan Page, London

Brown, S, Race, P and Smith, B (1996) *500 Tips on assessment*, Kogan Page, London

Charman, D and Elmes, A (1998a) *Computer based assessment (Vol 1): A guide to good practice*, SEED Publications, University of Plymouth

Charman, D and Elmes, A, eds (1998b) *Computer based assessment (Vol 2): Case studies in science and computing*, SEED Publications, University of Plymouth

Charman, D and Elmes, A (1998c) A computer-based formative assessment strategy for a basic statistics module in geography, *Journal of Geography in Higher Education*, **22** (3), pp 381–385

Charman, D and Elmes, A (1998d) Formative assessment in a basic geographical statistics module, in *Computer based assessment (Vol 2): Case studies in science and computing*, eds D Charman and A Elmes, SEED Publications, University of Plymouth, pp 15–19

Donkers, H H L M (1996) Computerized case-based testing: a modern method to assess clinical decision making, *Medical Teacher*, **18** (4), pp 294–299

Gibbs, G (1992) *Assessing more students,* Oxford Centre for Staff Development, Oxford Brookes University

Knight, P, ed (1995) *Assessment for learning in higher education*, Kogan Page SEDA series, London

Lloyd, A and Holden, C (1994) Computer aided assessments in pharmaceutical microbiology, *Active Learning*, **1**, pp 27–28

Mansen, T J and Haak, S W (1996) Evaluation of health assessment skills using a computer videodisc interactive program, *Journal of Nursing Education*, **35** (8), pp 382–383

Martin, J G, McCaffery, K and Lloyd, D (1996) The introduction of computer-based testing on an engineering technology course, *Assessment and Evaluation in Higher Education*, **21**, pp 83–90

Parrington, N, Ferguson, I, Hedges, S and Spence, L (1994) The use of hypertext and the World Wide Web in teaching and assessing software engineering, *Active Learning*, **1**, pp 39–42

Parshall, C G (1995) Practical issues in computer-based testing, *Journal of Instruction Delivery Systems*, **9** (3), pp 13–17

Paul, C R C and Boyle, A P (1998) Computer based assessment in palaeontology, in *Computer based assessment (Vol 2): Case studies in science and computing*, eds D Charman and A Elmes, SEED Publications, University of Plymouth, pp 51–56

Proctor, A and Donoghue, D (1994) Computer based assessment: a case study in geography, *Active Learning*, **1**, pp 29–34

Sensi, S, Merlitti, D, Murri, R, Palitti, V P and Guagnano, M T (1995) Evaluation of learning progress in internal medicine using computer-aided clinical case simulation, *Medical Teacher*, **17** (3), pp 321–326

Stephens, D (1994) Using computer assisted assessment: time saver or sophisticated distraction, *Active Learning*, **1**, pp 11–15

Thoennessen, M and Harrison, M J (1996) Computer-assisted assessment in a large physics class, *Computers and Education*, **27** (2), pp 141–147

Zakrzewski, S and Bull, J (1998) The mass implementation and evaluation of computer-based assessments, *Assessment and Evaluation*, **23** (2), pp 143–152

ACKNOWLEDGEMENTS

My work in CBA has been aided by funding from the University of Plymouth Technology Supported Learning Fund and the Science, Education Enhancement and Development project funded by HEFCE.

10

Computer-assisted peer review

Jennifer M Robinson

> In the English department at Harvard, my writing style was severely criticized and I was receiving grades of C or C+ on my papers. At eighteen, I was vain about my writing and felt it was Harvard, and not I, that was in error, so I decided to. . . experiment. The next assignment was a paper on *Gulliver's Travels*, and I remembered an essay by George Orwell that might fit. With some hesitation, I retyped Orwell's essay and submitted it as my own. I hesitated because if I were caught for plagiarism I would be expelled; but I was pretty sure that my instructor was not only wrong about writing styles, but poorly read as well. . . George Orwell got a B- at Harvard, which convinced me that the English department was too difficult for me.
>
> Crichton, 1988, p 4

INTRODUCTION

The ebb and flow of constructive criticism is important for learning. Universities conventionally put forward a top down model of criticism, much of which is linked to pointing out errors and assigning marks. The horizontal, student-to-student and self-critical aspects of this flow are rarely cultivated.

This chapter is about using networked computers to enhance the role of the horizontal flow in learning and give it official recognition as a vehicle for summative assessment, particularly for larger and more complicated assignments. Most of the chapter is about one form of horizontal exchange: multi-reviewer anonymous peer review. The chapter first develops the rationale for online anonymous peer review systems, then describes preliminary findings from two case studies, then outlines technical requirements for a system. It closes with suggestions and predictions for system development and thoughts on other forms of learning that might evolve using variants of the technology developed for anonymous peer review.

In this chapter, I use the phrase 'complex works' to refer to any substantial assignment (eg 20 per cent or more of the total mark) that defies simple objective assessment and places high demands on conventional marking techniques. The choice of words is an attempt to convey that the approach is broad and applies across many media and most disciplines.

RATIONALE FOR ANONYMOUS PEER REVIEW

Many employers want graduates who can do complex tasks with little supervision and create works that are at least close to professional standards. Thus it makes sense to base a substantial fraction of the mark given in many tertiary or final-year classes on complex works.

Complex works, however, are difficult to assess. Modern standards of accountability demand consistent and transparent assessment. Educational theory demands that the mark be accompanied by constructive feedback. If you try to live up to these standards, you are likely to find yourself spending 30 minutes to an hour processing a single assignment, and processing 100+ assignments becomes prohibitively time-consuming and expensive.

Peer and self-assessment have proven useful for formative assessment of complex works (Boud, 1995; Boud and Holmes, 1995; Campbell, 1996; Haaga, 1993; Horgan and Barnett, 1991; Jackson, 1996; Jenkinson, 1988; Marcoulides and Simkin, 1995; Rowntree, 1987; Sims, 1989; Stefani, 1994; Vatalaro 1990; Zariski, 1996). The approaches have many advantages. Firstly, spending an hour on the assessment of a single piece of work is feasible if you are only charged with assessing one or a few pieces of work. Secondly, student motivation to learn improves when students are respected and involved in the learning process. Furthermore, when the teacher's words go over a student's head, words from a fellow student may hit home. The student-assessors also benefit: being charged with assessment pushes students to think about the qualities that contribute to good work, gives them an additional incentive to learn material and helps them see the strengths and weaknesses of their own work in relation to that of their peers.

Peer and self-assessment, however, are problematic as a means for summative assessment of complex works. It has been shown that student markers can grade as consistently as professional teaching staff if standards are well defined and enough coaching is provided (Marcoulides and Simkin, 1995; Sims, 1989). These criteria can be satisfied for constrained works of low-to-medium complexity, for example marking essay questions on an examination where the points to be covered are well defined. However, for complex works of indeterminate form and content, there is no practical way to bring a class into consistent understanding of what constitutes excellence. In such cases, it is unlikely that marking based on a review by a single student will yield acceptable results.

Perception is also a problem. Students and outside authorities are likely to be uneasy with situations where marking could easily be affected by friendship, cheating, ego or low self-esteem. Discomfort may be overlooked for a few per cent of a student's mark but it is unlikely to be ignored for items with values of 20 per cent or more of the final mark.

ALTERNATIVE MODELS

Many institutions use peer-based evaluation in which input from multiple reviewers is synthesized by an editor, judge or chairperson. In the courts, trial by jury ensures against arbitrary judgments. In the arts and the artistic sports (dance, gymnastics, figure skating, etc), it is common practice to assess quality by pooling the opinions of a team of experts. In complex written works, anonymous peer review is the norm. In all of the above systems, pooling of opinions guards against arbitrary summative judgement and increases the credibility of the resulting evaluation.

The academic version of anonymous peer review is an especially interesting model because (in theory if not always in practice) it serves both summative and formative roles. Reviewers provide feedback that helps the author rewrite and improve the paper as well as providing the editor with a basis on which to evaluate the paper and make decisions regarding publication.

Conceptually, anonymous peer review, with the teacher serving as editor and the students serving as reviewers, offers most of the formative advantages of peer review, but provides a much stronger basis for summative assessment. Consideration of a number of peer reviews, overseen by a teacher, is at least as strong, in terms of legitimization, as review by a teacher, particularly in large classes where the 'teacher' is likely to be a paid marker of unspecified qualifications.

The barriers to adapting anonymous peer review systems in education seem to be physical and technical. Having students hand in multiple copies of their work, redistributing those works to two or more students and pooling and assimilating the lot and converting it to marks and organized comments to be returned to students is a daunting organizational task, especially in a large class.

However, all but the actual review part of the exercise can be broken down into parts that can be done using computers. Tracking several hundred objects and associated marks through a complicated exchange procedure is simple compared to many industrial and retail inventory systems. Increasingly, students are producing complex works in digital form and thus in a form that can be submitted electronically and stored on disk. If electronic products are funnelled through a network and logged on a networked database, very complex patterns of exchange can be implemented automatically. Reviews can likewise be electronically submitted, sorted and associated with the papers to which they pertain and delivered to the editor-marker in an orderly fashion for final determination of marks. Afterward, the marks can be attached to papers and returned, along with the reviewers' comments, over the network, to the students. Moreover, double anonymity systems, in which the reviewers do not learn the author's identity, and the author does not learn the reviewers' identity, are easy to set up and maintain and a process of rewrites and re-reviews could be implemented through minor modifications of the system. In short, all of the tedious paper shuffling that makes multi-reviewer anonymous peer review difficult with paper can be done instantaneously through a database-network system. What is needed is appropriate software, a network and computer access for all students and markers.

PRELIMINARY FINDINGS

Literature review turned up no instances of the use of anonymous peer review in education or of electronic implementation of anonymous peer review. Scanning the World Wide Web and participation in various newsgroups related to computers and education has turned up a few sites where student-authored Web pages have been reviewed and assessed through systems that gather responses online (Cox, 1998), and an evaluation of the learning value of collaborative hypertext (Makkonen, 1997). The Australian Research Council is doing trials on an electronic system for anonymous peer review of research proposals, but this will take several years to implement, and carries a five- or six-digit price tag (pers com., T. Rudd, Department of Employment, Education, Training and Youth Affairs (DEETYA)).

In 1997, I attempted anonymous peer review exercises in two units with no computer assistance other than the use of spreadsheets for tracking results. The intent was to gain design insight by studying student reaction to anonymous peer review and to bide time, waiting to find the right programmer or the right software to make an online system work. The first (Case 1) was a 2,000- word paper, written in a required second-year unit on atmospheric science with an enrolment of 160 students. The second (Case 2) was a simulated consultant's report looking at longer-term futures in a third-year unit entitled Coastal and Marine Management with an enrolment of 21 students.

In both cases, students reviewed two papers and had their work reviewed by two peers. The form of anonymity varied: in Case 1, both authors' names and reviewers' names were withheld; in Case 2, only reviewers' names were withheld. In both cases, reviews were marked and the respective assessed values of the assignment and the reviews were 20 per cent and 5 per cent of the total mark for the unit. In Case 1, two honours students served as editor/markers. In Case 2, I did all the editing.

Student response was monitored. In Case 1, a questionnaire was administered in class at the end of the semester. In Case 2, an hour was set aside on the last day of classes for students to provide verbal feedback on this and other aspects of the class.

The exercises were successful from the editors' perspective. It took the marker/editors about half as long to evaluate and synthesize peer reviews as it would to evaluate papers from scratch and they found the editing task much less stressful than conventional marking.

Student responses showed both positive signs and large margins for improvement. Perhaps the strongest outcome was an overwhelming preference for anonymity. In Case 1, 98 per cent of the students surveyed disagreed with a suggestion that it would be better to know whose work they were reviewing. In Case 2, where reviewers, but not authors, were anonymous, many voiced discomfort about marking the work of someone they knew, both during the assessment and in the *post hoc* feedback session. Students also agreed strongly that marking other students' work taught them valuable lessons.

In Case 1, the largest problem was probably the uneven quality of student feedback. A fair proportion, perhaps as much as half, of second-year students do not know the rules of grammar and have a poor notion of what a paper should look like. Thus, many of the reviews given were of limited value. Students who got two such reviews were unlikely to be impressed. It also appears that the exercise was flawed in not providing feedback to the reviewers on the quality of their reviews. Hindsight suggests some useful ways to overcome these problems, for example:

- Provide three or four reviews per paper and direct students' attention to the better reviews – which I would hesitate to do except in an electronically managed system.
- Add an unmarked practice round in which all students mark some sample works and are asked to compare their marking to models of good marking, which could also be done online.

In Case 2, I tried to provide students with feedback on the feedback they gave and found the exercise was a logistical nightmare on paper. The equivalent activity would be fairly simple on a well-configured database.

TECHNICAL ASPECTS

The basic components of an anonymous peer review system are a number of computer users (students and editors) interlinked by a server-side database through a network. The technical demands are not extraordinarily complex. The real difficulty is not in any one part of the system but in getting the whole thing to operate together in an institutional context.

Database

To handle the exchange, the software must be capable of handling many-to-many exchanges. It must also have reasonably good security, both in terms of protecting the operating system from hacking and in terms of preventing students from violating one another's privacy. Both demands are common in business applications and many software tools are available. However, the tasks are not recommended for beginners.

Network

Common Gateway Interface (CGI) software is needed to handle the interface between the database and the network. This needs to be capable of sending documents of any type that are likely to be assessed between any two computers that are likely to be on the system, which may raise some problems with mail systems and encoding. Off-the-shelf software does not seem to be able to provide such services in a multi-platform environment; thus the activity requires skilful systems programmers and/or administrators who can put adequate time into setting up and maintaining the system. Another alternative is to go to homogeneous systems (eg all Macintosh or all NT) and restrict the formats of the data that are to be exchanged in the assessment.

Hardware and software need to be matched with students, tutors and teachers who have adequate computer skills and adequate computer access to make use of the system. This is coming fast, but may not have arrived at many institutions.

PROSPECTS

The university computational environments are rapidly getting friendlier for the development of online peer exchange systems. In the early twenty-first century, it seems likely that they will be logical extensions of technologies that are in place, rather than items that require major software purchases and new systems. Thus, implementation is likely to be more a matter of meetings and institutional finagling and software grafts rather than *de nova* development. Facilitating developments include:

- **Growth of demand**. In my own institution, the secretarial costs of handling the work (papers, sound-clips, graphics, etc) of students taking online units of instruction have mounted to the point where development of an electronic assignment exchange system is cost-effective. We have a prototype running. This was explicitly created with a mind to supporting anonymous peer review down the line. It is, however, premature to document the system at this point. Our administration is getting increasingly serious about developing security measures required to build a student interface on to the internal records system. Computer ownership and network subscription rates are growing rapidly among students, hence access problems are shrinking and the amount that can be done without training is increasing.
- **Development of other tools to handle online teaching**. I would not be surprised to be in a position to say that tools for horizontal exchange have begun to be incorporated into one of the cheaper systems for online course management by the time this volume comes to print. Most of the tools for management of online courses now include some sort of database. To my knowledge, only Lotus Learning Space, which grew out of corporate training needs and is based on software that is used in commerce, has a full-featured Structured Query Language (SQL) database that could be manipulated to direct horizontal flows in the classroom. Learning Space is among the more expensive of the tools for online teaching, which restricts its adoption in university environments. It seems likely, however, that competition among vendors will result in the incorporation of more powerful and more accessible database facilities in future generations of software.
- **Growth of skilled workforce**. The explosion of electronic marketing and electronic data distribution has stimulated a burst in the number of software engineering students who can be counted on to link a database to a server. Meanwhile, proliferation of software tools has greatly increased the sophistication of what they can produce.

- **Improvements of self-help software tools**. Tools such as spelling, grammar and syntax checkers have improved to the point where much 'red ink' can be avoided, leaving assessors more time for higher-order questions such as quality of research, design and critical reasoning.

WIDER ADVANTAGES OF ELECTRONIC IMPLEMENTATION

Shifting text handling from paper to electronic media opens the way for many new forms of many-to-many exchanges and for breaking out of the top down mode of teaching. Anonymous peer review is but one of many possibilities.

For example, it may be that many students require guided practice before they function well as reviewers and that students with writing problems would benefit from a round of friendly reviews before submission of their papers. The fleetness of electronic media allows for activities involving review and rewrite before marking. A round of practice reviews, in which all students marked up the same text, could be added as a warm-up exercise before the peer review exercise. Likewise, informal paper exchanges of various sorts, anonymous, named, team-based or structured, between at-risk students and mentors, might precede submission for assessment. Review pools could be set up in which students could seek as many reviews as they wanted, provided they were willing to provide reviews in exchange. All limits are off on the geography of exchange: worldwide exchange is as easy as local.

Alternative systems, for example systems in which students first develop an outline or a proposal, exchange comments and go on to write their papers could be arranged. This might stimulate dialogue and thought in the conceptualization phase of writing; it would also make it hard to plagiarize, which has the potential to become a serious problem if a large volume of electronic manuscripts is in circulation. Team-writing projects could be arranged and the teacher could recede from the position of judge and jury to act as a monitor and facilitator whose job it is to help students help each other. Cascading exercises in which third-year students review the work of second-year students, and second-years review the work of first-years could be set up.

The technologies required for the above exercises are not things of the far-distant future. Every one of them is available today. What is lacking is integration. I have discussed the need to link databases to student work over the Web, with the assistance of security/authentication protocols. A larger need, however, is for educators to stop thinking of the Web in terms of broadcasting and newsgroups and begin employing it to structure and guide and facilitate interaction between and among students.

REFERENCES

Boud, D, ed (1995) *Enhancing Learning through Self-assessment*, Kogan Page, London

Boud, D and Holmes, H (1995) Self and peer marking in a large technical subject, in *Enhancing Learning through Self-assessment*, ed D Boud, Kogan Page, London, pp 63–78

Campbell, E (1996) Case study 32: research assignment, in *Assessing Learning in Universities*, eds P Nightingale *et al*, Professional Development Ctr, UNSW, Sydney

Cox, B (1998) Virtual school: taming the electronic frontier, George Mason University, http://www.virtualschool.edu/

Crichton, M (1998) *Travels*, Macmillan, London

Haaga, D A F (1993) Peer review of term papers in graduate psychology courses, *Teaching of Psychology*, **20** (1), pp 28–31

Horgan, D and Barnett, L (1991) Peer review: it works, Annual Meeting: American Educational Research Association, AERS, Chicago, p 11

Jackson, M (1996) Case study 53: peer reading and self evaluation, in *Assessing Learning in Universities*, eds P Nightingale *et al*, Professional Development Ctr, UNSW, Sydney, pp 219–20

Jenkinson, EB (1988) Learning to write/writing to learn, *Phi Delta Kappan*, **69** (10), pp 712–17

Makkonen, P (1997) Does collaborative hypertext support learning as a whole, EVTEK, Enable http://www.enable.evitech.fi/enable97/submissions/pekka.makkonen/paper.html (accessed November 1998)

Marcoulides, G A and Simkin, M G (1995) The consistency of peer review in student writing projects, *Journal of Education for Business*, **70** (4), pp 220–23

Rowntree, D (1987) *Assessing Students: How shall we know them*, Kogan Page, London

Sims, G K (1989) Peer review in the classroom: a teaching and grading tool, *Journal of Agronomic Education*, **18** (2), pp 105–08

Stefani, L (1994) Peer, self and tutor assessment, *Studies in Higher Education*, **19** (1), pp 69–75

Vatalaro, P (1990) Putting students in change of peer review, *Journal of Teaching Writing*, **9**, pp 21–29

Zariski, A (1996) Student peer assessment in tertiary education: promise, perils and practice, Teaching and Learning Forum, Perth, WA http://wwwtlc1.murdoch.edu/asu/pubs/tlf/tlf96/zaris189.html (accessed 31 March 1998)

11

Increasing learner responsibility and support with the aid of adaptive formative assessment using QM designer software

Christine Steven and Ian Hesketh

This chapter will review the creative development of the use of Question Mark (QM) in the area of formative assessments, considering its transformation from a static to a dynamic delivery mechanism. It will describe the interactive development of the current system and its evolution from being provider led to user led. This has manifested itself in an increase in learner responsibility resulting from this interaction between user and provider during the development of the application. The vehicle for the study has been a level 1 core module in computer science at the University of Luton.

The modular credit scheme at this university gives students the flexibility to build a programme of study from a range of modules within the scheme. The range is constantly updated to ensure programmes remain contemporary. Each module carries credit points which the students accumulate while they study. Brown and Saunders (1996) have discussed the merits of modular credit schemes and the university's scheme enhances its positive attitude towards non-standard entrants. Many students enter the undergraduate programme through a non-standard route and it is against this diversity of student body that the level 1 modules, particularly those which are core, have to ensure that the student interest, motivation and performance is maintained.

Two cohorts of students undertaking this level 1 core module in the field of computer science, also designated core for the fields of information systems and computer systems engineering, were canvassed for their experiences and expectations of computer-based assessment (CBA). Typically, the numbers of students taking this module are well in excess of 100. The students are a mix not only of entrance qualification, but also programme of study. Many of the students are mature, having entered via one of the non-traditional routes.

As Maier *et al* (1998) indicate, the diversity of the student body is one of a number of pressures within higher education. This exercise has partially met some of their solutions in that the tailored feedback has allowed the tutor to facilitate and increase student independence.

The university has an extensive computerized assessment system based on Question Mark Designer for Windows software. Question Mark allows the computerized delivery and marking of objective tests through an authoring shell (Dempster, 1994). While the system initially focused on the delivery of end-of-module examinations, its use to deliver formative and self-assessments has grown. It is this aspect which will be explored further. The ability of the software to provide instant and detailed feedback, using text and graphics, meant it was particularly suitable for use on this module, as tests could be designed to meet the needs of a large diverse group with a range of educational and computing experiences.

A mix of traditional lectures, tutorials and practical sessions are used to teach the module. Each lecture lasts two hours, during which time students receive handouts and are shown overhead slides. Because of the size of the group, only a limited time is allocated to questions and answers during the lecture. At the end of the lecture sessions, students are given short exercises, extracted mainly from the set text, to complete for formal assessment. Each set of exercises is associated specifically with the lecture material presented at that session. A number of these exercises have answers provided and students are expected to evaluate the applicability of these answers and encouraged to put forward their own ideas at all stages.

The first cohort of students was introduced to CBA and the testing method through the use of a series of short (10-question) computer-based tests (CBTs). This was repeated at regular intervals throughout the module and was intended to allow students to develop familiarity with the software and become accustomed to the types of questions that were to be used in the end-of-module examination. Research indicates that it is important to provide adequate training in CBA software (Bull, 1994; Proctor and Donoghue, 1994). Students were aware that a record was being kept of their use of the software and this enabled staff to assess the effectiveness of the introductory session. Although a detailed log of student use was not maintained, it was apparent that the substantial majority of the cohort had made use of the software. Use and effectiveness of the software was discussed in the drop-in tutorial sessions and any comments and feedback from students were noted and acted upon where appropriate.

These objective test questions included a basic level of feedback for the students, who were told their score for the question and whether or not they had chosen the correct response. The students completed a questionnaire both prior and subsequent to their use of the Question Mark package. In addition, as part of their directed learning, they were asked to comment on the tasters and also on the Question Mark package. They were required to write a brief report outlining the positive and negative points of both areas.

The second cohort of students were introduced to the Question Mark software through identical introductory sessions and written instructions. However, as a result of the comments made by this first cohort, the tasters were amended to provide a detailed level of feedback associated with each possible response to the question presented.

When looking to increase the sensitivity of feedback, the available default mechanisms were considered. It was quickly ascertained that these mechanisms were unable to provide the level of flexibility required, the on-screen feedback windows were too small to provide any worthwhile explanation and students were unable to retry multiple selection/response questions.

This was deemed unfortunate, as these questions, when used properly, can promote and assess deeper learning by forcing the student to consider the contextual framework of their responses.

With the principle of providing tailored feedback to all questions in mind, we were required to disable the default feedback mechanisms and substitute them with a mixture of generic confirmation and tailored feedback pages linked to individual question scores with navigation being controlled by the insertion of 'jumps'. A result of this was that options within the 'Test Caption' control information, ie *show question number*, *running score* and *number of questions answered so far*, were necessarily disabled to avoid student confusion. Additional on-screen information on question number was therefore required (Figure 11.1).

For the majority of questions, given the limited scope for incorrect selection in combination with the option of being able to retry, only two additional 'questions' were required.

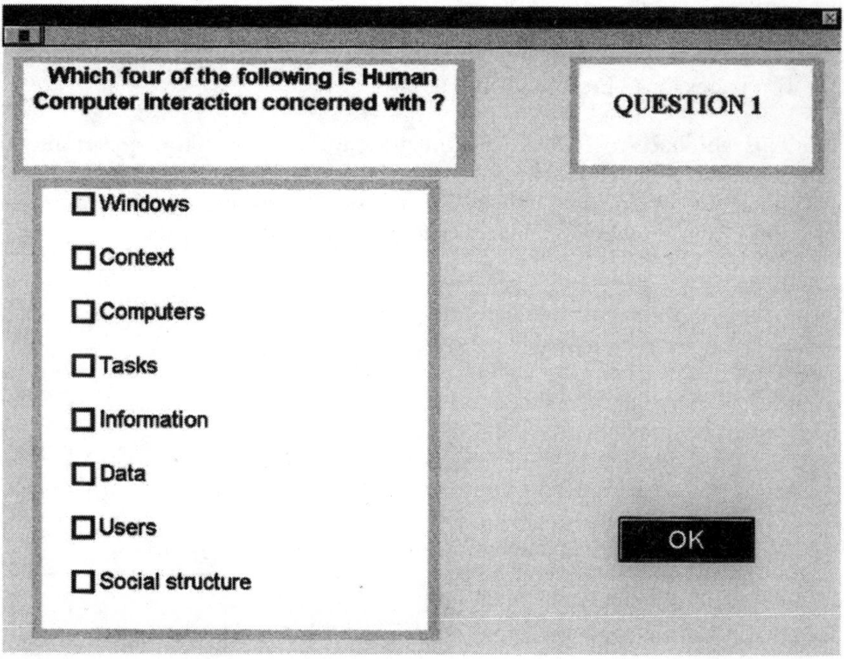

Figure 11.1 *Example of multiple response question*

At points within the CBA, multiple selection or response questions were inserted. The average number of correct responses required for these questions were four out of eight options. The number of possible response combinations were worked out using the formula:

$$\frac{n!}{k!\,(n-k)!}$$

Where: n = total number of answers to choose from
k = number of responses required

This calculation told us that we would have to provide 70 tailored feedback pages in response to answer combinations. This was quickly discounted as non-viable, not only in terms of software limitations but also in terms of utility.

To reduce the workload, a benchmark score for the question was determined and a differential scoring grid was created. This meant the main task was to highlight the wrong answers and if the least correct answers were selected (indicating lack of understanding of key principles, etc), even with three correct answers the benchmark would not be met. For the student to continue, they would need at least three out of the four (Figure 11.2).

By using the grid, a total of four tailored feedback pages were required:

- A page confirming correct selection.
- A page indicating the benchmark score had not been met, which would advise the student to undertake additional reading or study. This would end the test session with transportation to a generic reminder to take the advice.
- Two pages for point totals 5 and 6.

Students who had scored 5 or 6 on the question were given the opportunity to retry by making the feedback page a 'push button' question (non-scoring) linked back to the initial scoring question. This was possible as the correct combination of responses was not given, only an indication of the incorrect selection.

	RIGHT ANSWERS				***WRONG ANSWERS***				
					Nearly	Not close	Far away	Way out	
SCORE	Score for right answer = 2				0	−1	−2	−3	Total
4 of 4	Y	Y	Y	Y	N	N	N	N	8
3 of 4	Y	Y	Y	N	Y	N	N	N	6
3 of 4	Y	Y	Y	N	N	Y	N	N	5
3 of 4	Y	Y	Y	N	N	N	Y	N	4
3 of 4	Y	Y	Y	N	N	N	N	Y	3

Figure 11.2 *Simple grid for determination of combination score*

Below is an example of a question used with the first cohort of students using the standard feedback mechanisms. The same question was used for the second cohort and is also shown with its tailored responses and how the programming for a multiple response or selection question would look in the Designer software.

The structuring and manipulation of the feedback pages and 'jumps' within the Designer software is relatively straightforward, and while this was usually carried out linked to selection or multiple response questions, it would be possible to do this with the other available question types. However, the validity of this in terms of preparation time and the value to students given limited scope for incorrect responses is questionable.

In line with the approach to CBA at the University of Luton, the use of Question Mark in formative assessment has been developed progressively in conjunction with academic requirements and in response to student feedback. It is our view that the integration of formative assessment, as with the module under discussion, into the teaching process and curricula has accelerated the demand for ownership of the learning process.

Both cohorts completed the tasters in the same timescale together with similar short weekly exercises. They were also required to write a brief report on the Question Mark software and the effectiveness of the tasters.

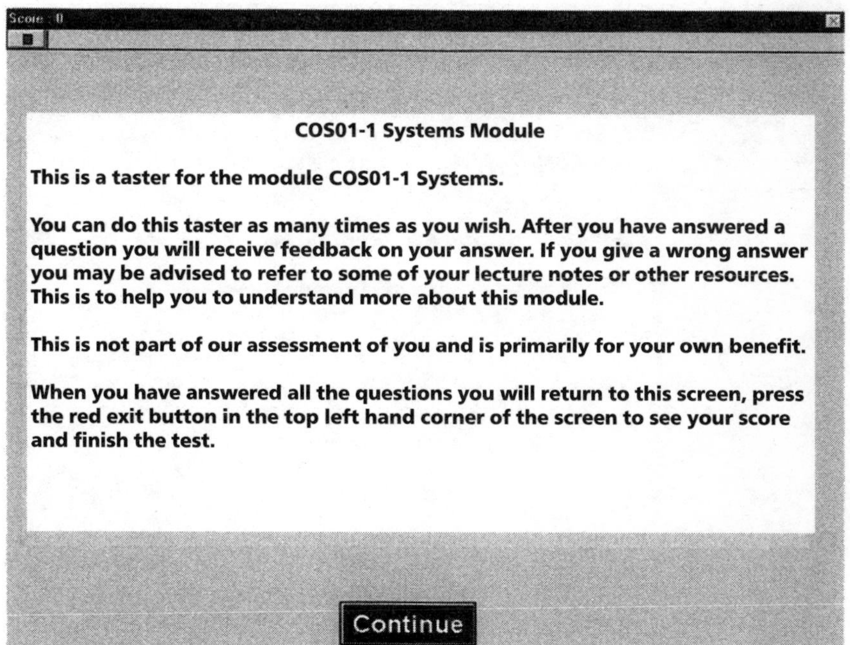

Figure 11.3 *Screenshot of 'Taster' introduction*

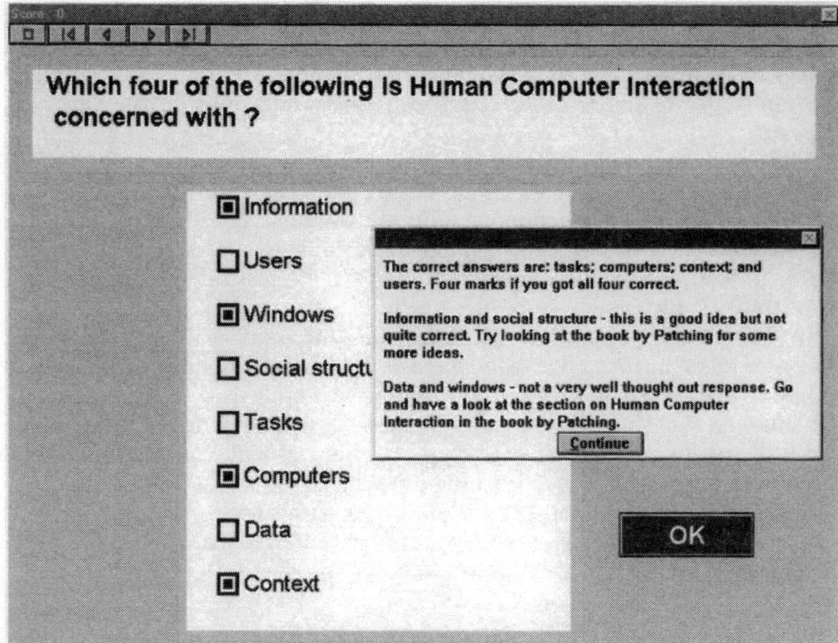

Figure 11.4 *Screenshot showing limitations of default feedback mechanisms*

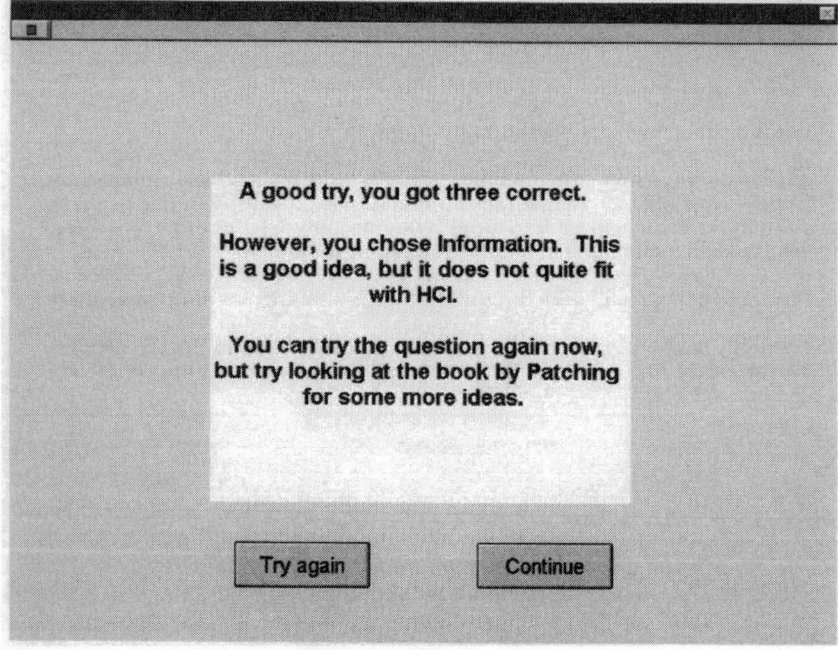

Figure 11.5 *Example of tailored feedback (score = 6)*

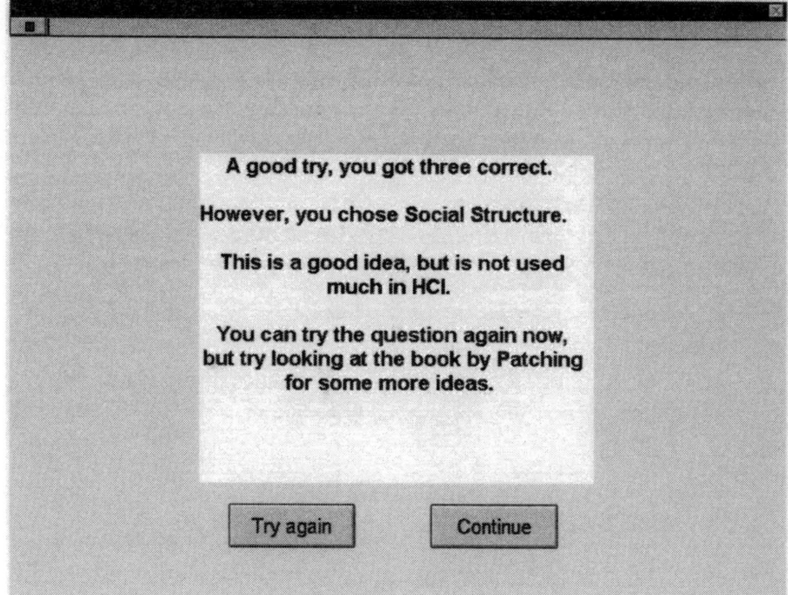

Figure 11.6 *Example of tailored feedback (score = 5)*

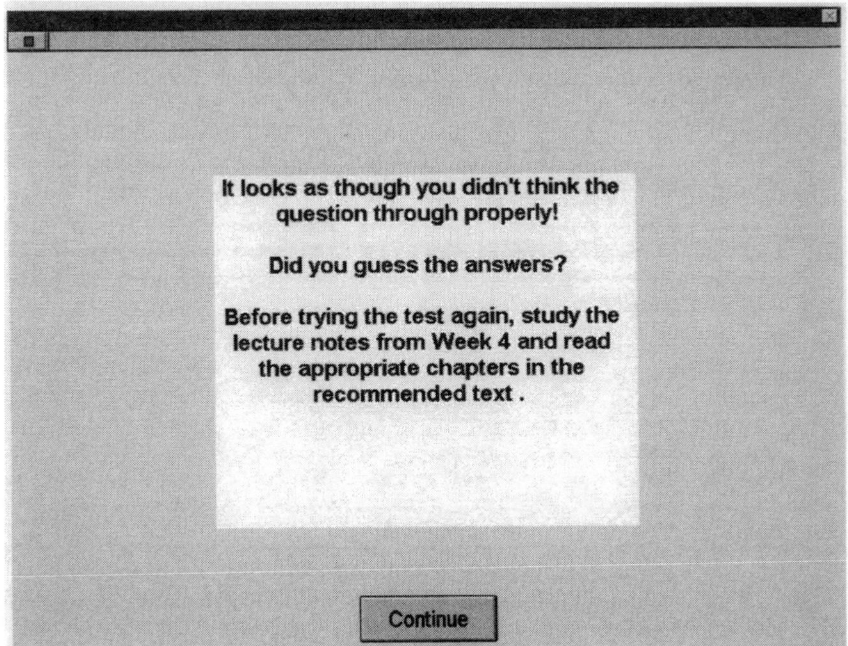

Figure 11.7 *Individual question score <5*

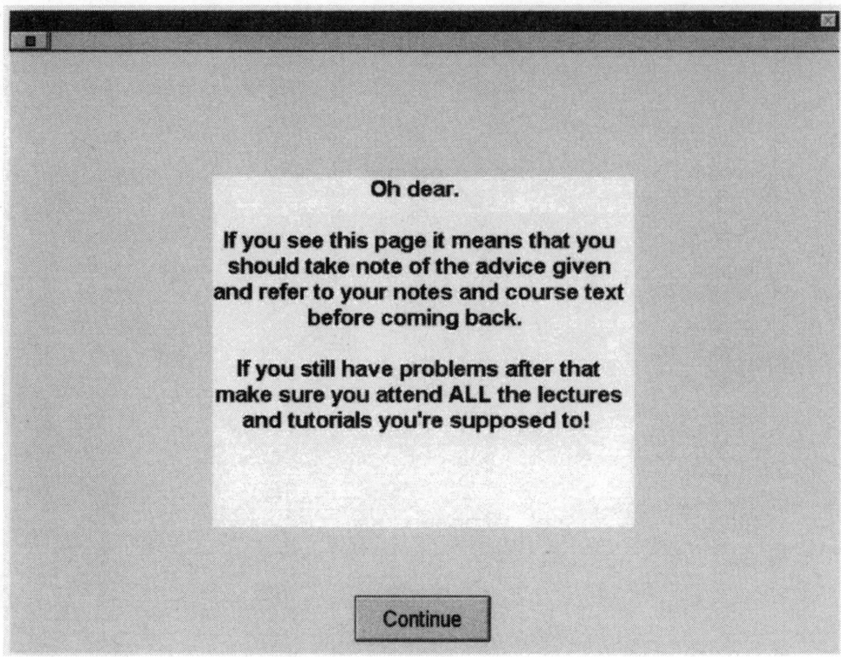

Figure 11.8 *Generic 'bomb-out' screenshot*

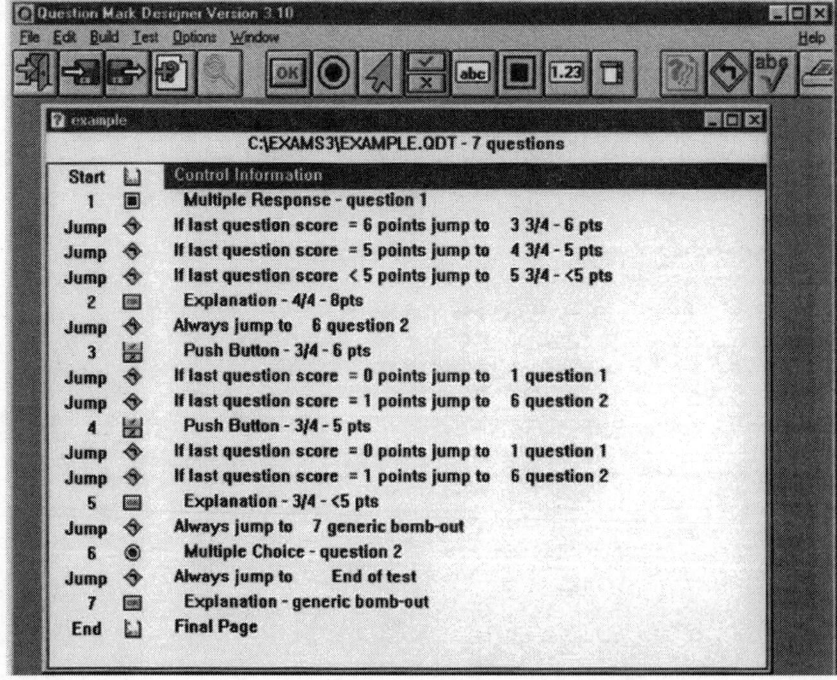

Figure 11.9 *'Programming' example for multiple-response question used*

Most of the comments concerning Question Mark and the tests obtained from the assignment were positive from both cohorts. The constructive comments, particularly those relating to feedback, were noted and alterations made. One student commented that the tasters were 'a valuable learning tool in that it reinforces vocabulary and graphical representation that are commonly used'.

Some of the students requested hard copies of both the questions and feedback, indicating a certain reluctance to accept assessments in a paperless format. Some students repeated the tests until they gained 100 per cent and although this was not the prime objective they countered by saying that it helped them to revise successfully. Twenty-seven per cent of the 96/97 cohort commented that the screen layout was dull; however, a few students elaborated and considered that the layout was acceptable for examinations, but that a more elaborate screen would be appropriate for formative tests.

Feedback was generally considered to be motivating. One student said it 'encourages you by giving positive reinforcement when a question is answered correctly, and also incorrectly, which keeps motivation levels up.'

Of the 95/96 cohort, 79 per cent of responses related to the feedback given through the tests. They appreciated the immediacy of the final score on completion of the test. Students also liked being shown the correct answer, but 42 per cent commented that an explanation of the correct answer would have been more useful. Others said it would be better to make them think about the answer, rather than immediately giving them the correct answer.

The major difference between the two sets of tests was the provision of detailed feedback, rather than basic correct/incorrect feedback. The 96/97 cohort valued the additional feedback, considering a major advantage of the tests to be the provision of instant feedback, and that the references and guidance notes given when their answer was incorrect were very valuable. Students made the following comments concerning the benefits of detailed feedback:

- '[Feedback] offers possible reading/resources, which guide you when things go wrong and tell you where to get help.'
- 'The comments did not put the user down in any way and tried to find out what was right about the answer rather than what was wrong. This together with a hint of humour made the package very enjoyable to use.'

The value in the more detailed feedback is reflected in the 88 per cent of the 96/97 cohort who stated that the tasters were useful for revision purposes, whereas of the previous cohort, only 47 per cent made this observation. The more discerning students requested tutorial packs as computerized objective test material, written in the same style as the tasters, for self-assessment.

Our results indicate that while students certainly benefit from feedback, the type and extent of feedback provided affects their perception of the course and can enhance their learning. To merely provide students with the correct response when they answer a question wrongly, or confirm their correct response, does not exploit the full potential of CBA. While this type of approach satisfies the need for immediate feedback, it does not necessarily make the feedback meaningful. Feedback that provides students with detailed explanations is far more valuable. In addition, that which encourages students to refer to journal articles or books, re-read their notes or explore other resources such as the Internet can motivate student learning in a way that can rarely be achieved by tutors of large classes.

Statistical analysis shows that the students in the 96/97 cohort performed statistically better in all their assessments than the 95/96 cohort. The 96/97 cohort were more positive about the benefits of the feedback given to them in the tasters and the majority considered that this helped them to revise.

After consideration of the positive comments made by both cohorts of students, a similar approach has been adopted in some level 2 modules. At level 3, the use of CBA is progressing with caution and forms only a part of the whole assessment process.

Students who have used this software for formative assessments have shown an increased awareness of the potential of software for teaching, learning and assessment purposes. This has impacted upon the research possibilities that they consider for their final-year projects. Student feedback has informed decisions about the visual presentation and layout for both formative and summative CBA.

Further work has now been undertaken to incorporate the use of the Internet and CBA into the module that has superseded that described in this chapter. The levels of sophistication of the assessments have been enhanced and these, together with the use of the Internet for extra course delivery, have led to a more integrated style of delivery. The results of this new venture have yet to be analysed fully but initial results indicate higher attendance at lectures and practical sessions and a general raising of motivation levels. The results of the newly introduced computerized phased tests, which give a good coverage of the module material, appear to be giving grades slightly higher than those previously obtained. However, whether this is statistically significant has not, as yet, been tested.

REFERENCES

Brown, S and Saunders, D (1996) The challenges of modularization in innovations, *Education and Training International*, **32** (2), pp 96–105

Bull, J (1994) Computer-based assessment: some issues for consideration, *Active Learning*, **1**, pp 18–21

Dempster, J (1994) Review: Question Mark Designer for Windows, *Active Learning*, **1**, pp 47–50

Maier, P, Barnett, L, Warren, A and Brunner, D (1998) *Using Technology in Teaching and Learning*, p 39, Kogan Page, London

Proctor, A and Donoghue, D (1994) Computer-based assessment: a case study in geography, *Active Learning*, **1**, pp 29–34

12

Computer managed learning as an aid to formative assessment in higher education

Leith Sly and Léonie J Rennie

INTRODUCTION

Computer managed learning (CML) systems for assessment and student tracking have advantages in managing large numbers of student assessments. If lecturers are to use CML as one part of their assessment programme, it is important that they use effectively all of the information available. The tests generated using the CML system provide feedback relating both to student performance and the effectiveness of the questions in the question bank, hence the information can be used for either formative or summative purposes. In this chapter, the features of CML that promote opportunities for formative assessment are explored.

FORMATIVE AND SUMMATIVE ASSESSMENT

Scriven (1967) first used the terms formative and summative in the context of curriculum evaluation, but they now have wide currency in assessment. However, formative assessment does not have a strictly defined meaning. Black and William (1998, p 7), in their review of the literature on classroom formative assessment, interpret it as 'encompassing all those activities undertaken by teachers, and/or by their students, which provide information to be used as feedback to modify the teaching and learning activities in which they are engaged'.

Sadler (1998, p 77) refers to formative assessment 'that is specifically intended to provide feedback on performance to improve and accelerate learning'. Rolfe and McPherson (1995) see it as a testing method without academic penalty that reveals shortcomings in students' understanding while allowing them to take responsibility for their own learning. In all cases, the aim is to improve a process at a stage where change can be made rather than to appraise a finished product.

In contrast, summative assessment is generally an end-point assessment that contributes to students' grades. The terms formative and summative refer to the purpose of the assessment rather than to the methods used (Brown and Knight, 1994; Rowntree, 1987), thus the same test is regarded as formative when it provides only feedback on performance, but summative when the mark contributes to the final grade.

COMPUTER MANAGED LEARNING SYSTEMS

Computer managed learning systems are software packages with several common features, including generating tests from banks of questions, marking of tests generated, analysis of the results and keeping records of students' marks and progress. Feedback to students on their responses is common.

CML systems usually hold many banks of questions, each of which can be categorized into smaller components, such as topics, learning outcomes or objectives. Often questions can also be coded on a variety of characteristics, for example degree of difficulty and cognitive content. So, we have test banks, which can be subdivided into component parts, made up of questions which themselves can be categorized.

The key function of a CML system is to generate tests. It has a template or a course-map where the parameters used to generate any test are stored. There is a range of available options, depending on the specific CML system in use. Some tests may be generated using the same questions for all students, while others may be set to select questions randomly – but to take them from specific parts of the bank of questions. In the latter case, students are more likely to have unique tests, depending on the number of questions available for selection. Another option could include the coding of individual questions as a variable, for example a test could be set to draw a specified number of questions from selected objectives but to take only those questions coded at a particular difficulty level. Again, the test could specify that certain questions are mandatory. Most systems are able to generate tests that use multiple-choice, true-false, short answer, matching and calculation questions.

Most systems also have the ability to give students immediate feedback on incorrect answers and supply them with the correct response. Some give students additional information in the form of comments on their response. Because systems retain students' answers to questions, they are able to produce a report of the distribution of question responses and students' marks. This feedback can alert lecturers to problem areas in terms of question quality and also student performance. Because CML retains information about incorrect as well as correct answers, lecturers can be made aware of common misconceptions held by students and are then able to address these before summative assessment.

COMPUTER MANAGED LEARNING AT CURTIN UNIVERSITY OF TECHNOLOGY

The CML system at Curtin University uses primarily multiple-choice questions, drawn at random from a test bank according to parameters requested by the lecturer. While the system handles all question types mentioned earlier, most lecturers select multiple-choice. Although advantages may exist for using questions that require written answers, that is constructed response items (Birenbaum and Tatsuoka, 1987), increasing student numbers and lecturer workloads have been associated with the use of multiple-choice questions, which are marked by the system. Students access both practice tests and assessed tests, but only the assessed tests contribute to the overall grade. The typical contribution of CML tests to the overall assessment is 20 per cent.

Standard procedures for CML testing

Students come to the CML lab at their booked time, are marked off the booking list and proceed to a terminal. They select the appropriate subdirectory for their particular subject, identify themselves to the system, using both their identification number and password, and their test is randomly generated. A paper copy of the test is printed with the student identification number and students are required to produce photo identification to verify that they are collecting the correct test. They complete the test under supervision in the CML lab, then enter their answers on the terminal. Again students are required to identify themselves with both ID and password and they are then prompted for answers to their specific test. Before answers are finally marked, the student is able to review and change any answer. No feedback is given at this stage. This review and change process can be repeated as many times as students require.

When students indicate they are satisfied with their answers, the test is marked and immediate feedback given on incorrect responses. Students are encouraged to print this feedback, which consists of the correct response to any question the student answered incorrectly, and use this 'error summary' in conjunction with their printed test paper to examine their errors. Students may take their error summary from the lab but test papers are retained so as not to compromise the test bank. Writing is disallowed on the error summary, though students are able to query any question or answer and request that their test paper be sent to their lecturer for comment. In this case, students usually make an appointment to meet with the lecturer to discuss the test.

THE CONTRIBUTION OF COMPUTER MANAGED LEARNING TO FORMATIVE ASSESSMENT

As the type of assessment used at university level has the potential to influence student grades (Brown and Knight, 1994; Heywood, 1977; Nightingale *et al*, 1996; Piper *et al*, 1996; Webster, 1992), the contribution of formative testing to improve student performance will be discussed in the context of CML testing. The features of the CML system used for formative assessment are the possibility of a practice test, the feedback to students and feedback to lecturers. Some lecturers allow students to do a practice test that is computer marked and, although the results are available to lecturers, these scores do not contribute to students' grades. Importantly, feedback is available to the student on incorrect responses and students are encouraged to review their test papers and error summaries under supervised conditions in the CML lab. Often lecturers provide a textbook that can be used for reference in this review process.

Two kinds of feedback are provided to lecturers. They receive a statistical analysis of the responses to questions and also a performance report, which lists all students enrolled in their subject with their test marks. The performance report alerts lecturers to students who are falling behind and the statistical analysis is useful in identifying those content areas in which students are experiencing difficulty.

Currently, a practice test is used only in some subjects, but it is used in a variety of ways. Some lecturers make the test compulsory while others leave it as optional. Some practice tests cover the same content as the assessed test, while others select only part of the assessed test content. It is common for students to be offered a practice test before the first unit assessment test, but not before any additional unit assessment tests. In all cases, the practice test is used as formative assessment and scores do not contribute to grades.

INVESTIGATION OF THE EFFECT OF THE PRACTICE TEST

Because the practice test adds to the workload and expense of running the CML system, research has been undertaken to investigate the influence that the practice test has on student performance. There are two ways a practice test may contribute to enhanced performance in later CML tests. Firstly, if the practice test covers similar content then feedback on performance may diagnose areas of weakness and assist students' revision for the assessment tests. Secondly, the practice test allows students to familiarize themselves with the CML system and may allay anxiety during the assessment tests.

This chapter reports the results of two studies of first-year university students – one group in economics, the other in psychology – which investigated the effect of the practice test on performance in later CML tests. In each case, the CML component of the subject assessment consisted of a practice test and two compulsory unit assessment tests. In economics, the practice test and first assessment test covered identical topics and were of equal length, but in psychology, the practice test covered only half of the topics and was half the length of the first assessment test. The practice test was optional for the economics students but compulsory for the psychology students. The second assessment test in both subject areas was also randomly generated, but there was no practice test to precede it. This test was drawn from a different part of the test bank, so no questions would have been encountered previously by any student. Students received feedback on their responses to questions on all tests.

Results of the economics study

Table 12.1 reports test results for the population of 277 economics students. The percentage means show that those students who sat the optional practice test increased their mean mark from 56.65 to 71.78, which is a statistically significant difference (dependent $t=12.66$, $p<0.001$) with a substantial effect size of 0.98. Effect sizes are the difference between means divided by the pooled standard deviation (after Hedges, 1981). Effect sizes for correlated comparisons are calculated following Dunlap *et al* (1996).

On the first assessment test, this group of students also performed better than those who had not sat the practice test. The difference was statistically significant (independent $t=4.38$, $p<0.001$) with an effect size of 0.54.

Table 12.1 *Mean scores (%) on the CML assessment component for economics students*

	Practice test group			*Non-practice test group*			
Test	*N*	*Mean*	*SD*	*N*	*Mean*	*SD*	*t*
Practice (optional)	152	56.65	16.1				
Assessment 1	152	71.78	14.45	125	63.56	16.36	4.38**
Assessment 2	150	63.73	17.26	117	57.35	17.03	3.02*

* $p<0.01$, ** $p<0.001$

The practice test group also outperformed the non-practice test group when compared on the second assessment test, even though there was no practice test before this test. Again, there was a statistically significant difference in the means with a modest effect size of 0.37.

It is possible that their superior results were a consequence of the more able group selecting the practice test but there were no independent data available to test this hypothesis. Subsequently, the study was replicated with a different group of first-year economics students in another semester (Sly, in press). Here, similar results were obtained and, based on the performance score used for university entry, no relationship was found between ability and selection of the practice test. Taken together, these findings suggest that the practice test does enhance later performance, but the reason for this is not clear. The next study investigated the effect of the content covered in the practice test.

Results of the psychology study

In this study, the compulsory practice test was half as long as the first assessment test and covered only half of its content. The results from the first assessment are divided into two equal parts. Part A covers topics examined by the practice test, and Part B covers topics not previously examined. Table 12.2 reports the percentage mean scores on the different tests for a sample of 323 psychology students.

Table 12.2 *Mean scores (%) on the CML assessment component for psychology students*

Test		*Mean*	*SD*
Practice		70.90	16.44
Assessment 1 (total)		75.76	12.18
Assessment 1	Part A	77.51	12.95
Assessment 1	Part B	73.98	15.97

The percentage mean scores in Table 12.2 show that students performed better overall on the first assessment test than they did on the practice test. In particular, they performed better on Part A (topics that were included in the practice test) than on Part B, which was new work. The effect size for the difference between the practice test and Part A is modest at 0.45 and between the practice test and Part B is small, at 0.20. Both of these differences are statistically significant ($t=7.12$, $p<0.001$ and $t=2.98$ $p<0.01$, respectively). These results suggest that performance is more likely to be enhanced when the practice test covers similar material. As students had received no feedback on the content of Part B questions, they had no opportunity to test their own knowledge and revise weak areas. This could account for the difference in performance on parts A and B of the unit assessment test for these students.

This conclusion receives tentative support from analysis of results of a group of 53 psychology students who, for various reasons, did not take the practice test. Although the results need to be interpreted cautiously, there was no statistically significant difference between the scores of these students on parts A and B of the first assessment, suggesting that Part B was of equal difficulty to Part A.

DISCUSSION

The results from both studies suggest that the practice test had a positive effect on later test results, as is borne out in Charman's chapter in this volume. The purpose of the practice test in both studies was as formative assessment and students were aware that their marks were used only as a guide for them and not for their overall assessment. They were provided with practice in using the CML system and were given feedback on incorrect answers.

There are a number of possible explanations for the findings of these studies. First, perhaps the more able or more motivated students were the ones who chose to do the practice test in the economics study. However, data from another economics group (Sly, in press) found no relationship between ability as measured by the university entrance score and student choice to do the optional practice test. A second possible explanation is that the group became familiar with both the computer system and the procedure for sitting CML tests. This may be part of the explanation for improvement as students performed better in both parts A and B of the unit assessment test for psychology. The best performance was on Part A, where the practice test provided students with feedback on the content. A third possibility is that the practice test served to decrease student anxiety. However, an additional aspect of the psychology study measured anxiety before both the practice test and the first assessed test and found no relationship between anxiety and CML test performance.

The results of the two studies suggest that the practice test makes a difference and feedback helps to improve student performance on subsequent CML tests. Two likely explanations for improvement following the practice test are, first, that students use the feedback they receive on incorrect responses to assist in their learning of the topic and, second, that increased familiarity with the CML system may contribute to a better performance the next time.

For students to gain the maximum benefit from formative assessment, adequate feedback and review procedures need to be designed. By giving students feedback on incorrect answers, they have the opportunity to diagnose areas of weakness and increase the effectiveness of their study. Of course, no one form of assessment is ideal for all students, so a variety of assessment methods other than CML need to be used. In this context, computer-assisted assessment is a very useful tool, making a particular contribution to formative assessment. The key features include practice tests providing feedback to students and feedback to lecturers. Feedback to lecturers has considerable potential benefit that requires investigation. Unfortunately, we have found little evidence of it being used.

REFERENCES

Birenbaum, M and Tatsuoka, K K (1987) Open-ended versus multiple-choice response formats – it does make a difference for diagnostic purposes, *Applied Psychological Measurement*, **11**, pp 385–395

Black, P and Wiliam, D (1998) Assessment and classroom learning, *Assessment in Education*, **5** (1), pp 7–74

Brown, S and Knight, P (1994) *Assessing Learners in Higher Education*, Kogan Page, London

Dunlap, W P, Cortina, J M, Vaslow, JB and Burke, M J (1996) Meta-analysis of experiments with matched groups or repeated measures designs, *Psychological Methods*, **1**, pp 170–177

Hedges, L (1981) Distributed theory for Glass's estimator of effect size and related estimators, *Journal of Educational Statistics*, **6**, pp 107–128

Heywood, J (1977) *Assessment in Higher Education*, John Wiley & Sons, New York

Nightingale, P, Wiata, I T, Toohey, S, Ryan, G, Hughes, C and Magin, D (1996) *Assessing Learning in Universities*, University of New South Wales Press, Sydney, Australia

Piper, D W, Nulty, D and O'Grady, G (1996) *Examination Practices and Procedures in Australian Universities: Summary report*, Australian Government Publishing Service, Canberra

Rolfe, I and McPherson, J (1995) Formative assessment: how am I doing? *The Lancet*, 345/8953, pp 837–839

Rowntree, D (1987) *Assessing Students: How Shall We Know Them?* Kogan Page, London

Sadler, R D (1998) Formative assessment: revisiting the territory, *Assessment in Education*, **5** (1), pp 77–84

Scriven, M (1967) *The Methodology of Evaluation*, AERA Monograph Series in Curriculum Evaluation, No. 1, pp 39–83, Rand McNally, Chicago

Sly, L and Western, D (1998) Practice tests improve student performance on computer managed learning, proceedings of the 1998 Forum on Teaching and Learning, University of Western Australia, Perth, WA

Sly, L (1999) Practice tests as formative assessment improve student performance on computer managed learning assessments, *Assessment and Evaluation in Higher Education*, **24** (3), pp 339–43

Webster, F (1992) Thinking strategically: a subject group's attempts to maintain quality with reduced resources, in *Teaching Large Classes in Higher Education: How to maintain quality with reduced resources*, ed G J Gibbs, Kogan Page, London

SECTION THREE: Learning from Experience

13

Optical mark reading (OMR) as CAA: experiences at Loughborough University

Myles Danson

INTRODUCTION

An optical mark reader (OMR) is a machine for reading 'tick box' information from printed forms into a computer without using a keyboard; in essence, a mark reading data capture technology. While the technology has been used in marking multiple-choice questions since the 1950s, we have found that OMR CAA can become a vital tool in the implementation of modern CAA. Linking to modern PCs can provide new facilities, such as exporting OMR-captured results to existing databases or to statistical analysis packages. The trade-off compared to other modern CAA techniques is in question types supported. OMR is ideal for rapid and accurate scoring of multiple-choice questions. OCR (optical character recognition), being text recognition, is not discussed here.

HOW DOES OMR WORK?

A simple pen or pencil mark is made by the candidate on a pre-printed paper form to indicate each selected response. The completed forms are scanned by an OMR that detects the presence of a mark by measuring the reflected light. The OMR then interprets the pattern of marks into a data record and sends this to the computer for storage, analysis and reporting.

HARDWARE

The choice of OMR is usually between a hand-fed reader, semi-automatic reader or a fully automatic reader. The choice of reader will depend on your budget and how many forms an hour you want to read. As an example, high-speed fully automatic readers from DRS (http://www.drs.co.uk/), at the time of going to press, read 2,400 A4 forms per hour. While this specification may seem unnecessary to process the typically smaller batches of CAA forms for a single assessment (usually in the region of 100–300 forms in UK higher education, one form per candidate) this does offer benefits. The time to process a test can be as little as a minute or two. The service offered at Loughborough has proved popular for this reason and a trained operator offers a while-you-wait service to academic staff. It is desirable, and possible, to keep the turnaround time from students' completion of the scripts to the feedback stage to a minimum. The alternative of hand feeding is popular elsewhere and allows rates of around three hundred scripts per hour to be achieved.

BENEFITS AND LIMITATIONS OF OMR

The OMR CAA System at Loughborough is not the definitive solution to automated assessment. It is one tool suited to certain scenarios. Different CAA systems are utilized to meet other requirements such as LAN-based (Local Area Network) and Web-based CAA.

The major drawback is that supported question types are currently limited to multiple choice. Creative and careful question design has been shown to yield good discrimination in assessed skills and knowledge. The advanced reporting facilities allow the examiner to analyse the performance of the test itself and hence improve the test and question design for the future. These reports are discussed in more detail later in this chapter.

On the positive side, OMR CAA is user-friendly for students. Students must be prepared in advance of the assessment. We have minimized the failure rate through the use of standard verbal and written instructions and typically see only 1–2 per cent of rejected scripts. These must be hand-marked by the internal examiner concerned. The popularity of the National Lottery in the UK may have gone some way towards familiarizing candidates with the process of completing OMR forms.

Integration with established, traditional assessment facilities and protocols has proved to be achievable. Through liaison between the university CAA officer, examinations office and senior management, institutional acceptance has been forced. Service-level statements and a code of practice for OMR CAA examinations have been put in place and go some way to ensuring quality assurance and risk minimization.

The system is paper based and, by addressing a few specific details, OMR examinations are run alongside, or as part of, a traditional examination in the same location. This means there are no extra concerns in examination timetabling. Examination halls are utilized and the traditional invigilation system has proved to be adequate. While not insisting, we do currently make a strong recommendation that the internal examiner invigilates his or her own OMR examination. At the time of writing, OMR CAA penetration is far from complete and we cannot assume that all academic invigilators are familiar with the nuances of this type of assessment.

A clear benefit of the scenario outlined is that there is no reliance on client computers, network infrastructure or file servers. No technical support is necessary and no special arrangements need be made such as a back-up test.

PREPARING STAFF

In order that the system is utilized correctly, a code of practice has been developed. This was put in place prior to the system being offered as a service to all academic staff. The entire code is not repeated here. In summary provision is made to:

- Insist on a one-off training session to be undertaken by the internal examiner. At present, the CAA officer provides training, along with a handbook for reference. This session is often unpopular with academic staff but, in our experience, all trainees are pleased that they made the effort to attend. The session is designed to highlight areas of risk and potential pitfalls, to explain the analyses available and to provide a forum to discuss any operational issues that may arise.
- Explain the roles of the CAA officer, the examinations office, computing services and the internal examiner.
- Outline the procedure for the processing of scripts.
- Insist that any forms rejected by the system are hand-marked by the internal examiner.

The processing at Loughborough is handled by computing services staff and a service-level statement has been negotiated to regulate this area. In particular, the statement covers the following:

- Arranging an appointment.
- Signing in and out of forms.
- The required input, ie the material that should be submitted.
- A monthly diagnostic check of the hardware.
- An insistence that the internal examiner waits for the job to be completed.
- This latter point is extremely important. The turnaround time for a test should only be a few minutes – the time needed to physically put the sheets through the OMR and for the reports to be printed. By waiting until the job is completed, we ensure that no student answer sheets can be misplaced or lost.

Once this training is completed, we require only the following details of future assessments before the stationery is dispatched:

- test date;
- module code;
- internal examiner contact details;
- department;
- number of candidates;
- number of student answer sheets;
- type of test (formative, diagnostic, coursework summative, examination summative).

We have recently begun to record the percentage allocated to the OMR assessment in terms of the overall credit for a particular module.

THE STATIONERY

The forms used in OMR may be designed in house and printed using traditional techniques. The alternative is to buy software that allows in-house design and printing, or to pay a commercial company to supply the forms for you. Commercial programs such as Print and Scan from Trax UK (http://thor.prohosting.com-1-zephron/) offer these features, while DRS (http://www.drs.co.uk/) offers form design and print services. It should be noted that paper tolerances have an effect on the efficiency of automatic OMR feeders.

At Loughborough, we use four types of form for CAA.

One answer sheet for each student

We have two types of answer sheet: an anonymous one for examinations and another for coursework with a space to write the candidate's name. Our examination policy of double blind marking is still applied to OMR CAA. Though we are convinced that the machine is impartial, a final quality control check requires that a sample of the OMR scripts should be hand-marked by another member of academic staff.

It is often the case that the candidate name is a machine-readable part of the form. This consumes a good deal of the space available as each letter of the alphabet must be represented. At Loughborough, this area is not machine-readable. Instead, we use the student identification number, a unique seven-digit identifier for each student. At the processing stage, our system extracts the corresponding real name from a central student records database. We also add the programme code of the candidate. Since a cohort of students taking a particular module may be composed of many programmes, we can analyse the performance of these groups. This is clearly an important part of the form. If a candidate fails to complete this area, the script is still marked, but no name can be ascribed automatically. We put much effort into avoiding this, but do see a very small percentage of occurrence. In the case of a coursework test, the name has been supplied as non-machine-readable on the answer sheet and may be added to the reports manually. In the case of an examination, we include the seat number that relates to the seating plan of the examination hall. This is the last line of defence and it is emphasized to internal examiners through the code of practice that they should invigilate their own examination and take steps to ensure that the student identification number (SIN) is present on each script.

Lastly, the form has a question response area: a series of 60 question numbers with 5 choice boxes (A,B,C,D,E) against each. This is the final part of the answer sheet that is read by the OMR.

One lecturer answer sheet for each test

This is the sheet containing the correct answers, to be completed by the lecturer. It is similar in format to the student answer sheet. One lecturer answer sheet is required for each set of answers. At present, only one correct answer is permitted per question, though this is likely to change with future development.

A batch header sheet

This sheet provides additional information used for marking and reporting. It includes spaces for writing in the department name, lecturer name, examination/test title and test number. There are also spaces for the following machine-readable information to be entered by the internal examiner:

- Department code. At Loughborough, this is two alphabetic characters, eg CM (chemistry), MA (mathematical sciences).
- Module code. One alphabetic character (A,B,C,D,F or P) followed by three digits. This uniquely identifies the module.
- Date of test. The format for this is dd/month/yy.
- Number of forms returned. The number of student answer sheets submitted. We recommend that the internal examiner counts manually and that the system also makes a count, giving us a double check that no forms are missing.
- Test number. A two-digit number. If the test is one of a series in a module, this will identify the test to which the results refer.
- The marking schedule. A set of three fields that will enable the internal examiner to specify how the test is marked. Each of the fields can be set at any number from +5 to -5. These are the mark for a correct answer, an incorrect answer, null response or multiple responses to a question. At present, the marking schedule applies across all questions in the test.

At Loughborough, we do not print the assessment questions on to the OMR answer sheet. Instead, a traditional test paper is set by the internal examiner within the restraints of the OMR system (currently a maximum of 60 numbered questions with up to 5 choices per question, the choices being labelled A,B,C,D and E). Our OMR CAA service is institutional and would require a substantial labour cost to offer this service for every assessment taking place. A benefit of this approach is that central control of form stock ensures that only the current version is in circulation at any one time. A disadvantage is that it is desirable to retrieve the questions for re-use. Since the test paper has been issued to students as a separate document, the mechanism for retrieving the questions is again the responsibility of the internal examiner.

We have found that the purchase of a counting device has proved essential in managing OMR CAA stationery. The device at Loughborough counts by weight and has proved to be extremely accurate.

THE REPORTS

We offer seven reports as standard, with the option to have both the raw data and processed results on disk. This allows provision for those who wish to process their own results through an analysis package, or direct entry of processed results into a spreadsheet or database. In reality, very few clients use this facility, preferring the standard paper reports below.

Student results by student number

This is a simple report giving the full test details of module code, test number, marking schedule, numbers of papers received and processed and the test date and process date. There are gaps for the lecturer to fill in a module title and test title if desired. The report details student number with the corresponding results. This is anonymous and may be placed directly on to a notice board for dissemination.

Student results in alphabetical order

This report provides details of student names, ID numbers and results as percentages ordered alphabetically according to surname. The full test details are covered as above.

The report can be used for investigating any individual student's results or performance.

Student results ranked from lowest to highest

Here we provide the results as percentages, along with the candidate names and student ID number. This report is useful to check the spread of results. With the weakest candidates listed first, at a glance one can identify the names of any recurring poor performers.

Student results in order of processing

We use this report to locate any answer forms without the student ID number completed correctly. These scripts will have been marked but, without an ID number, the system cannot query the central student records database. No identity is assigned to the result. As long as the order of the forms has not been changed since the processing, it is straightforward to locate the problem answer sheets. The candidate names are determined and manually written into the processed results printout.

Full results report
This report gives the full test details along with a list of individual responses ordered by candidate number and programme code. The report allows trends in candidate answers to be identified quickly, a process previously impractical using hand-marking methods. Common errors become apparent and these may be attributed to a lack of student knowledge, misunderstanding or question error. Results are also listed by programme code with number of students, maximum score, minimum score, mean and standard deviation. This allows a comparison of programme performances for a particular module.

Question analysis and test summary report
The question analysis records, for each question in the test:

- the correct response (A–E);
- the percentage of students choosing A, B, C, D, E;
- the percentage of students answering correctly;
- the percentage of students answering incorrectly;
- the percentage of students selecting no answer;
- the percentage of students selecting more than one answer.

The analysis can be used to identify questions that may be too easy, too difficult or ambiguous. If the question is found to be appropriate then a low percentage 'low percentage correct' response may indicate an area of knowledge within the student cohort that needs further attention. The summary information includes the mean, minimum and maximum percentages for the group, the question facility, question discrimination, test reliability and the standard deviation for the test.

MAINTENANCE

The reliability of any automated assessment system is of premium concern. A diagnostic check of the system should be undertaken regularly and most modern machines offer an automated mechanism for this. In terms of the marks on scripts being correctly read, we have found that OMR scanners are extremely reliable and, if properly configured, provide full error-trapping facilities.

We continue an annual maintenance contract with the hardware suppliers. This takes the form of a site visit to service the machine. On delivery, the hardware comes complete with a dust cover. It is important that this is used in order that the optical reading head is kept in a clean condition. Any dirt on the head can result in misreading.

APPLICATIONS

An example of large-scale diagnostic testing through the OMR CAA service is undertaken by our mathematical sciences department annually. The complete findings are published elsewhere (Armstrong and Croft, 1999). The test was given to the majority of the engineering faculty student intake. This is in the region of 700 candidates, hence CAA was an ideal mechanism. The new students were tested prior to receiving any new mathematics teaching. This ruled out using any PC-based CAA. Students would not yet be familiar with the location of computer laboratories. The large group size could not have been accommodated in our centrally managed PC labs. Furthermore, at this early stage in the academic year, it was unlikely that students would have the required username and password to access the university network.

Coursework testing through the OMR CAA system for the first semester of 1998/99 has involved 54 assessments of around 5,600 candidates.

Summative OMR CAA examinations numbered 13 for the examination period of the first semester of 1998/99. Purely formative testing through OMR takes place to a lesser extent.

FUTURE DEVELOPMENTS

In the future, linkage to the central student records database may be utilized to upload candidate results automatically, removing the need for manual data entry.

There is a strong demand from our clients to support a more flexible marking scheme. This should allow different weightings to be applied to different questions. We are also looking into supporting multiple-response question types.

SUMMARY

- OMR can be used to determine pure performance (summative assessment) but may also be used as a dynamic teaching device (formative assessment).
- OMR can be easily incorporated into existing assessment methods provided steps are taken to provide the appropriate infrastructure.
- Both academic staff and students must be trained in the methodology, and formal documentation such as a code of practice should be put in place. Statements of best practice require collaboration between departments such as the examinations office as well as senior management.

- The need to seat hundreds of candidates for an examination is an issue for many university courses. This may be impossible in an IT suite due to a lack of workstations, while the reliability of the computer network may be questionable when put under such pressure. However, an OMR examination may take place in a conventional examination hall and can be run alongside other traditional examinations that may be timetabled for the same time and location. This is a general advantage of OMR over online assessment. The risks of catastrophic failure inherent in electronic keyboard entry assessment methods and consequent candidate hostility are avoided.
- OMR is a friendly system for candidates. A paper-and-pencil methodology is still far more familiar to students than keyboard, mouse and monitor.
- The test itself may be considered and often improved. Item analysis is possible, highlighting ambiguities in the wording of questions and allowing a level of difficulty to be assigned to individual questions.

REFERENCES

Armstrong, P K and Croft A C (1999) Identifying the learning needs in mathematics of entrants to undergraduate programmes in an English university, *European Journal of Engineering Education*, **24** (1)

DRS Data & Research Services plc (http://www.drs.co.uk/)

http://international.ncs.com/international/locations/uk.htm

http://www.cardiffsw.co.uk/gnome.html

Second annual computer-assisted assessment conference (1998) *Optical Mark Reader Discussion Group Summary*, pp 158–159, Loughborough University, ISBN 0953321010

Trax UK (http://thor.prohosting.com/zephron/)

ACKNOWLEDGEMENTS

I would like to acknowledge the efforts of Janine Mascia, Derek Stephens, Max Hunt, Lynne Render, Jane Easton, John Feather and Winnie Wade.

14

The computer-assisted assessment of practical IT skills

R D Dowsing

INTRODUCTION

Computers are becoming an essential part of everyday life, requiring most of the population to become skilled in the use of common information technology (IT) tools such as word processors and spreadsheets. Many institutions offer tuition in these skills and many examination boards offer appropriate qualifications, for example CLAIT (CLAIT, 1996), offered by the Oxford, Cambridge and Royal Society of Arts Examination Board, and European Computer Driving Licence (ECDL, 1998), offered by the British Computer Society. The problem for examination boards and other bodies, such as further and higher education establishments that assess large numbers of candidates, is that assessment is a costly and time-consuming process.

IT tools require the use of a computer, so it is natural to ask whether the assessment of IT skills can be computerized. This chapter explains some of the benefits and problems of computerizing such assessment and illustrates the type of assessment tool that can be produced by reference to one that we have developed to assess basic word processing skills.

Although the material in this chapter relates specifically to the assessment of IT skills, many of the points made are applicable to other applications of computer-assisted assessment (CAA).

THE BENEFITS OF COMPUTER-ASSISTED ASSESSMENT OF IT SKILLS

One of the major problems of assessment using human examiners concerns the reliability and consistency of the results. Human beings make mistakes and, when faced with the often tedious, boring and monotonous task of marking, they make frequent mistakes (Panko, 1997; Norman, 1981; Reason, 1990). Computers are ideally suited to simple, repetitive tasks since they do not get bored, tired or lose concentration (see Charman elsewhere in this volume), making CAA more reliable than the use of human examiners.

However, computers – or, more frequently, computer software – make mistakes because of errors in design or implementation, for example (Pressman, 1982). Software mistakes are usually consistent, so if an assessor has been programmed incorrectly it will consistently make the same errors, while human examiners tend to make mistakes in a more random fashion. Some degree of human error is tolerated whereas a computer is often expected to be infallible. A complex computer-assisted assessor is likely to contain residual errors and thus an examiner using such an assessment system must be aware that the results may contain errors.

In most cases of summative assessment, candidates do not see their marked paper; they are only given the result. Indications from UK quality assurance agencies suggest that this will not be acceptable in the future and that it will be a requirement that candidates have their marked work returned to them. Candidates could then appeal against a result and this requires a different examiner to re-mark the script in question. Computerized marking will always give the same result, so an appeal could be dealt with by a human examiner checking the computerized marking. The computerized marking can be provided in detail on the script in many different ways to aid human checking and explain the reasoning underlying the assessment. The example given later illustrates one technique for marking the candidate script.

Dealing with large numbers of students is now a fact of life in education, especially higher and further education. Assessment therefore takes up a substantial (and increasing) percentage of the teaching process, consuming a considerable amount of faculty time. CAA can reduce faculty involvement in assessment as well as speeding up the assessment process. As an example, CAA of a professional word processing examination script can be performed in less than one second on current hardware.

THE TYPES OF ASSESSMENT THAT CAN BE APPLIED TO IT SKILLS

Assessment is based on an educational model of learning and the model cited by most authors is that of Bloom (1956), whose taxonomy is based on a hierarchy of six educational objectives as discussed in Pritchett's chapter in Section One. The simplest objective, and the lowest level of the hierarchy, relates to the ability of a student to remember and recall knowledge. Higher levels in the hierarchy relate to higher-level skills, for example the fifth level in the hierarchy is synthesis, which relates to the ability of a candidate to create a new object from a set of components. Competence has to be assessed at each level and the assessment process (setting challenging and appropriate questions and assessing the results) becomes more difficult the higher the level.

Traditionally, CAA has been synonymous with multiple-choice questions (MCQs) (Heywood, 1989). MCQs are good for assessing knowledge at the lower levels of the hierarchy but it is far more difficult to construct questions that deal with the higher levels. One of the reasons for this is that MCQs normally only test whether the answer is correct or not, not the degree of correctness. Assessment at higher levels of the hierarchy relies on grading the candidate answer depending on the number and type of errors produced rather than a simple correct/incorrect assessment.

The equivalent of MCQ tests in the IT skills domain is function tests. These are tests of a candidate's ability to use a specific function of the IT tool, for example to select a word or to copy a cell's contents. These types of test are seldom, if ever, used for summative assessment but are frequently used for formative assessment to reinforce learning. Many examples of function tests are to be found in tutorial packages for IT tools, for example OWL Microsoft Word 97 Training Package (OWL, 1998).

Full skills tests involve assessing a candidate undertaking a typical 'real world' task using an IT tool, for example producing a letter or a spreadsheet. Such assessment is aimed at the synthesis level of the Bloom hierarchy and hence assessment is comparatively difficult. This is the type of assessment discussed in the remainder of this chapter.

THE ASSESSMENT MODEL

The model of assessment we have adopted in our work mirrors the way in which human-based assessment of IT skills is performed. Firstly, an examiner produces a suitable test and model answer(s), bearing in mind the assessment objectives and assessment criteria. The candidates sit the test and attributes and/or outcomes of their performance are collected for assessment. The assessment proceeds by comparing the model and candidate answers to produce raw differences and these raw differences are further processed to relate them to the assessment criteria. Grading is performed using a set of rules provided by the examiner to relate the number and type of errors discovered to a numerical score or pass/fail criteria.

For simple assessment criteria it is possible to completely automate the assessment but for more complex criteria total automation may not be possible or desirable. Human examiners and computer-assisted assessors are complementary; they have different strengths and weaknesses. Human examiners are poor at simple tasks that require a high level of concentration whereas computer-assisted assessors are excellent at detailed, simple tasks but are poor at exercising the same judgement as humans in complex cases since it is difficult to build 'intelligence' into a computer program. Thus, for complex assessment, it is often better to regard the computer-assisted assessor as an aid to a human examiner, one that assesses attempts with only simple errors and filters out the more difficult attempts for assessment by a human examiner (Dowsing and Long, 1997). In terms of the assessment model given above, the computer-assisted assessor is very much better than a human examiner in determining the raw differences between the candidate answer and the model answer since this is really a simple (but tedious) pattern-matching process. Relating the raw differences to the assessment criteria is a more difficult task requiring judgement, and this is where the automated assessor may require help from a human examiner. The computer-assisted assessor can highlight the position of the errors in the text before being passing them to a human examiner, thus removing the most error-prone part of human examiner assessment.

WHAT CAN BE ASSESSED?

In general, two attributes of the candidate's performance using IT can be assessed; outcome and method. Outcome is the traditional form of assessment and assesses the output of an IT test, usually in the form of a printed document. Method is assessed by observing a candidate undertaking a test and assessing the actions taken. This is generally too expensive to undertake using human examiners, but it is feasible by computer and there are two types of information which can be collected and assessed. The simplest type of method assessment relies on the formatting information stored in the saved copy of the candidate's output. This type of information can be used to determine how the formatting has been carried out, for example whether the centring command has been used to centre a heading or whether spaces, tabs or indents have been used. Collection of the event stream (the sequence of user interactions with the IT tool) allows analysis of the method used in finer detail, for example whether the candidate selected a word and then deleted it or whether he or she deleted the word character-by-character. This latter type of assessment can be used to detect the efficiency of the method used by the candidate and is more common in formative assessment.

Most current IT skills tests are assessed by human examiners marking printed output on paper. Computer-assisted assessment is most naturally carried out on the stored file containing the output and assessing the same attributes as the printed version, but this can be difficult, especially where format and layout is concerned. Using the example given above, there is no difference in the printed output if the candidate has used spaces, tabs or the centring command to centre text whereas the file contents will differ depending on which method has been used. Should different methods be assessed differently? If several people are to work on the same document then it is important that standards are maintained and that the intended format and layout is maintained in different environments. For these reasons, use of the centring command is to be preferred in the example given and this should be reflected in the assessment criteria. This illustrates the important point that criteria designed for paper-based assessment by human examiners should not be used for file-based computer-assisted assessment criteria without careful consideration. Examiners rightly believe that technology should not drive assessment criteria – but, conversely, human examiner failings and limitations should not drive computer-assisted assessment criteria.

IMPLEMENTATION OF A COMPUTER-ASSISTED ASSESSOR FOR IT TOOLS

There are two ways in which IT skills exercises can be implemented, either using a 'standard' IT tool or using a specially written generic IT tool for a given skill. The advantages of using a 'standard' tool is that this is the software that the candidate is familiar with and is likely to use in future work. The disadvantage is that the environment in which a 'standard' tool works is very flexible and may allow the candidate to perform actions that could undermine the security arrangements for the examination. Examples of the types of action that need to be guarded against include e-mailing someone outside the examination room for help and submitting a pre-prepared answer. The alternative approach of producing a special version of the IT tool specifically for the test can remove these problems since it can be written to reduce or remove many of the security problems by restricting candidate access to computer resources. Examination centres which use the former approach have to take draconian measures to ensure that candidates do not cheat, for example by using stand-alone computers for examinations and removing floppy disk drives so that candidates cannot load data into the computer. The major problem with the simulation approach is that considerable effort is required to continually update the tool to reflect the ever-increasing functionality of 'standard' IT tools.

Another consideration is the attributes of the candidate's result that need to be collected for the assessment. If outcome is to be assessed, an online assessor can examine the internal data structures of the IT tool at the end of the test or examine the contents of a file of the output which the examiner has saved. An offline assessor, which assesses the candidate's output some time after the test, can only use the latter method. If several different IT tools can be used for the test (eg any of a number of word processors), it is convenient to standardize on a single file format for output rather than supporting several different ones. Similarly, an online assessor can examine the internal structure of the document to determine the formatting. Detailed assessment of method for efficiency is more difficult as the data can only be collected as the candidate sits the test. A generic approach allows the writer of the software to instrument the code to collect the user interaction and either assess it immediately or store it in a file for later assessment. Collecting the user interaction using a 'standard' IT tool is more difficult as this involves interrogating the IT tool to collect the user interaction details. The data that can be collected depends on the particular IT tool and the ease of interrogation.

ASSESSMENT OUTPUT

For summative examinations, results have to be integrated with the institution's mark-recording system. The interface between the computer-assisted assessor and the mark-recording system is critical in ensuring that the management of the examination, which consumes a considerable amount of human examiner and administrator time, is reduced to a minimum. The results are confidential since they relate to all the candidates taking the test and thus they must be hidden from the candidates by encryption and other security measures. To ensure that they can be used by a large number of institutions using a wide variety of different administrative systems, the interface needs to be made as general as possible. In the assessors we have produced, we have adopted a simple approach of producing the results file in an encrypted Comma Separated Value (CSV) format which can be read by the majority of spreadsheet programs and database tools used by management systems.

EXAMPLE

Our group, the Computer-assisted Assessment of IT Transferable Skills (CATS) group at the University of East Anglia, have developed a wide range of IT skills assessors. An outline of the WordTask (Dowsing, Long and Sleep, 1996) word processing assessment system is given here as a simple example of an IT skills assessor.

The WordTask assessor was built to assess basic word processing skills in a HE environment. It is intended to be useful in a first IT skills course and hence uses only basic assessment criteria. Because the assessment criteria are simple, the assessment can be fully automated; no human examiner intervention is required.

The candidate is presented – on paper – with a document containing text that has to be edited according to given instructions. An excerpt of an example is shown in Figure 14.1.

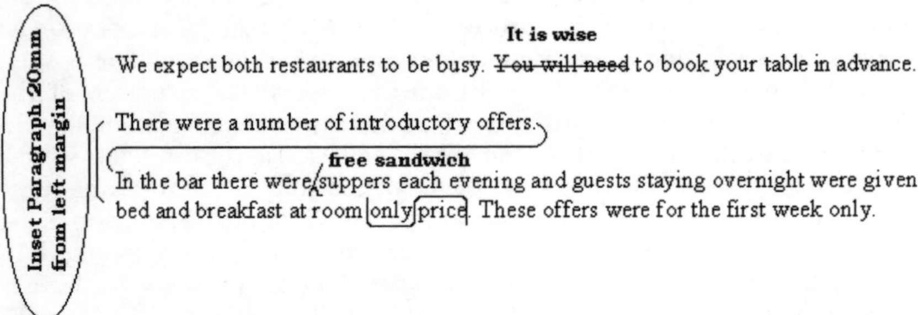

Figure 14.1 *Excerpt from a word processing exercise*

There are two versions of the assessor; an online version that uses a generic word processor and an offline version that assesses RTF files output from any 'standard' word processor. Both versions compare the output from the word processor with model solutions produced by the examiner and record the differences. The differences are classified into textual errors and formatting errors and the numbers in each type reported via a CSV results file. The examiner can generate a pass mark or grading scheme by applying suitable formulae to the error counts using any spreadsheet program. A coloured version of the candidate's submission is generated showing where the errors have occurred and a log file is generated detailing the errors. The model answer for the exercise and a sample candidate answer are shown in Figure 14.2(a) and Figure 14.2(b). Part of the detailed output produced by the assessor is shown in Figure 14.3.

We expect both restaurants to be busy. It is wise to book your table in advance.

> There were a number of introductory offers. In the bar there were free sandwich suppers each evening and guests staying overnight were given bed and breakfast at room price only. These offers were for the first week only.

Figure 14.2(a) *Excerpt from model answer for the given exercise*

We expect both restaurants to be busy. It is wose to book your table in advance.

> There were a number of introductory offers. In the bar there were free suppers each evening and guests staying overnight were given bed and breakfast at room price only These offers were for the first week only.

Figure 14.2(b) *Excerpt from a candidate answer to the given exercise*

The overall results of the assessment for this document extract are as follows:

Word accuracy errors	=	2
Word separator errors	=	1
Char format errors	=	0
Paragraph/Page errors	=	1
Accuracy errors	=	2
Presentation errors	=	1
Total errors	=	7

A detailed error report is available. The relevant parts are given below:

WORD DIFFERENCES:
REPLACE: [.<s>It<s>is<s>[wose]<s>To<s>book] with: wise
INSERT: [<s>were<s>free<s>[sandwich]<s>suppers<s>each]

WORD SEPARATOR DIFFERENCES:
REPLACE: [<s>room<s>price<s>[only]<s>These<s>offers with: only.

PARAGRAPH FORMAT DIFFERENCES:
Matched Paragraph 6: Inset Diff

Figure 14.3 *Part of the assessor output for the candidate of Figure 14.2(b)*

A tutor's module is provided to allow examiners to tailor the tests to their particular requirements, for example to generate new tests and to determine the amount of feedback given to students.

This assessor is now in use at a growing number of FE and HE institutions.

REFERENCES

Bloom, B S, ed (1956) *Taxonomy of Educational Objectives Handbook I: Cognitive Domain*, McKay, New York

CLAIT (1996) *Computer Literacy and Information Technology – Stage 1, Syllabus and Tutor's Handbook (L706)*, RSA Examinations Board, Westwood Way, Coventry CV4 8HS, England

Dowsing, R D and Long, S (1997) *The Do's and Don'ts of Computerising IT Skills Assessment*, proceedings of 14th annual conference of ASCILITE, Perth, pp 115–19

Dowsing, R D, Long, S and Sleep, M R (1996) The CATS word-processing skills assessor, *Active Learning*, **4**, pp 46–52

ECDL (1998) *European Computer Driving Licence*, British Computer Society, 1 Sandford Street, Swindon, Wilts SN1 1HJ, England

Heywood, J (1989) *Assessment in Higher Education*, John Wiley, Chichester

Norman, D A (1981) Categorisation of Action Slips, *Psychological Review*, **88**, pp 1–15

OWL (1998) Microsoft Word 97 Training Package, On With Learning Inc, 131 Bridge Street, Arroyo Grande, CA 93420, USA

Panko, R R (1997) A Human Error Website, (http://www.cba.hawaii.edu/panko/papers/humanerr/) University of Hawaii, Honolulu, HI,

Pressman, R S (1982) Software testing and reliability, in *Software Engineering: A practitioner's approach*, McGraw-Hill, New York

Reason, J T (1990) *Human Error*, Cambridge University Press, New York

Rowntree, D (1987) *Assessing students – how should we know them?* Kogan Page, London

ACKNOWLEDGEMENTS

Stewart Long was responsible for most of the implementation of WordTask and has contributed considerably to the development of IT assessors at UEA.

15

Assessment in a cognitive apprenticeship-based learning environment: potential and pitfalls

A Patel, D Russell and Kinshuk

The cognitive apprenticeship-based learning environments (CABLE) approach to designing tutoring systems is very popular, especially within the applied domains where learning is more concerned with the operational knowledge. Since CABLE can accommodate both the 'instruction' and 'construction' of knowledge and involves active engagement it has been more successful, as demonstrated by the popularity and wide acceptance of simulation-based tutoring systems. A CABLE-based intelligent tutoring system (ITS) provides powerful learning and assessment opportunities, as we show later in the chapter. We will also, based on our experiences, caution that merely tagging assessment functionality on to a system designed for learning may be unsatisfactory and the assessment system needs to be considered separately. We would like to emphasize that the assessment system dominates the overall context within which teaching and learning takes place and needs much care in its design regardless of whether it employs technology or traditional methods to achieve its goals. In the case of applied disciplines, we argue that the assessment process benefits from extending CABLE to include the general purpose software tools. This approach not only enables the students to experience more authentic situations but also to break the interface-based visual syntactic links that are unavoidable when conceptual manipulations are achieved through interface objects. Though the use of information and communication technology (ICT) for assessment has come a long way, we believe that there are even more exciting possibilities ahead, provided we are cognizant of the possible pitfalls arising from the manner in which the technology is employed.

It is useful at the outset to distinguish between the formative and summative aspects of assessment. The former helps the students in their learning activities by providing mechanisms for self-testing. The latter attempts to sum up the skills and knowledge gained at the end of a period of learning to ensure that the required learning has indeed been achieved. Norman (1986) presented the notion of the necessity to bridge the two gulfs, the 'Gulf of Execution' and the

'Gulf of Evaluation' while discussing human-computer interaction. We believe that this notion also applies to the learning of any new concept, which benefits from the different types of formative assessment helping to bridge these gulfs between the learner and what is being learnt. The formative assessment also bridges the distance between the learning and summative assessment. The diagram in Figure 15.1 captures these relationships between learning and assessment.

Formative assessment using identical conditions reduces the cognitive load on a novice learner and enables experimentation with the newly acquired concepts, possibly in a gradually expanding problem space and with an immediate feedback on student actions. In case of the use of ICT, the identical conditions also includes the user interface so that the student attention isn't diverted towards making sense of a new interface. As the students gain confidence, they should be exposed to far from identical conditions to enable abstraction of the concepts learnt and generalization of their applicability. The summative assessment could take either of these roles of using identical or far from identical conditions.

THE IMPORTANCE OF FORMATIVE ASSESSMENT IN LEARNING

Traditionally, the students would study a problem and work through its given solution to firm up their grasp of the concepts and to understand their application, relying on self-explanation and revisiting the study texts or consulting a peer learner/teacher in case of an impasse. With the interactive computer

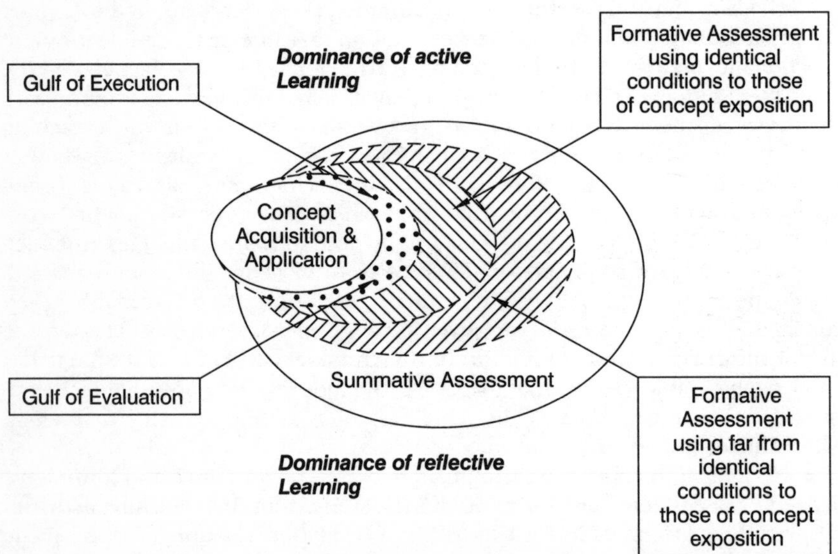

Figure 15.1 *Role of assessment in learning*

systems this approach was replaced by formative assessment accompanied by dynamic feedback, to the extent that it would not be incorrect to say that formative assessment was at the heart of the intelligent tutoring systems. We will demonstrate the usefulness of formative assessment in ICT-based learning systems through a brief discussion of the CABLE model employed by us. It is based on the cognitive apprenticeship framework suggested by Collins, Brown and Newman (1989), which is considered suitable for both academic and situated learning. It guided the design and implementation of the intelligent tutoring tools (ITTs) developed by Byzantium, a project funded under the Teaching and Learning Technology Programme of the Higher Education Funding Councils of the United Kingdom. The interactive learning screen from an ITT for learning about marginal costing is shown in Figure 15.2. The students see the whole problem space while attempting a solution to any part of it through backward or forward chaining.

In the given problem, the system has randomly picked four out of fourteen variables and generated a random value for each within the bounds specified in the software. The student has filled one variable correctly and is now attempting to find the value of fixed cost. Since the value cannot be determined directly from the available data, the system advises the student

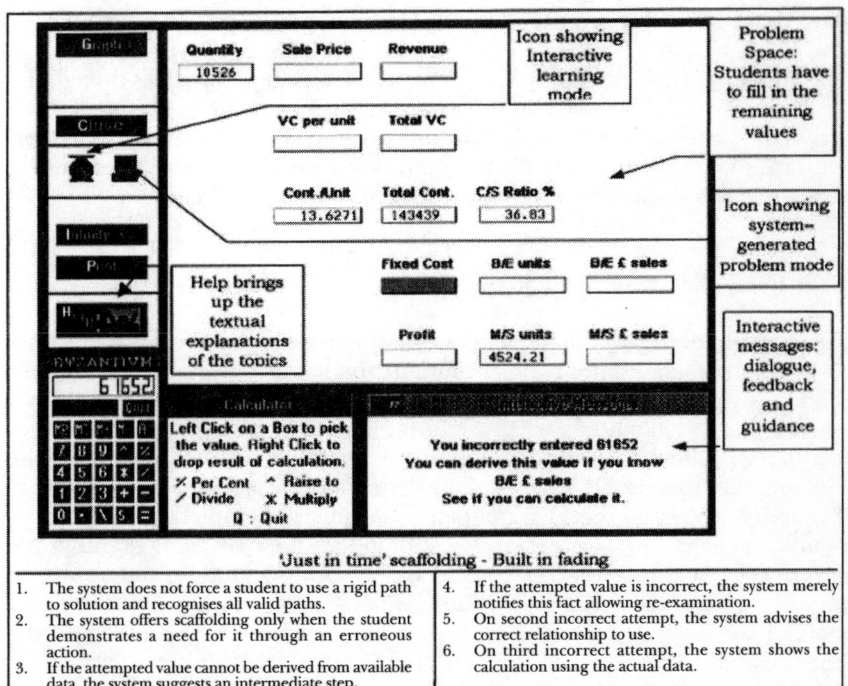

Figure 15.2 *Interactive learning interface*

to first obtain the value of another variable that can help in determining the value of fixed cost. This feedback is based on the system's path to the solution. At this point, the student has the option of either pursuing the suggested path or examining the data again with a view to finding another variable whose value may be derived from the available data. Actually there are four variables (sale price, revenue, B/E units and profit) whose value can be derived. If the student realizes that B/E units is the difference between the quantity and M/S sales and obtains it, this provides an alternative feasible path to obtaining fixed cost. If the student now enters an incorrect value in the fixed cost, the system will advise that the value can be derived and the student should try again. Thus, the system allows the student to attempt any variable in any order and adjusts its feedback in line with the work done by the student. So, the mainstay of the Byzantium ITT is formative assessment accompanied by intelligent feedback. After an initial exposure to the concepts through a lecture or through reading a textbook, the students try out a few problems to improve their understanding of these concepts. For more details on the architecture of the Byzantium ITT, please see Patel and Kinshuk, 1997.

The Byzantium ITT also provides an 'enter your own' problem mode where the students are given an example in a narrative form and they have to interpret the narration to derive the given values. This mode encourages the acquisition of meta-cognitive skills of identifying and drawing out relevant information from data that might contain a lot of superfluous information. This mode is provided mainly for summative assessment purposes though the students may use its restricted formative assessment version to prepare for the summative assessment. The Byzantium project also developed a 'marker' software to complement the ITTs to create an intelligent assessment workbench (for details please see Patel, Kinshuk and Russell, 1998a).

THE INTELLIGENT ASSESSMENT WORKBENCH

The diagram of the overall intelligent assessment workbench is given in Figure 15.3. The students submit their solutions for test problems that are either randomly generated by the ITTs, loaded from a test question bank created by a teacher or handed out in a narrative form. In case of the system-generated or test bank problems, the independent variables are already filled and the students have to derive the values of the dependent variables. On submission of the student solution, the ITT compares the values attempted by the student against the values in its expert model and judges their correctness within the permissible tolerance that may be required due to rounding differences at various stages of the solution. For the questions given out in a narrative form, the ITT's expert model (local expert model in Figure 15.3) is based on the student's interpretation and the ITT is able to assess the correctness of the procedures applied.

For the randomly generated and test question bank problems, the marker software simply uses the ITT's evaluation of performance for further adjustments.

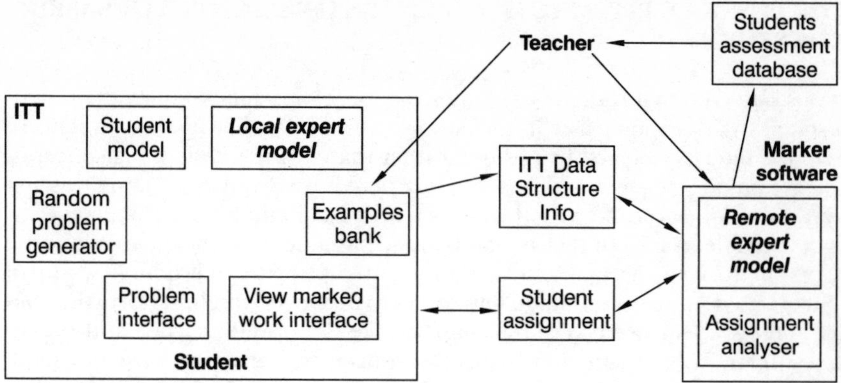

Figure 15.3 *Intelligent assessment workbench*

Such adjustment is required for late submission penalty or where an ITT has different constituent parts within it, for restricting the assessment only to the required tasks. For the problems in a narrative form, the marker performs a further comparison with the model answer provided by the tutor (remote expert model in Figure 15.3). This comparison enables the marker to assess the correctness of data interpretation and assign a partial score for correct procedure but incorrect interpretation. The tutor can set the various parameters for implementing these adjustments.

THE POTENTIAL OF INTELLIGENT COMPUTER-BASED ASSESSMENT

The above discussion demonstrates that it is possible to achieve many aspects of the assessments traditionally carried out by human tutors. It is possible for the students to attempt questions given out in the traditional narrative form or as a part of a case study and to intelligently assess them, discriminating between a completely incorrect attempt, correct interpretation but application of incorrect procedure or incorrect interpretation but application of correct procedure. Though the ITTs currently use only the overlay model, we would like to enhance it by introducing process monitoring. The ITTs provide a calculator interface and allow picking and dropping of values by left-click and right-click of the mouse respectively on the variable containers. By constraining the interface so that a student has to always use the calculator interface, the system can keep track of a student's problem-solving process. It can thus monitor the relationships actually used rather than inferring the student's understanding from an outcomes-based overlay model. Process monitoring would provide the computer-based assessment system with the same information that a human tutor sees when going through a student's workings.

THE POSSIBLE PITFALLS IN IMPLEMENTING COMPUTER-BASED ASSESSMENT

It was observed that the sole use of abstract problems generated by the system resulted in a static interface in the case of some ITTs, allowing the students to map the interface objects by position rather than by their underlying concepts. Their thinking degenerated into 'the box here is obtained by dividing this box by that box', based on visual memory and syntactic learning rather than conceptual learning. In the pen-and-paper-based tests, such students found it necessary to draw the screen layout before attempting the solution. Assessment that is based on the same static interface produced very high performance but the same students were very reluctant to take the traditional pen-and-paper-based tests. This observation led to the concern for ensuring better generalization and far transfer of knowledge and resulted in plans for further enhancements and a recommended implementation and integration framework as shown in Figure 15.4.

As Sutherland (1996) has observed, in order to achieve coherent, transferable expertise, one needs to acquire a set of linked hierarchical models in which the emergent properties at one level become the primitive properties of the next level and which thereby ground the higher-order abstractions. The recommended learning path, therefore, consists of transition through observation, interactive learning, simple testing, learning and testing involving multiple contexts and/or interpretation of rich narrative and finally extending the learning process to integrate the essential tools of trade, such as spreadsheet,

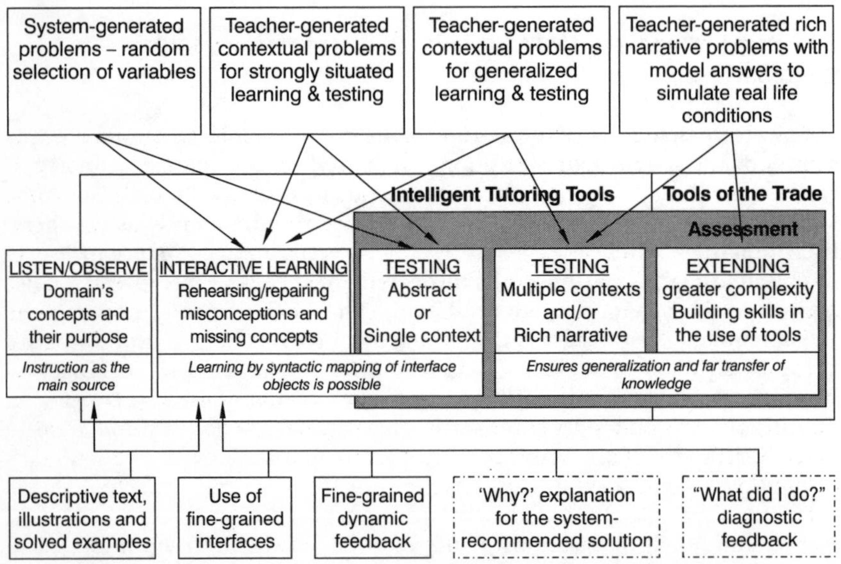

Figure 15.4 *ITT implementation and integration framework*

database and statistical packages. The tools in themselves are not good vehicles for initial learning, as they divert the attention to their own operational requirements at the expense of the topic being learnt. Since they are geared towards providing ready solutions once the parameters are set, the tools fail to provide adequate opportunity for rehearsing. However, beyond the initial learning, they provide powerful opportunities for efficiently handling further complexity. By using their knowledge along with such tools, the students are able to handle more complex and more authentic problems. Systematic integration of such tools is very important as it also provides the skills necessary for the workplace.

We believe, however, that the real breakthrough will come through Internet-based intelligent authoring shells for rapidly creating, customizing and linking intelligent tutoring applications/Hyper-ITS (see Patel, Russell and Kinshuk, 1998b). Since the Internet enables sharing of both the development efforts and the developed applications, it is possible to create the large number of applications that are required to cover the numerous topics at different levels of abstraction. The link-based architecture would also make it easy to move between fine- and coarse-grained representations. The flexible architecture would also enable mixing and matching of various techniques/topics for the purpose of computer-based assessment.

However, learning through a gradual shift from simple to complex and from smaller to larger clusters of concepts requires time, practice and patience but we notice that students are increasingly driven by the requirements of coursework as an end in itself. They engage in assignment hopping and adopt a just-in-time approach to learning. This makes it critical that we examine the role of summative assessment in providing an overall context for the learning activities.

SUMMATIVE ASSESSMENT AS AN OBJECTIVAL CONTEXT OF LEARNING

It is interesting to compare the objectives of the traditional approaches to planning for teaching and methods of assessment. For planning of teaching, a syllabus is drawn up consisting of all the subject knowledge that is considered essential. This syllabus acts as an indicative teaching plan and excepting some small variations, a teacher endeavours to cover as much of the syllabus as possible. The teaching is thus implicitly based on the necessity of knowing most of the discipline's 'essential' subject matter. On the other hand, the assessment methods may only cover 30 per cent to 60 per cent of the syllabus. Student performance in a typical assessment may be distributed across a range of, say, 20 per cent to 80 per cent, where a 50 per cent score may indicate a pass mark. Thus, for an assessment based on, say, 40 per cent of the syllabus, a student needs to achieve a 50 per cent performance, ie a 20 per cent proven knowledge of the whole syllabus to pass!

This situation raises some interesting questions about the overall objectives of the educational system (Patel *et al*, 1998). Is it to encourage acquisition of the facts and rules constituting the knowledge of a discipline or is it to encourage acquisition of meta-learning abilities? Is it to expose a student to various subject disciplines with a view to experiencing different types of situations with different priorities, perspectives, problems and ways to solve these problems? While the divergence between the implications of the teaching and assessment methods may raise issues about the quality of assessments, it also raises questions about what and how much of it we are trying to teach within a subject syllabus. For instance, is there a need to look at the combination of the subjects studied by a student in an integrated fashion and build each syllabus to provide complementary skills? Looking solely at the objectives of a teaching and learning system does not reveal the real objectives of an educational system.

Since the acquired knowledge can only be demonstrated through summative assessment, the assessment strategy strongly influences the students' learning activities and provides an overriding objectival context that can undermine the objectives of a teaching and learning system. A badly designed summative assessment system can cause widespread adoption of shallow learning approaches. Since the development of any non-trivial computer-based system is time and cost intensive, there is always a pressure to tag a simplistic assessment system on to the learning system. It may be necessary to use such summative assessment, if only to encourage the students to carry out adequate amounts of formative assessment. But major reliance on such simplistic assessment would encourage shallow approaches to learning.

In conclusion, we would like to examine the possibility that perhaps the students are instinctively adopting a correct approach to education. The rapid technological changes affecting all areas of our lives require that we need a just-in-time approach to learning that is supplemented by lifelong learning. Perhaps we need less summative assessments and more formative assessments to help those who may be motivated at any stage of their life to learn – either out of curiosity or out of the requirements of an imminent application. We need an infrastructure that supports ease of access and facilities for lifelong learning.

REFERENCES

Collins A, Brown, J S and Newman, S E (1989) Cognitive apprenticeship: teaching the crafts of reading, writing and mathematics, in *Knowing, Learning and Instruction*, ed L B Resnick, pp 453–494, Lawrence Erlbaum Associates, Hillsdale, NJ

Norman, D A (1986) Cognitive engineering, in *User-centred System Design: New perspectives on human-computer interaction*, eds D A Norman and S W Draper, Lawrence Erlbaum Associates, Hillsdale, NJ

Patel, A and Kinshuk (1997) Intelligent tutoring tools in a computer-integrated learning environment for introductory numeric disciplines, *Innovations in Education and Training International Journal*, **34** (3), pp 200–207

Patel, A, Kinshuk and Russell, D (1998a) A computer-based intelligent assessment system for numeric disciplines, *Information Services and Use* (IOS Press, Amsterdam), **18** (1,2) pp 53–63

Patel, A, Russell, D and Kinshuk (1998b) Collaborative teaching in distance education – an innovation in intelligent tutoring, *Exploiting Learning Technology: Issues for Learners and Educators* (Institution of Electrical Engineers, London), **98** (453), pp 21–29

Patel, A, Russell, D, Kinshuk, Oppermann, R and Rashev, R (1998) An initial framework of contexts for designing usable intelligent tutoring systems, *Information Services and Use* (IOS Press, Amsterdam), **18** (1,2), pp 65–76

Sutherland, R (1996) New technologies for modelling science and mathematics, in *Advanced Educational Technology: research issues and future potential*, ed T Liao, pp 114–122, Springer-Verlag Berlin, Heidelberg

16

Online assessment: creating communities and opportunities

Meg O'Reilly and Chris Morgan

INTRODUCTION

Since Rowntree (1977) coined the term 'the de facto curriculum', the literature of assessment in higher education has, with growing consistency, delivered the message that assessment is the key to learning, that student assessment is at the heart of an integrated approach to student learning. With this in mind, it is an important time to review the role of assessment as the use of information and communication technologies (ICTs) and online teaching and learning gathers pace. While there are many new opportunities and some new constraints, which we outline in this chapter, there is also a need for educators to reconceptualize their assessment practices using these new media. It is argued that there are as many losses as there are gains in online assessment, unless we employ a pedagogically driven, student-centred approach in our educational design.

This chapter examines a small sample of current online assessment practices gathered from the UK, Australia, South Africa and the Netherlands, which capture some major themes in online assessment and which illustrate a convergence of the on-campus, off-campus and off-shore student groups. We also examine new models of assessment with respect to open and flexible learning and point to the growth of online learning communities resulting from changing assessment practices.

RECONCEPTUALIZING OUR ASSESSMENT PRACTICES

We usually have strong ideas about the most appropriate ways to assess in our disciplines, and what works and what doesn't. Online learning, however, offers us new opportunities. When using the Web to teach on-campus students, we can reduce contact hours and offer learners the opportunity for more flexible and self-paced study. With the resources of the Internet at the learners' fingertips, the pressure we experience as resource providers is reduced and the opportunity is created for learners to more independently explore content areas.

For distance learners, the new opportunities are even more pronounced. Learners previously working in isolation can now interact and collaborate with teachers and peers in discussions, teamwork and problem solving. The diversity of discussions generated by students have the capacity to deepen students' approaches to assessment tasks, encouraging less reproductive learning and supporting more critical and reflective work.

Ideally we are aiming for teaching and learning encounters that capture the best of face-to-face teaching, with its immediacy and shared endeavour, in conjunction with the flexibility and openness that characterizes distance education. However, we need to ensure that we are really using the new medium to advantage and that the limitations of the old pedagogies that emphasize the transfer of content at the expense of process (either by distance or face to face) are not thoughtlessly replicated. On the one hand, we will want to be relying on lessons from the past to inform our progress; on the other hand, as educators we do not want to be 'walking into the future backwards' (Turoff, 1997).

We need to find new ways to think about assessment rather than transfer the issues of traditional, face-to-face or distance assessment to Web-based courses. Does the use of traditional terminology and assessment models result in assessment practices that do not address the characteristics and possibilities of the online medium? Are we able to adopt a flexible approach to teaching and learning while maintaining openness in requirements for entry and participation? To consider some of these questions we will now present some case studies that illustrate new ways of conceiving of teaching, learning and assessment.

OPPORTUNITIES IN ONLINE ASSESSMENT: SOME CASE STUDIES

During 1998, we embarked upon a project to examine the assessment practices within open and distance education contexts. Before too long it was apparent that not only have ICTs had a pronounced effect in off-campus assessment, but they have also expanded the range of strategies for assessing on-campus students. A number of case studies were collected, covering a broad range of learning outcomes, which can be successfully assessed at a distance or via computer-mediated means (O'Reilly and Patterson, 1998).

The creation of a 'community of learners' seems to be an important outcome in many of these case studies. Through online learning and assessment, we are developing a culture of shared endeavour, critical and reflective thinking and democratic and negotiated processes. The case studies presented here illustrate the four main pedagogical principles that support the development of a community of learners: conferencing, reflection, collaboration and a global community (Foley and Schuck, 1998).

1 Discussion, conferencing and constructivist activity

The pedagogy of constructivism has been popularly adopted in Web teaching and learning. In its most basic form, it is seen in the plethora of course discussion lists that encourage debate, exchange and negotiation of meanings in relation to course content. Taken further, we find constructivist activity such as shared decisions and solutions, group reports, prototypes, models, consultancies and projects. Klemm and Snell (1996) argue for the use of computer conferencing to 'raise the intellectual level of group discourse by requiring student groups to produce tangible products, not just opinion comments' (p 1).

Where conferencing is undertaken as a teaching strategy, not only does it need to be well integrated into the course content (Collins and Berge, 1996), but it will also be of greater purpose to students if it is assessed (Day, 1998). Research concerning online discourse (Holt *et al*, 1998) has found that the 'actions of a moderator are peripheral instead of central' (p 11) and should aim at facilitating and supporting discussion between students.

The example presented here illustrates a case where learners actively participate in workplace-based online discussion to solve a consulting problem over one study period.

Practicum strategy and organization, Open University of the Netherlands
Dr A M M Vijverberg and Dr K Schlusmans

In this subject, students study at a distance from the university and interact with their academic 'coach' via e-mail. The focus for the consulting project is selected from among the problems identified by students with respect to their own organizations or outside networks. One of the criteria used for selection of a problem is the existence of a body of knowledge concerning the problem within a variety of management and business areas.

Teams of four students are then allocated to provide consultancy services to the chosen client organizations. Conferencing between students and clients is in the face-to-face mode, though e-mail and an electronic logbook of activities are extensively used by all parties as it would be in the networked organizational environment.

The consulting process, which takes six months, is problem based and client driven, although students are allowed as consultants to override the clients' perception of the organizational problem. A logbook of transcripts from the electronic dialogues occurring during the consulting period is developed. The logbook activities are structured according to the ten steps of consultancy which students must complete. At the completion of each step, academic coaches accept the submission of logbook entries from each student.

The problem to be solved is always placed in a larger context that requires the team to investigate from a number of perspectives. The team operates in an advisory capacity and develops skills in 'getting things done without being in charge'. Interaction is sustained and includes the use of computer conferencing for communication within the client organization.

The features of constructivism in this example include the way students are encouraged to build their understanding and to make decisions on the basis of information obtained. Through the use of the ten-step consultancy approach, the client organization is also empowered to learn from the experience of managers, staff and students involved in the projects. Students' contribution to the client organization is thus not a 'simulation' but has the elements of a real solution to the identified problem, in the style of action research.

The final contribution is assessed by the client, the students in the team, the coach and the examiner.

2 Student-centred, peer and reflective self-assessment

In a student-centred approach, assessment cannot be a unilateral activity. Stefani (1998) also argues that assessment is an episode in learning where there is a shared understanding of the learning task and the assessment criteria. Online technologies enable agreements to be readily reached between teachers and learners regarding assessment.

Opportunities also present themselves for learners to structure their learning around immediate needs in their own lives and working environments. This 'authentic' assessment approach further enables learners to have a sense of ownership of the assessment tasks and encourages them to effectively transfer and test academic knowledge in real life or work situations (Nightingale *et al*, 1996). The identification of needs also requires reflective processes both in regard to oneself as well as others and reflection is enriched by asynchronous online communication.

Traditionally, peer assessment and self-assessment have been seen as unreliable and cumbersome to administer. Arguably, any graduating student needs the ability to self-evaluate and to make considered judgements of others' work. For some discipline areas and assessment techniques, peer assessment is not only appropriate but is a positive enhancement in terms of motivation and a sense of community. Self-assessment is a process of reflection that encourages learners along the path towards independent and autonomous learning.

The key issues in peer and self-assessment include ensuring the appropriateness of this approach, validity of students' judgements, shared understanding of assessment criteria and reliability (Gibbs, 1995). These issues still remain in the online medium. However, fresh approaches are being taken and can be seen in the following example of the power of ICTs for facilitating reflection.

IT and Society, Open University, UK
Nick Heap and Janet MacDonald
'IT and Society' is an undergraduate distance course that provides an electronic environment for resource-based learning. Students are supplied with resources in print and a library of articles on CD ROM. They are required to link to the Internet for further resources and for the purpose of conferencing with peers and tutors. The course is assessed by a variety of assignments, some of which are online.

One assignment requires students to contribute to an online conference on a given topic, over a period of several weeks. They use the conference to discuss their interpretation of various readings and are required to submit printed transcripts illustrating their online contributions, together with a summary of the debate as a whole.

The final assignment is an online collaborative project in which students are required to produce a critique of a fictional newspaper article. The main part of the resulting report is an individual effort, but students collaborate online to produce a group summary and conclusion. The exercise is designed to develop critical thinking, analytical skills, information-handling skills and online collaborative skills.

Building on experiences with the use of peer review and assessment for formative support in campus-based universities, it was decided to experiment with these ideas, using computer conferencing (Macdonald, Mason and Heap, in press). Students were required to grade and comment on a peer's script, and then to review their own script. The electronic medium facilitated a rapid turnaround of scripts and guaranteed anonymity.

3 Group projects and international collaboration

According to Harasim *et al* (1995, p 191) 'the key concept in network teaching is to facilitate collaborative learning'. Group projects are an outcome of collaboration where both the process and the outcomes of learning are based on interdependence among students (Klemm and Snell, 1996).

The opportunities for group projects and international collaboration that have emerged from Internet technology (indeed, were the driving forces behind its inception) are an exciting development for many disciplines. Students now have opportunities to learn directly about other cultures through shared learning tasks (Alexander and McKenzie, 1998). Collaboration between students from far-flung institutions around the globe can considerably enrich the experience and broaden the contextual perspectives of each participant (Muchnik in Day, 1998). Excellent examples can be found of international collaboration and online groupwork, particularly in the areas of communication, marketing, politics, psychology and physiotherapy, just to name a few.

The following example illustrates collaboration through groupwork by off-campus students.

Environmental psychology, University of Pretoria, South Africa
Prof A C Fiedeldey
The MA (Research Psychology) at the University of Pretoria is a fully online programme that leads to professional registration as research psychologist with the Professional Board of Psychology in South Africa. Students also complete an internship and a thesis after successful completion of their first year of postgraduate study.

The topic selected for groupwork assignments in the subject of environmental psychology is agreed early in the course and arises from individual assignments dealing with different perspectives on the selected topic. The groupwork assignment provides an opportunity for students to work in collaboration with peers and integrate their individual assignment topics into a report that reflects their combined knowledge and understanding of the topic.

The abilities being assessed include the ability to share work, interpersonal negotiation skills and the ability to integrate and synthesize students' own work with that of others.

The ability to share work is seen as important in the field of research psychology, where work undertaken in both the electronic and research domains commonly occurs within a team context. This concept of sharing work impacts upon students at either end of the achievement spectrum. Further to this, students need to demonstrate interpersonal negotiation skills in order to identify their individual contributions for inclusion, choose a conceptual approach, negotiate roles and delegate tasks.

The integration of different areas of content from different contributors is also seen as a core skill to be developed in the field of research psychology. The group assignment mark is thus allocated for integration of individual assignments into one report and covers the conceptual, methodological, technical and research aspects of the assignment. Marks are also allocated for the clarity of written work, its length and timely submission.

Collaboration is thus evident in the groupwork through the sharing of individual efforts, effective and sustained communication via e-mail, conflict resolution and delegation, so that the final report is completed by consensus.

4 Creating a community online

Probably the most significant opportunity online is the new forms of interaction and dialogue available through the synchronous and asynchronous communication tools such as e-mail, discussion lists and computer conferencing. Providing the learner has access to these tools through a computer and modem, opportunities open up for learners to be part of wider professional or vocational discourses. This can occur via the ever-expanding number of specialized public access e-mail and Web forums but it can also be facilitated through creative assessment.

The development of an online community relies principally on text-based discussion. Discussion can take many forms and, depending on the content area, can take place between pairs or larger groups with the inclusion or exclusion of the academic coordinator or subject expert. Twenty-six techniques are outlined in Paulsen's (1995) 'Online report on pedagogical techniques for computer-mediated communication'. Many of these are evident from case studies gathered, such as notice boards, public tutorials, seminars, debates, simulations, team presentations, project work, informal socializing and community decision-making.

The example presented here illustrates the development of an online community over the course of a first-year foundation subject called 'Science and Communication' in a traditional on-campus university.

Science and Communication, University of Melbourne
Dr Glyn Rimmington
Students develop a Web page in the first two weeks of semester. This forms the basis for communication about the organizing and hosting of a scientific conference to occur at the end of semester. Committees are formed through self-selection and arrangements begin via e-mail to find a theme, invite keynote speakers, develop a programme and undertake all the administrivia of conferences.

The development of a Web site occurs in support of the live conference event. The programme is published, registrations are taken, abstracts are published and peer reviewed and finally the proceedings are published, all online. Each of these steps carries a weighting towards assessment. The final component of assessment requires students to submit a self-evaluation of the value of their contribution to their community of peers.

As an *ad hoc* online community in the field of science, this example illustrates a wide range of communication methods relevant for the discipline, that is collaboration, preparation of abstracts and full papers for publication, reviewing written work of peers, presenting and evaluating the presentations of others. The development of a community of scholars is represented here by a real life conference event. Not only is the event attended by keynote speakers with expertise in the chosen conference area, but it also draws an audience of peers, family and friends on conference day. Publication of conference details on the Web site further disseminates the information designed, developed and published by the students to potentially an unbounded audience.

This unit is offered as an undergraduate on-campus unit but there are no attendance requirements other than the conference day. In principle, if students were able to travel to attend the conference, this could be taught internationally. The conference would be thus opened up to a stimulating mix of cultural and inter-disciplinary exchange.

TOWARDS NEW MODELS OF ASSESSMENT

The above case studies suggest that new models of assessment are being forged, building from a reconceptualization of pedagogy, combined with an informed use of ICTs and the online medium. A considered use of ICTs can ensure a flexible approach where the inherent advantages of both on-campus and open and distance learning are not lost. Some of the building blocks of these new assessment models are highlighted below.

MAINTAINING OR EXPANDING OPENNESS

As we have seen, online learning has the potential to increase access by learners to programmes and to provide flexible, student-centred options for learners. This is a challenging prospect to institutions that have been relatively 'closed' in terms of their student entry criteria and assessment practices. Teachers will find themselves assessing students with a wider range of needs, interests, work contexts, levels of ability and cultural backgrounds – to mention only a few of the variables. Flexible responses to assessment will be required to meet these needs, involving new levels of individual negotiation or choice in assessment modes and topics. It may be that in a truly flexible programme students will choose their subject, select the medium for delivery and participate in establishing the assessment tasks for themselves or the team. They will also negotiate the marking criteria, their grades and the grades of student peers from around the world.

Those moving from traditional distance education to online teaching and learning will already be familiar with many of these issues, but will be presented with challenges in maintaining openness in their programmes. Traditional distance learners, who are familiar with studying at places and times to suit, will be challenged by new assessments requiring weekly discussion, collaboration, teamwork and debate. Given their busy working and family commitments, it may even preclude their participation. Online educators will need to strike a new balance between the needs of those seeking interaction with those who prefer to 'go it alone'.

OVERCOMING DISTANCE

On-campus teachers are now facing the prospect of off-campus learners or a blended cohort that includes local and international students. The knowledge and expertise gained over the past 20-odd years in distance education has much to inform online learning. The structure of open and distance study materials have for decades been designed as 'tutorials in print' (Rowntree, 1986) that optimize the reflexive experiences of critical thinking and the application of knowledge to real life settings.

In particular, assessment practices in open and distance contexts have at times very creatively handled the factor of isolation from the institution and student peers. Through use of local mentors, study groups, workplace learning and applied exercises based upon interaction, students have been assisted to see themselves in the context of their own local or workplace community. As shown by the case studies in this chapter, these features can be readily transposed and developed for the online environment, enabling the design of dynamic, interactive and integrated assessment tasks.

EQUITY AND ACCESS

In terms of student-centredness, this question arises: 'Who are the learners we will be connected with online?' The figures released in Clemente's (1998) American-based investigation of who is using the Web show that 'academic users represent the smallest segment of the total user population with. . . 6% of the total user population' (p 116). This indicates that students remain a select proportion of the population. Whether or not this statistic is representative of all users around the world is debatable. However, what it does show us is that online activity is various and more prolific than the educational environment might suggest.

The question of computer-ownership and on-demand access to networks and the Web is also a slippery one. Australian statistics show an overall penetration rate of 18 per cent of full dial-in access to the Internet (Australian Bureau of Statistics, 1998). This currently represents quite an inequitable situation and, although constantly changing, the ability of students to access the Web must not be ignored in our efforts at making learning interesting, satisfying and shared.

Once set up and connected, learners may still find the online experience less than desirable, with problems reported such as 'system downtime', 'problems logging in', 'difficulty posting responses', 'group size too big', 'uneven contributions' and 'too many opinions' (Foley and Schuck, 1998, p 131).

It takes the right set up and some practice to make the most of being part of an online community. The broader range of assessment provided by online options allows learners to gravitate towards personal preferences, for example peer discussions, team work, international collaboration or print-based and online private study.

ASSESSING NEW SKILLS

For students who have experienced difficulties in accessing information and resources, the Internet offers a considerably expanded opportunity. Online course materials may now embed numerous hyperlinks to other units, courses and relevant information sites. Learners are encouraged to also undertake their own searching in areas of specific interest to their study and assessments. The new challenge for learners, and indeed for all of us in the so-called 'information age', is to be able to quickly and critically evaluate the value of the information to the task at hand and to sift adeptly through the numerous links and pointers that may take us off in any range of directions.

New models of online assessment provide opportunities for the achievement of an expanded range of learning outcomes which include the accessing and managing of information, managing and developing oneself, and communication (Nightingale *et al*, 1996). Such opportunities allow the broadening of assessment methods beyond the regular use of essays and exams.

MERGING OF SUMMATIVE WITH FORMATIVE ASSESSMENT

It appears that the merging of formative and summative assessment processes is an important outcome of effective online assessment. The facility to provide speedy formative feedback in a series of incremental assessments that build upon each other means that the critical formative function of assessment can be maximized.

AUTHENTICATION

How do we know whose work is being submitted for assessment? This is a familiar issue for distance educators, although a less familiar one for those who have relied on invigilated exams. In distance education, the use of incremental assignments and personalized or workplace projects have been used as a means of ensuring that students do their own work and that teachers can familiarize themselves with individual students' work. For objective testing methods, such as multiple-choice and short-answer questions that utilize testing software, the issue is more thorny. US colleges that utilize this kind of testing frequently have resorted to photographic capture of the keyboard operator and even iris scanning as a means of authentication. To address this issue effectively, it is suggested that educators need to reconceptualize their assessment methods rather than devise new methods of surveillance of students.

ACADEMIC DEVELOPMENT AND WORKLOAD

Online assessment design requires careful consideration for the impact upon academic workload. Concerns have been expressed that while some online assessment activities have enhanced the learning environment, they are simply unsustainable in the longer term. This has particularly been the case for distance educators moving online, who must now deal with a significantly increased volume of individual communications from learners and the facilitation of sometimes very large and active discussions among the community of learners.

With an eye to workload, academic staff need to undertake some role in the team-based development of study materials for online teaching and learning. Such projects may enhance the quality and integrity of the study materials as a package, but ultimately the responsibility for teaching and assessment remains with the academic subject specialist. This brings into question changes that may occur to academic workloads as a direct result of implementing a technology mediated assessment system. What is sustainable and how can staff can be supported?

A recent study conducted of Australian universities showed that where staff development was provided in the strategies for online teaching, traditional methods were used and a limited range of activities provided. The majority of universities that responded to the survey stated that in 1997 they could not meet the training needs of staff (Ellis *et al*, 1998). Further data is needed of academic skills and requirements for the new opportunities presented by ICTs.

RELIABILITY IN MARKING

While collaborative learning, groupwork and online discussion have been readily adopted as methods of online assessment, there is a range of concerns regarding reliability and consistency in marking students' work, as well as ascertaining the performance of individuals within a group. These issues are not new to assessment. However, in online environments there is sometimes less opportunity for teachers to observe and mediate these processes.

GENERALIZABILITY OF ADOPTION

It is not surprising to find that early adopters of ICTs have been in the discipline areas for which the online medium is a more natural supplement to existing forms of course delivery. Numerous case studies have been found from the disciplines of education, information technology and communication. Maintaining alignment in the online environment between objectives, content, teaching and learning strategies and assessment has thus not been particularly onerous. The questions remain: will this translate to other discipline areas, and how? This highlights the need for a meaningful educational rationale for the move to online teaching rather than just perceived economic or marketing imperatives.

The case studies presented suggest that in disciplines where conferencing, reflection, collaboration and the sense of a community of peers is important, the online medium has a lot to offer in expanding the experiences of assessment.

CONCLUDING REMARKS

Our examination of a range of international case studies has not resulted in new models of online assessment as such. Rather, it throws light on the willingness of educators to undertake a process of reconceptualizing existing pedagogies in the light of new opportunities which Web-based teaching and learning offer. Some of the best examples of online assessment have stimulated the development of online communities of learners and exploited new opportunities for debate, dialogue, groupwork, peer assessment and so on. The move to successful online learning in these instances has usually involved quite a radical rethink of past practices and a willingness to reconceptualize their pedagogy in light of issues raised above.

The more ordinary examples of online assessment are where this reconceptualization has not taken place. Face-to-face teachers moving on to the Web may tend to replicate the old within the new: paced weekly classes, a focus on coverage of content, objective testing and end-of-term exams. This may come as a shock to distance learners who are familiar with higher levels of control and choice in their learning. Similarly, distance educators moving to the Web may simply want to mount their printed study guides with enhancements such as hyperlinks and discussions lists, but keeping the traditional assessments and general 'distance' experience intact. Thus, learners may lack the incentive to go online at all if print-based options are still available to them. Opportunities for interaction are sometimes resisted by students, particularly when the idea of dialogue, teamwork and collaboration seem unrelated to their core purpose of study.

We do not suggest that teachers lack the imagination to really use this new medium. A major rethink along these lines is a risky business for educators who are already struggling with large classes and shrinking budgets, added to which are the very real concerns about student access to the Internet. These first, often tentative steps to Web teaching represent a first phase of development in which both teachers and learners are familiarizing themselves with the landscape and the opportunities it presents in their discipline areas. An end goal, in many cases, is not entirely clear. For the time being, we can focus on designing and conducting online courses that are pedagogically driven, student centred and sustainable.

We argue that a central goal of online learning is to support students from dependency to independence and, ultimately, to an interdependent community of learners. While ICTs enable a range of learning activities and assessment tasks to be innovative and broad ranging in their measure of student achievement, this chapter advocates a considered use of ICTs to ensure that the inherent advantages of face-to-face, open and distance learning are not lost while employing the benefits that the technologies allow. We also argue that the familiar educational quality assessment practices can be maintained using these new technologies. In seizing the opportunities offered by these technologies, the principles that underpin openness and flexibility need to be preserved.

REFERENCES

Alexander, S and McKenzie, J (1998) *Evaluation of IT in University Learning: the CAUT Experience*, Australian Government Printing Service, Canberra

Australian Bureau of Statistics (November 1998) http://www.statistics.gov.au/websitedbs/d3110125.nsf/4a255eef008309e44a255eef00061e57/d69a87dffa39a58aca2566c600800f16?OpenDocument

Clemente, (1998) *The State of the Net,* McGraw-Hill, New York

Collins, M and Berge, Z (1996) 'Facilitating interaction in computer mediated online courses', http://star.ucc.nau.edu/mauri/moderate/flec.html

Day, I (1998) 'Communication and the media' (10701), report on Web delivery trial, http://www-p.roma.unisa.edu.au/10701/index.htm

Ellis, A, O'Reilly, M and Debreceny, R (1998) 'Staff development responses to the demand for online teaching and learning' (ASCILITE 98), Wollongong University Press, pp 191–201

Foley, G and Schuck, S (1998) Web-based conferencing: pedagogical asset or constraint? *Australian Journal of Educational Technology*, **14** (2), pp 122–140

Gibbs, G (1995) *Assessing Student Centred Courses*, Oxford Brookes University

Harasim, L, Hiltz, S R, Teles, L and Turoff, M (1995) *Learning Networks*, MIT Press, Massachusetts

Holt, M E, Rees, F, Swenson, J D and Klieber, P B (1998) 'Evolution of evaluations for critical, reflective and deliberative discourse: national issues forums on-line', http://www.coe.uga.edu/adulted/faculty/mholt/paper1.html

Klemm, W R and Snell, J R (1996) 'Enriching computer-mediated group learning by coupling constructivism with collaborative learning', http://www.usq.edu.au/electpub/e-jist/klemm.htm

Macdonald, J, Mason, R and Heap, N (in press) Refining assessment for resource based learning, *Assessment and Evaluation in Higher Education*, probably **24** (3)

Nightingale, P, Wiata, I T, Toohey, S, Ryan, G, Hughes, C and Magin, D (1996), *Assessing Learning in Universities*, UNSW Press, Sydney

O'Reilly, M and Patterson (1998) Assessing learners through the WWW, *Computer Networks and ISDN Systems*, **30** (1–7), pp 727–29

Paulsen, M (1995) 'The online report on pedagogical techniques for computer-mediated communication', http://www.hs.nki.no/morten/cmcped.htm

Rowntree, D (1977) *Assessing Students: How shall we know them?* Kogan Page, London

Rowntree, D (1986) *Teaching Through Self-instruction*, Kogan Page, London

Stefani, L (1998) 'Assessing in partnership with learners', http://www.ouh.nl/open/fdo/eecae98/assessme.htm

Turoff, M (1997) 'Alternative futures for distance learning: the Force and the Darkside', keynote presentation at UNESCO/Open University International Colloquium, April 27–29 (Virtual learning environments and the role of the teacher), Open University, Milton Keynes

ACKNOWLEDGEMENTS

The authors would like to acknowledge, with thanks, the assistance of the contributors of the case studies.

17

Delivering automated innovative assessment in a varied curriculum

Roy Seden

INTRODUCTION

Subject differentiation and definition is a major factor in higher education (HE) policy and practice. Compare the range of subject groupings used in the UK Research Assessment Exercises (RAE) and the Quality Assurance Agency (QAA) teaching quality assessments, and the differing ways in which universities organize themselves in response to their cultural and market environment. The redefinition of subjects such as 'History of Art and Design' into 'History of Art and Material Culture', the rise of inter-disciplinarity in general and market-based moves, exemplified by that from explicit engineering subjects into implicit technology subjects such as music or theatre technology – all re-emphasize the rise of more wide-ranging modular programmes in form and content. There is also an emerging widely held concern with coherence in modular provision, especially in vocational education.

The impact of information and communication technologies (ICTs) is another major factor in HE policy and practice for it has led to a high level of relatively uncoordinated activity in electronic learning and assessment. I suggest that it is possible that such activity has often not been built on secure pedagogical foundations. Much software has little usage in educational delivery, barring notable exceptions such as AUTOCAD, which is an industry standard. The third round of the Teaching and Learning Technology Programme (TLTP) is focusing on embedding software into the delivered curriculum for this very reason. One TLTP project entitled 'Built Environment Appropriate Technology for Learning, (BEATL), in which I am involved through De Montfort University (DMU) being a partner, uses a strong research methodology with a view to developing secure transferable information regarding using ICTs to achieve assessed learning outcomes.

These issues of coherence and pedagogy lead me to consider that functional simplification, relating to the purpose of a programme or module, is crucial. Issues of standardization then follow in terms of module commonality and the use of ICTs in the curriculum at sub-module level for learning and assessment.

Computer-assisted assessment (CAA) can also be valuable in its contribution to resource-effective programmes where integration and coherence is delivered in an explicit way. I shall refer to evidence supporting this assertion for a varied programme delivery area, so presenting one test of this thesis for HE more generally.

AUTOMATED ASSESSMENT IN STRUCTURES

Construction education is wide ranging in its content, forms and assessed learning outcomes. The ways students are assessed profoundly influence the ways they learn (Atkins, Beattie and Dockrell, 1993; Tang, 1993), so assessment strategies are best designed to reflect clearly the real ethos, aims and values of a programme as well as the subject being assessed. On wide-ranging programmes, such strategies can tend to lead to a high level of continuous assessment and students can have difficulties in terms of the purpose of a particular assessment on the programme and the assessment feedback. Equally, staff can have problems in terms of volume of assessment and the pressure to reduce assessment levels and this may compromise the quality of assessed learning outcomes.

I suggest that automated assessment strategies, when correctly placed within a programme, can not only assist in solving problems relating to student feedback, staff workload and assessed learning output, but can also be valuable in supporting the entire programme. In any varied education, such as construction, they help to solve the problem of how to spend more assessment time in the heart of a wide-ranging programme. They also assist in terms of university policy and practice by clarifying how coherence in modularity may be handled.

Aspects of continuous assessment may be usefully automated, as illustrated by a case study from DMU, involving structure assessment and studio assessment on the BSc (Hons) Construction Technology and Management (CTM) programme. I have developed an integrated learning and assessment suite of software for structures teaching on year-one modules delivered to 80 students on three programmes at DMU.

The software I have produced (Seden, 1993a, 1993b) includes load assessment (DMLOAD), forces in trusses (DMTRUSS), forces in beams (DMSHEAR) and section properties (DMSECT). Design features include a mouse-based graphical calculator, 'rubber band' measurement, extensive colour coding, speedy definition of examples, immediate feedback and mouse-based mimicking of hand techniques. A standardized regime of user interface, software structure, graphical routines, colour coding and activity routines between different software items all ease student access at the university, work and home.

Except for DMLOAD, all the software is multi-modal and is delivered in seamless learning and assessment modes (eg DMTRUSSA). I use a proprietary programme (DMSUPER) that enables me to log, weigh, grade and print student assessment results. These depend on the easy/medium/hard balance of examples for the subject and the weightings for different stages of the structural analysis, as specified by myself. The results for each subject can then be calculated, graded, aggregated with other subjects where required and printed out. The distance learning version (eg DMTRUSSD) is a truncated combination of the learning and assessment versions.

The explicit rigour means that it is important to reinforce student learning. Feedback through the software's 'show' facility gives an immediate and focused remedial context where the learner can choose to be shown the solution for the current stage of the structural problem they are attempting, plus a range of options for viewing the structural problem, the development of the process and/or the final product or solution, often in weighted colour-coded form. These facilities place as much power as possible in the learners' hands to shape and pace their learning experience, especially as they know the precise basis of the assessment. Feedback occurs throughout the software and has proved very popular.

AUTOMATED ASSESSMENT METHOD

The principles underlying the computer-based assessment methodology are:

- Assessment examples are presented in the same way as learning and practice examples.
- The technique being assessed is transparent in terms of structural principles.
- The technique being assessed is broken down into appropriate stages so that: the error of a learner who is being assessed is penalized only at that stage; tutors can weight different stages as they see fit.
- The generic assessment example files are individualized through random number generation of loads and dimensions.
- The generic examples can be graded easy, medium or hard at the discretion of the tutor.
- Degree and diploma/certificate assessments are differentiated through distinct combinations of easy/medium/hard examples.

The advantages of the methodology are that: assessments are robust as all students are required to complete them; plagiarism is limited; I am not exhausted; the student time involved is very low; and the assessment requirements are rigorous in terms of the levels of assessed learning outcomes.

Typical results (Seden, 1997) for the automatic assessment method show that the assessed learning outcomes of over 250 students not only maintain existing standards of achievement in this subject, but also measurably enhance them. They also show that:

- differing admissions levels between degrees lead to differential achievements at level 1;

- HND and HNC students perform comparably with each other and the equivalent degree students, suggesting that the differential assessment strategies adopted are about right;
- results are very consistent over the four years reviewed, indicating the ability of automated assessed learning outcomes to maintain standards in the face of considerable changes in the design and delivery of programmes and the diminution of the unit of resource.

While I have inevitably encountered problems, it is clear that robust learning, practice and assessment techniques have been successfully developed to support an automated innovative assessment strategy. Such techniques are transferable in principle to any subject area that also involves staged sequential analytical procedures. In reality, this would require considerable input by the tutors to ensure the rigour of the assessment method and the seamlessness between learning and assessment through practice. The automated assessment strategy has been used as part of a continuous assessment strategy as briefly outlined below.

SEMI-AUTOMATED ASSESSMENT METHOD

Six degree and HND programmes have used DMLOAD in year one as part of the structures work in the Building Technology 1 modules. Over 200 students have been assessed using material piloted on 50–70 students per year over four years on the CTM degree and an HND.

A data file on DMLOAD generates a framed structural morphology, while DMSUPER allocates each student a randomly generated reference number giving the specific dimensions of their structure. The students receive a print out of a range of beam and column loads, load patterns and reactions and they are required to justify these by using their specific dimensions, thus ensuring individual work. The submission requires interpretation of computer output, calculations, text and sketching.

My results for this method are similar to those for other multi-mode assignments. Their value lies in the rigour given to the nature of the assessment by the automated component.

STUDIO ASSESSMENT: THE EFFECT OF ICT IN THE VARIED CURRICULUM

The studio in each study year is the focus of the CTM programme, supplying much of its ethos and providing a continuous spine through each year by explicit coherence and integration. In most semesters of the programme there is a central integrative studio module in which a portfolio of work is developed from a range of assessments. In early years, it consolidates and brings together the different subjects to help fulfil the principal course aim. In later years, it supplies much of the integrated honours challenge of the CTM programme. It is the workshop of the programme and contains a series of carefully organized tasks that solve construction industry-related problems arranged around the studio theme of the year. The studio assessment strategy is not automated and it is unlikely it ever will be.

A sense of overall purpose and course identity is established as space and time is given to allow the full circle of learning (Lyons, Seden and Ashton, 1995) to be experienced time and again. Motivation and purpose come from the strong design link between learning, assessment and feedback. Assignment delivery is by means of a cycle of briefing, input, tutorials and assessment feedback, to which all tutors contribute during the year. Staff feedback is an important part of the overall learning strategy that requires much staff time. This can be released to some extent by automated assessment techniques, which thus support the overall programme delivery as well as the subject assessment.

The studio succeeds as the opportunity for continuity and the development of thinking processes over a long period. Central to any success is the time and attention given by tutors to encouraging the students, assessing their submissions, presentations and portfolios and giving them valuable feedback on their efforts. This cannot be automated to any significant extent. The assessment methods adopted for the studio work are congruent with the studio's place at the heart of the programme. It is vital that those parts of the curriculum that can be assessed automatically are assessed in such a manner, so releasing staff to give personal attention to assessment and feedback where it is most needed.

OVERALL DESIGN AND PURPOSE OF PROGRAMMES OF LEARNING

ICT-supported learning normally covers a limited syllabus area within a module. However, an important variable is the nature of the programme(s) the module serves, especially in terms of assessment strategies. While some programmes are composed of wholly 'stand alone' modules, others are not, so the module design must be simplified to fulfil this function, implying a more balanced relationship between module and programme than is often the case.

The CTM programme is designed around the integrating studio, which has a workshop-based problem-solving ethos encouraging inductive learning styles. The programme is at least 75 per cent coursework assessed and the structural work is 100 per cent coursework assessed. This is demanding of both staff and student. The value placed on the studio module places particular pressure on the subject modules and their content time. Thus, the learning delivery and assessment profile in the structural work in the building technology subject module reflects one of the most analytical, precise and experimental parts of this wide-ranging course, which highly values integration and the solving of multimodal problems. Student-centred learning delivery leads the module contact time in physical and electronic laboratories and this self-paced, resource-based learning and assessment is the main focus of the structures work in the module that carries the pressure from the studio.

FORMS OF INNOVATIVE AUTOMATED ASSESSMENT

What are the appropriate means by which authentic assessment may be achieved? (Atkins, Beattie and Dockrell, 1993; Seden and McArthur, 1996) Authentic assessment is integral with the underlying algorithms and as seamless as possible with the learning experience of the learner, who knows the precise basis of the assessment. Tutors are as free as possible to apply their own value judgements in respect of weighting different parts of an assignment and different assignments within an overall assessment. Finally, the learner receives the assessment material in the manner of the learning material.

In the first form, the assessment process is wholly automated and self-contained. It is interesting that students' self-expectations continue to be very high when faced with being assessed by CBA. My experience is that they require constant reminders that the pass level is 40 per cent, not 90 per cent. This reflects the way in which CBA can have a focal/iconic mode to it. Students sense there is no extraneous subject matter, that they are being rigorously confronted and that all they do has some useful purpose, given that they must learn a particular technique/algorithm.

In the second form, the software generates individual assessment examples automatically from a common source file, which are assessed by the tutor manually using standard feedback sheets. Nonetheless, ICT is integrated into an assessment that is wide-ranging in its modes, one of which is electronic. This is an example of software being used to support more general, assessable work.

A third form practised at DMU (Seden and McArthur, 1996) uses an optical mark reader (OMR) to help produce effective, self-motivated, self-directed and self-paced studies in construction science. The OMR cards are processed by commercial analysis and reporting software. This close link between learning and assessment benefits students and staff in ways already outlined for the structures delivery. In particular, the tutors have a reduced marking workload and receive feedback about the performance of each test question in terms of facility, selectivity and reliability, so helping to evaluate the students, the assessment and the delivery. In this respect alone, the CMA method outlined above has proved its worth. The automated assessment strategy has been used as part of a continuous assessment strategy elsewhere in the construction materials science curriculum on modules involving over 200 students from four programmes each year. The techniques have also been transferred to diagnostic/formative and evaluative/summative parts of the assessment profile of a year one module introducing the built environment to over 200 students from six programmes.

> OMR *facility* is the proportion of those being assessed who correctly answer the questions, and a good overall test will have questions covering a wide range of facility. *Selectivity* is a measure of the correlation between those who answer a particular question correctly and those who do well in the test overall. *Reliability* is simply the product of facility and selectivity and is a measure of the overall effectiveness of the question. If an average facility and a high selectivity are achieved then the question could be argued to be very reliable at differentiating between good and poor overall candidates.

LEARNING AND ASSESSMENT CONTEXT OR CULTURE

The first 'software embedded' level of learning and assessment context is provided by its design. For example, DM software is structured on identical graphical routines and uses colour coding widely. Detailed examples include: green/red/yellow indicating solved/currently active/unsolved parts of the structure within a solution; learner activity routines focusing on 'full screen' graphical calculators that include all current symbols as mouse-operated buttons.

The second 'software interactive' level is provided by immediate and focused remedial feedback in stages. It is an especially valuable form of reinforcement for the weaker learner, who is taught to use it in an anticipatory way. In the DM software, if the learner is lost at any stage in the solution input then they can be 'shown' the solution for that stage at once. If the learner's attempts at a stage of the solution are wrong then he or she is allowed further attempts beginning, where possible, from the first incorrect input. Finally, students can 'view' the final solution while in the middle of developing the solution for themselves. Such responsive and secure features place as much power as possible in the learners' hands to build confidence regarding assessment and shape and pace their learning experience within the overall guidance of the tutor for the learning unit.

The third 'software usage' level is provided by the way the software is embedded and used in a learning session. My experience is that the most effective learning sessions have been those when the learners have truly used the computer as a tutor and moved readily between their own predicted calculations and sketches and the feedback provided by the software. The levels of activity, responsiveness and curiosity seem to reflect closely the levels of achievement.

It is salutary for a student whose wider context is studying multi-faceted processes of, say, construction management to be challenged by the precision of a method of solving force systems in trusses. This is commented on regularly by the students, who have a wide range of learning styles (Seden, 1993b). However, they comment equally on the fairness of the automated assessment method because it is based on the nature of the algorithm, it is delivered in stages and marks can be made highly technique-orientated by the tutor. Students see this as fair and reliable, as assessment criteria and learning outcomes are so closely linked, and they view this type of assessment favourably as compared to other less explicit assessments on the programme. This is valuable, especially when the module is 100 per cent coursework assessed within the context of a high level of such assessment within a programme of study.

CONCLUSIONS

My experience over the last ten years suggests that automated innovative assessment strategies can be valuable in enhancing student learning, assessment and feedback. They can also assist in reducing tutor input without lowering the quality of assessed learning outcomes.

Functional simplification allows us to put automated assessment where it belongs, in curriculum areas which lend themselves to just such an approach. This enables us to give greater attention to assessment, where it belongs, at the design heart of a programme.

The use of computers to support innovative assessment can offer measurable benefits in terms not only of assessed student outcomes, but also in a range of other outputs including module viability and overall programme design. However, there is still much to do, not least at the higher levels of educational management, even in the most supportive HE environments.

REFERENCES

Atkins, M J, Beattie, J and Dockrell, W B (1993) *Assessment Issues in Higher Education*, Department of Employment Report, University of Newcastle upon Tyne

Lyons, A, Seden, M R and Ashton, R (1995) 'Implementing information technology on built environment courses: strategies and student learning styles', from the proceedings of the CIB W89 symposium on construction/building education and research, beyond 2000, University of Florida, Orlando, pp 805–814

Seden, M R (1993a) 'Structural computing for built environment learners in a changing educational environment', Civil-Comp 93, paper presented at the fifth international conference on civil and structural engineering computing: developments in structural engineering computing, Heriot-Watt University, Edinburgh, pp 431–438

Seden, M R (1993b) 'How to sweeten a scientific pill for a less than scientific palate', paper presented at the international conference on computer-based learning in science, Technical University of Vienna, pp 567–576

Seden, M R (1997) 'Ten years on: an evaluation', CBLIS 97, paper presented at international conference on computer-based learning in science, De Montfort University

Seden, M R, Davenport, P E and Ashley, M J (1995) 'Course design, course ethos and the industrial context, proceedings of the CIB W89 symposium on construction/building education and research, beyond 2000, University of Florida, Orlando, pp 581–590

Seden, M R and McArthur, H (1996) 'Automated innovative assessment', paper presented at conference on innovations in student assessment, Quality Support Centre, The Open University, Milton Keynes

Tang, C (1993) 'Effects of modes of assessment on students' preparation strategies, paper presented at symposium on improving student learning, Oxford Brookes University

18

A structured approach to mass implementation of computer-based assessment (CBA)

Stan Zakrzewski

INTRODUCTION

The purpose of this chapter is to put forward a framework that recognizes the 'openness' that can be achieved in systems for computer-based assessment and to suggest a generic, structured model for their development and implementation. In the broadest sense, a 'system' is a collection of components that interact together to accomplish specific tasks. Computer-based assessment systems are 'systems' in which management, academic staff, support staff and students work together to deliver summative or formative assessment using computers and their networks. The success of such systems will depend on a range of factors including their technical, operational, pedagogic and financial feasibility.

WHY DEVELOP SUCH SYSTEMS?

One reason is that the request for computer-based assessment arises because of identified needs of the academic staff. The need may be pedagogic; in other words, it may simply arise because objective testing is the most suitable form for testing specific knowledge and skills within a particular part of a course. It may be the most efficient and effective means of reducing the marking load, especially for very large classes, and thus enable academic staff to pursue other areas of academic interest. Time saved, however, may represent a redistribution of workload and careful evaluation should ensure that this is not only appropriate but also acknowledged. Perhaps fast feedback or results will enable academic staff to plan more effectively. It may be seen as a way of saving costs in a time where a diminishing unit of resource is constantly with us or it may be quite simply that students benefit. The system's aims and objectives are its reason for development and implementation. Successful computer-based assessment systems enhance the quality of the learning experience for students and are not there just to demonstrate the value of sophisticated technology. Computer-based assessment systems are 'open' and not isolated. Objective tests, for example, are subject to external examination.

USING QUESTION MARK DESIGNER AT LUTON

At the University of Luton, the computer-based assessment system centred on 'Question Mark Designer for Windows' was originally implemented in the spring of 1993, and it continues to expand. In the academic year 1998/99, over 10,000 student sittings for summative and 3,000 for formative assessment took place.

The computer adviser of the university invited management, academic and support staff to a demonstration of the software. The demonstration involved describing what the software could achieve and a 'hands on' element. The participants undertook a test in travel and tourism. At the end of the test, the results were read out to the participants within five minutes of finishing the test. The success of the demonstration was reflected in the willingness of some of the academic staff to undertake a pilot. In June of that year, the pilot was launched with 150 comparative psychology students (Pritchett and Zakrzewski, 1996). The students took a summative assessment in seven local faculty computer areas. At that time, each faculty area had its own dedicated network of computer workstations. The results were collated from all the networked areas as soon as the examination had finished. The examination duration was one hour and the question types predominantly multiple-choice. Objective test delivery grew in the psychology department over the next few years and its administrative staff were trained to convert examinations to Question Mark format. Other departments began to take an interest, including politics and public policy, biology and computing. Each year, more and more departments were using their local facilities to deliver objective tests. Formative assessments began to grow out of the summative system and central support was provided to help develop the system more widely.

CENTRALIZING THE IMPLEMENTATION

The learning resources centre (LRC) at Luton University houses some 200 workstations in one large central complex. A modular credit scheme supports the student programmes of study. At the end of each semester (in January and June), the central complex is used for two weeks to facilitate computer-based summative end-of-module examinations. These examinations are timetabled by the exams office, which is also responsible for assigning academic invigilators to the system, and technical support is provided by central computer services. The system is integrated as far as possible with the traditional examination procedures. The LRC is also reserved for phase tests (summative examinations taken during the semester) eight times a year. Formative examinations are taken on an open-access basis in the centre throughout the year. In the academic year 1998/99 modules in accounting, economics, leisure, travel and tourism, design, material sciences, biology, computing, mathematics, social sciences, midwifery, psychology, media, languages, law and history used computer-based assessment as part of their assessment portfolio.

DESIGNING AN OPERATIONAL FRAMEWORK

The success of the system prompted the design of a generic framework for the implementation of computer-based assessment. An efficient and effective framework reflects planned sustainable growth. The framework consists of four developmental stages, in which roles and responsibilities, the feasibility of what is being attempted for summative or formative assessment and a review of the outcomes are essential components (see Figure 18.1). Pedagogic, technical, operational and financial feasibility must be established, not only for the strategy in the short term, where a demonstration or a pilot is likely, but also in the medium to long term, through the reporting mechanism, if expansion is to take place. The framework gives a good indication of where the assessment strategy is heading over a period of time.

The objective of stage 0 (Figure 18.1) is to demonstrate the potential of the system, provoke academic debate on the suitability and feasibility of objective testing and gain management support for this new initiative. But who is the instigator? Many academic institutions have now established learning technology departments which interact very closely with academic staff using technology in teaching, learning and assessment and act as an interface between academic staff and computer support staff. In many institutions, they may bridge the gap between the academic and support staff who may see priorities and goals differently. In other institutions, it may be a single person, a computer adviser, who would act in this capacity. Whether responsibility lies with a department or a single person, the awareness of what can be achieved must lie with them.

PILOTING

A demonstration must have impact and if the impact is sufficient then some academic staff may express interest in using the system. Managers are more likely to lend their support for a demonstration that will lead to an official pilot of the system in a specific course.

The objective of stage 1 is, therefore, to implement a pilot. The decision as to whether to pilot with summative or formative assessment (or both) should be led by the needs of the curriculum with reference to the technical and operational capabilities of existing computer systems. It is the curriculum that is the driving mechanism and staff development in effective objective test design is essential. Summative assessment systems obviate the need for marking formal examinations and require less design input as no tailored feedback needs to be designed. Nevertheless, some institutions may adopt what they consider to be a more prudent approach and will start with formative testing before making the transition to summative examination. In any event, whether summative or formative, a formal system test will need to be conducted before the pilot is launched and there are no better testers of systems then the students themselves. After the pilot has been conducted, a formal review of the system should be undertaken before any further expansion takes place. Particular attention should be given to integration with existing assessment procedures, effective question design, student experiences and the views of the academic and support staff of the system operation. Management should be informed of the costs and benefits so that the planned approach to expansion can be properly supported and resources can be distributed appropriately.

EXPANDING INTO DEPARTMENTS

Stage 2 (Figure 18.1) is concerned with departmental expansion. Additional personnel will be involved, documentation to support the system will need to increase and a strategy to accommodate multi-assessments will need to be evolved. Staff development will play a more active role. Questions should become more challenging so that they begin to test or develop higher-order cognitive skills. A user group could be formed to exchange good practice and learn from the experiences of external consultants or guest speakers. Administrative tasks will increase and it may be necessary to train departmental personnel in the correct procedures that facilitate integration and the production of the tests in electronic form. It is likely that summative and formative examinations will flourish and the assessment system will need to address key issues in both. A senior member of staff in each department may be given the responsibility for controlling test production and delivery and managing the quality assurance processes. A formal review of the system should take place at the end of the academic year.

INTO THE WHOLE INSTITUTION

Whereas stage 2 can be viewed as expansion, stage 3 is a significant system change as the move is made from a number of de-centralized departmental systems to a centralized university-wide system. The systems at this stage would be fully integrated with the traditional assessment system of the university. A central examinations office would be responsible for timetabling and scheduling the examinations and a quality assurance department would take responsibility for monitoring the quality of the processes. A large centralized system may very well be supported by a research-based assessment team. Again, a formal review of the system should take place at the end of the academic year.

The generic framework offers a snapshot of the life or the system. It emphasizes the system's degree of openness and its own boundaries over time. The assessment system will interface with both internal systems (computer services, staff development, learning technology, quality assurance and examinations) and external systems (consultants, external examiners and teaching quality assessments). It reflects the importance of planning with staff from many areas within the institution and gives an indication of new roles and responsibilities that will be central to the system's success. In short, computer-based assessment systems will be viewed as complete systems and not just a piece of software running on workstations.

TURNING A FRAMEWORK INTO A SYSTEM

The framework is a good starting point, placing importance on planning, but it does not detail the plan itself. It does not generate the detailed procedures that, when put into operation, will deliver a quality system. We may be able to use or refine an established approach to systems analysis and design. Most learning technology models are 'waterfall' in nature (LTDI, 1996) with a sequential progression from analysis to design to implementation and finally review, but it needs to be asked whether they are appropriate for computer-based assessment. Let us turn back to the implementation of CBA at Luton. There, a pilot was discussed with the possibility of evolutionary development to departmental and university-wide systems. What is necessary is a model that at each stage implements a complete system. 'Prototyping' is therefore perhaps not appropriate as it implies partially finished products that will continually be refined. Complete systems are required at evolutionary stages.

The framework places importance on feasibility, but this should be questioned. Assessment is a risky business: academic staff are uncertain of the pedagogic value of objective testing and computer support staff will be concerned with reliability and security of their computer networks. Implementation teams need to ask what would happen if the servers break down. Will the institution be tied up all summer dealing with student appeals? Is it really worth it? Computer-based assessment systems are often not implemented because managers are reluctant to take the financial risks, academic staff the pedagogic risks and support staff the technical risks – yet the benefits of a successful assessment system will outweigh the costs (Zakrzewski and Bull, 1998). If we are to design a successful system, it must eliminate or at least reduce the likelihood of risks occurring and minimize their impact in the event that they do so. A generic model for computer-based assessment must therefore be based on the assessment and management of risks.

In 1988, Boehm developed the risk or spiral model for engineering large software systems. The model has four quadrants in which setting objectives, risk assessment, engineering the product and review are dominant activities. These quadrants are revisited as large software systems reach completion and a risk analysis is conducted before the next version of the software is designed and implemented.

In order to adapt the model for computer-based assessment (LTDI, 1999) the original engineering quadrant is replaced with evolutionary development of the stages in the framework and 'quality design of objective questions'

(Heard, Nichol and Heath, 1997) is added before development of each stage commences. The planning and review components of the framework map into the first and last quadrants in Boehm's model. The risk analysis is conducted prior to objective test design and remains the second quadrant in the model. It is the risk analysis that generates strategies for risk elimination or reduction that in turn generates the detailed procedures necessary to implement successful computer-based assessment systems. The detailed procedures that characterize the system play a pivotal role in its success and therefore must be derived from the elimination or reduction of risks.

Let us take two examples. It may be perceived that introducing a new method or assessment may cause student anxiety and must be viewed as a pedagogic risk. It is not appropriate to simply confront students with an entirely new form of assessment. Strategies must therefore be deployed to eradicate this risk. One strategy may be to introduce 'taster questions' on the network well before the examination starts. These tasters, perhaps seven or eight questions, would be available to students on an open-access basis and would serve a dual purpose. Firstly, they would be used to introduce the students to the differing question types and, secondly, to enable students to familiarize themselves with the technology. The tasters would have to be accompanied by an instruction set. This strategy can be translated into a formal system procedure:

> Four weeks before the commencement of examinations, all tasters will be mounted in the central IT suite by computer services. The learning technology department will provide student instructions that will be made available behind the counter in the IT suite.

The second example involves storage of answer files. It may be perceived by computer services that the loss of an individual answer file is a technical risk and must be eliminated. The strategy to eliminate the risk may involve the use of a checklist. A flag must be set in the test control information to store the answer files and a formal systems test must be carried out to ensure that the answer files are being stored before the students enter the examination. Again, this strategy may be translated into a formal system procedure:

> The learning technology department will use a checklist to ensure that answer file flags are set for each test in the test control information block. This checklist will be signed by the head of the learning technology department. The learning technology department will conduct a formal test to ensure answer files are being stored on the examination day. This test will be conducted 15 minutes prior to the students entering the IT suite. A formal count will be made 5 minutes after the start of the examination and the number of students sitting the examination matched with the number of answer files. A computer seat number and student identification number will uniquely identify and pinpoint a mismatch if it occurs and the student will be asked to restart the examination.

The success of the computer-based system at the University of Luton is due to academic and support staff working together to achieve the aims and objectives of the system through a planned approach to design and implementation that eliminates risks.

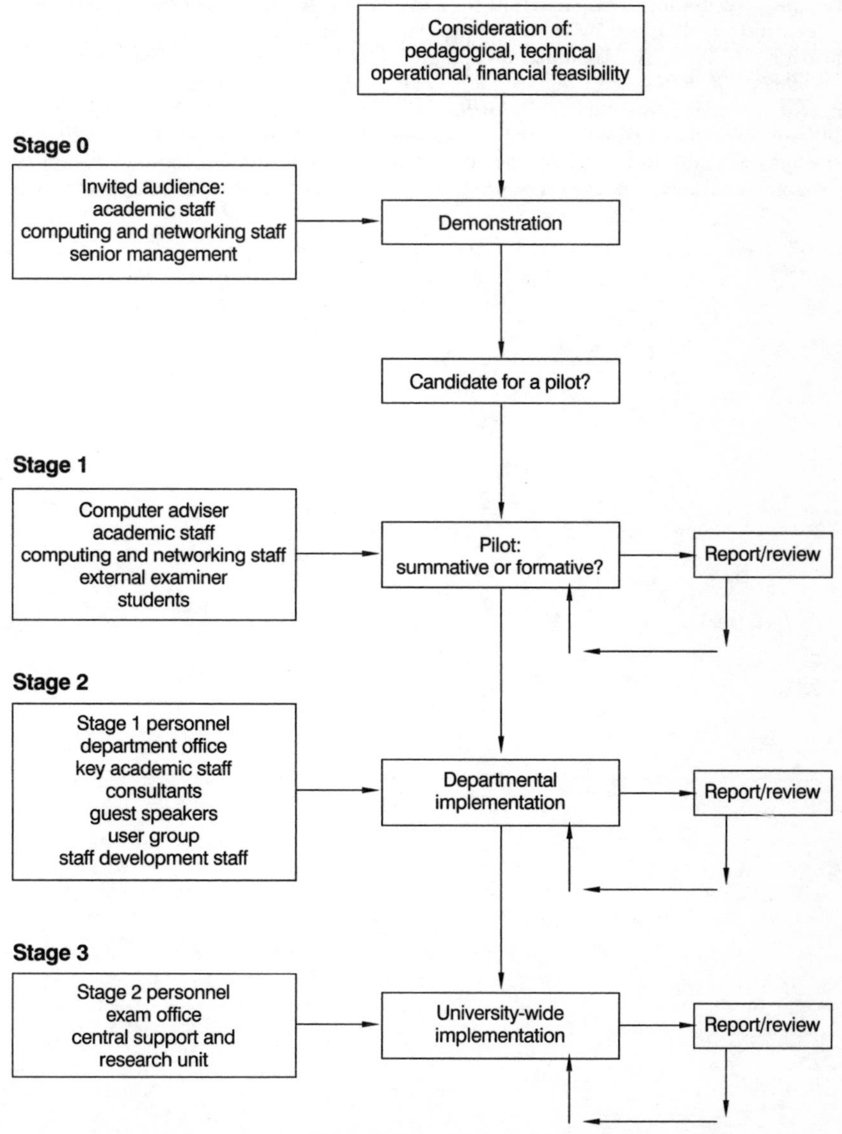

Figure 18.1 *A framework for computer-based assessment*

REFERENCES

Boehm, B (1988) A spiral model for software development and enhancement, *IEEE Computer*, **21** (5), pp 61–72

Heard, S, Nichol, J and Heath, S (1997) *Setting Effective Objective Tests*, MERTal Publications, University of Aberdeen

Learning Technology Dissemination Initiative (1996) *Implementing Learning Technology*, Learning Technology Dissemination Initiative, Edinburgh

Learning Technology Dissemination Initiative (1999) *Learning Technology Dissemination Initiative CD ROM*, Learning Technology Dissemination Initiative, Edinburgh

Pritchett, N and Zakrzewski, S (1996) Interactive computer assessment of large groups: student responses, *Innovations in Education and Training International*, **33** (3), pp 242–247

Zakrzewski, S and Bull, J (1998) The mass implementation and evaluation of computer-based assessments, *Assessment and Evaluation in Higher Education*, **23** (2), pp 141–152

19

Student perceptions of the learning benefits of computer-assisted assessment: a case study in electronic engineering

Kay Sambell, Alistair Sambell and Graham Sexton

INTRODUCTION

This chapter is based on the findings of an exploratory study that investigated the impact of introducing computer-assisted assessment (CAA) onto a range of undergraduate programmes within the context of electronic engineering education. This formed part of a developmental project funded by the University of Northumbria, 'Using communication networks to disseminate teaching, learning and assessment', undertaken by the division of electronic and electrical engineering. It considers the extent to which generic assessment software, used both formatively and summatively, promotes effective teaching and learning, as defined by a recent review of educational practices within the discipline. In particular, it illuminates student perspectives on the impact of this alternative form of assessment and relates them to the development of competency in self-evaluation.

BACKGROUND

Recent developments in IT are often seen to promise 'a radical transformation of higher education' and to offer significant pedagogical benefits (Light and Light, 1998). Computer-assisted learning is often advocated on educational grounds, but is still somewhat under-used (Barnard, 1998). Educational research has consistently highlighted the pedagogical value of providing detailed, timely feedback to students, but tutors find themselves having to cut down on the number of chances for students to engage in one-to-one formative assessment opportunities and are often faced with having to reduce, rather than increase, the level of tutor-feedback offered. Computer-based learning and assessment packages are offered as one solution (Knight, 1996). Computer-assisted communication, for instance, is promoted as an attractive opportunity to develop practical schemes that may support traditional teaching programmes and provide improved levels of feedback (Light, Colbourne and Light, 1997).

There is also growing recognition that the increased pressures brought to bear on lecturers (eg increasing tendencies to offer places to non-traditional students, the diminishing unit of resource and considerable demands on their time with growing student numbers) mean that there is an urgent need to re-evaluate tutors' working practices with students. The quality of the learning experience in higher education must not be compromised and universities seek to develop realistic teaching and learning methods that enable students to learn successfully by encouraging deep rather than surface approaches to learning. In this chapter we explore the ways in which CAA may be used as a viable and valuable option to provide ample opportunities for formative assessment and feedback.

DESCRIPTION OF THE PROJECT

The project introduced computer-assisted assessment points on a range of undergraduate programmes (at levels one and three) and in a number of different ways. In each case a generic assessment software package was used to develop computer-marked tests. The software allows the lecturer to determine content knowledge, set appropriate tasks and provide plentiful qualitative feedback as well as marks, which students can access immediately they have performed the test. Although some test items were multiple choice, the package is interactive, allowing students to respond by inputting data, at the end or at points during a question. (For a fuller description of the assessment materials see Figure 19.1.) Each test was run over the Internet, so students could access practice tests from remote sites and in their own time, if desirable. Marking large numbers of students' work was rapid and easy. Lecturers were able to immediately receive information about how many students took the tests and the marks they achieved. This acted as diagnostic feedback that helped lecturers to perceive any problems which students experienced and adapt teaching accordingly (Nitko, 1995).

In most cases the tests were used in summative contexts, representing up to 40 per cent of the overall unit mark. Most involved high levels of student interaction, typically in the form of mathematical calculation and manipulation. They were designed to encourage students to develop and apply their understanding to problems.

In all the cases, however, students were given the opportunity to undertake a series of formative 'practice' tests. These were made available at the outset of the unit. They were voluntary and not timed, and students could choose when to take them. They could be revisited several times and briefings made clear that the anonymous marks sent to tutors did not 'count'. These practice tests placed emphasis upon the provision of detailed and timely feedback.

Supporting interactive material was also made available via the Internet, which was designed to act as a resource that would enhance learners' capacities to become fully and realistically involved in the assessment of their own learning via the 'practice' tests. For instance, students could access worked examples and seminar solutions (exemplar), which the lecturer could choose to make immediately available or to phase on to the Web as the unit progressed. The aim was to fully integrate assessment into the learning process; to enable learners to access materials in their own time and at their own pace; and to allow students to exercise considerable control over their own learning.

THE ROLE OF ASSESSMENT IN STUDENT LEARNING

The role of assessment in the learning experience is crucial. A growing body of literature makes the case for a timely shift in our assessment paradigms, arguing that carefully designed assessment can usefully be seen as a tool for facilitating learning (Brown and Knight, 1994; Birenbaum, 1996).

'Whereas in the past, we have seen assessment only as a means to determine measures and thus certification, there is now a realisation that the potential benefits of assessing are much wider and impinge on all stages of the learning process.' (Dochy and McDowell, 1997, p279)

Birenbaum (1996) has called this a shift from a 'testing culture' to an 'assessment culture'. In the former, teaching and assessment are viewed as separate activities and the level of control exercised by the teacher is high. The latter strongly emphasizes the integration of assessment and learning, with students playing a far more active part in the construction and evaluation of their learning. In this context, assessment has new goals and functions, which are importantly student-centred, predicated upon the notion of active learning. Alternative learner-centred approaches to assessment, such as peer review and self-evaluation, are being explored accordingly, on the grounds that they encourage students to engage continuously and foster a deep approach to learning, equipping learners with lifelong learning skills (Moerkerke, 1996; Sambell and McDowell, 1997).

The project sought to use CAA to get students more fully involved in the assessment of their own learning. We felt that the formative 'practice tests' could act as a potent integrated tool to enhance the teaching process (Birenbaum and Dochy, 1996). Developments were based on the assumption that students' commitment to learning is likely to be strengthened when they are equipped with adequate mechanisms and take more responsibility, in collaboration with their tutors, for monitoring their own progress, evaluating their own strengths and weaknesses and for collectively devising future strategies for improving their learning outcomes.

Student self-evaluation is central to the learning process (Klenowski, 1995). The process of self-monitoring engages students in identifying how successfully something is being done, perceiving the gaps in knowledge/ability that need to be addressed and deciding upon an action plan to move their learning forward. This tends to ascribe value to the *processes* by which learning occurs, as well as just the content being studied (Brown and Dove, 1992). A key element is feedback, that is, information about how successfully something is being done. For us, feedback includes the provision of explicit information and discussion about learning objectives (Erstad *et al*, 1997), assessment criteria and expectations, as well as specific comments about a piece of work. All these aspects of assessment combine to provide vital information, which allows students to enhance their self-knowledge in a particular context and leads to appropriate action.

Researchers have begun to investigate the impact of assessment software which integrates learning and assessment systems in order to support learning (Dochy and Moerkerke, 1997). The CAAs used on the project described here were employed and evaluated from this perspective. The remainder of the chapter considers student perspectives of the value of these CAAs and support materials. It particularly concentrates upon the learning benefits of the 'practice tests' because we discovered that these were extremely well received by all the students consulted. In-depth interviews with student groups were conducted by an external researcher with a view to describing, analysing and interpreting the processes involved in student uptake of the assessments being offered. The interviews were also supported by data from a questionnaire administered to all learners on the relevant units.

Definitions of effective educational practice within the discipline (McDowell, 1995) were used as one means of analysing the data.

EFFECTIVE TEACHING AND LEARNING IN ENGINEERING, SCIENCE AND TECHNOLOGY

In a literature review that identifies effective practice in UK engineering foundation courses, McDowell (1995) highlighted the following consistently appearing educational approaches designed to accommodate student diversity, encourage deep approaches to learning and develop many skills that employers demand from graduates:

- Assessment strategies that reduce anxiety, are clear, appropriate and are likely to encourage students to fulfil the aims of the course.
- Opportunities for active learning.
- Help in learning and study skills.
- Opportunities for collaborative learning.
- Provision of clear goals and structure.
- Feedback on progress.

We will take each as a point of analysis to explore how far, and in what ways, students felt CAAs facilitated their learning.

STUDENT VIEWS OF COMPUTER-ASSISTED ASSESSMENT STRATEGIES

The hidden curriculum

It is widely recognized that assessment implicitly issues important messages to students about the aims of the course and the type of learning being valued or rewarded (Wolf,1993; Sambell and McDowell, 1998). In other words, the assessment system itself supplies the student with vital information about how they should behave. Snyder (1971) has called this the 'hidden curriculum'. The way in which students interpret these messages heavily influences their learning behaviour.

We found evidence that the practice tests encouraged students to study effectively, putting effort into understanding the course content as the unit progressed, rather than 'cramming' for exams at the last minute:

> To revise for [the summative CAA] you had to do as much as normal, go through your notes and work through practice examples. But with this you'd been doing that revision all along, having a go at the questions [in the practice tests] and that.

One student felt the practice tests had helped him develop a sense of the process of tackling engineering problems, which his normal revision techniques did not readily allow him to do:

> Also, when you revise normally you tend to look at past papers, but they don't have the solutions and they don't show you how they get there. With this you can get to see how to go about it from the word go.

Factors associated with 'positive assessments'

McDowell also suggests that 'positive assessments' (Berry and Whitworth, 1989) that reduce anxiety, are continuous throughout the course and provide good feedback on progress are potent factors in encouraging students to adopt deep approaches to study. These factors were all mentioned in interviews. In terms of summative usage of the software, students appreciated accruing marks as they went along (where that occurred):

> It's good to know you've got a certain per cent under your belt. . . takes the pressure off.

When used as a summative instrument, most reported that it was less stressful than traditional exam room contexts:

> It didn't feel like an exam. I go to pieces on exams. Like, I knew it was a test, and you had to revise and that, but it didn't seem as much pressure. It's less daunting.

This was partly associated with the less formal laboratory setting and with the variety afforded, which dispelled traditional phobias of the exam hall:

> This is different, more unusual. You don't sit down and you're not being told: 'You've got two hours to do this. Start!' [Said threateningly.]

It was also cited as a useful alternative to writing for dyslexic students and those working in a second language. Students were, however, overwhelmingly positive about the formative tests:

> I'd like to see the assessment software used more. It helps you revise, it's different and it's more, sort of, friendly.

This was associated with the feeling of being freed from 'high-stakes' assessment and being enabled to develop confidence:

> With this I can learn from my mistakes.

'Doing badly' was often associated with facing the unknown in terminal exams, which did not then fairly allow students to demonstrate their abilities. One described how he got over his initial panic during the summative computer-assisted test because he had already practised similar ones:

> When I first looked at it the fear of God struck me! But after looking at it the second time, I realized it wasn't that bad, and I was nervous, but practising allayed a lot of the anxieties I had.

Some saw the practice tests as 'friendly' because they interpreted that the tests were there to help them learn more effectively, rather than test them:

> It's refreshing to find a lecturer using IT to see how it can actually help us to learn better, how it can actually add something to teaching, and realizing that it can help us, rather than just sticking things on the Web because they're supposed to be using it and it's all over the prospectuses.

OPPORTUNITIES FOR ACTIVE LEARNING

McDowell highlights the ways in which, although some students are active in lectures, many perceive it as a passive learning medium and become too readily locked into a transmission view of learning, which in turn lends itself to a view of knowledge as accumulation, with note-taking simply a matter of recording to remember. To become effective learners, students need to be actively involved and learn to apply their knowledge.

In each case, the practice tests were integrated into a series of learning tasks. They were designed to act as a signal to students that they needed to know (and be prepared to answer questions or tackle problems on) the material being gathered. Practice self-testing was a means, therefore, of prompting students to actively and purposefully seek information, ascribing value to the process of learning rather than simply viewing it as content 'delivered' in a lecture.

The take-up of the voluntary self-test was very high, and students appeared to use them as tasks to guide their learning. In the following quote, a student explains how doing the practice tests helped him to improve the quality of his notes:

> If I saw that I'd gone terribly wrong on one question, or if I'd got completely stuck on another, I just went away and looked it up. I checked through my notes, made my notes better if I had to, by referring in more detail to stuff in the library, that sort of thing.

This learner does not assume that facts must simply be recorded and committed to memory, but has been encouraged, via the information provided during formative assessment, to test out his understanding. This enabled him to build on it in the future.

Other students' comments suggested they were learning from the tests by being actively engaged in the process of evaluating their own achievements. Some valued the test because it prevented them from having to constantly seek out tutors if they got 'stuck', because the test provided sufficient guidance, via the elaborate feedback and support materials, for students to see for themselves where they were going wrong, or by suggesting fruitful ways forward. (See Figure 19.2 for an example of the feedback made available to students.)

> About the formative test – it's really good to get the feedback because the past exam papers have been put on the Internet now, but you just get the questions and you don't always have all that, all the answers, and how you get there, that you're sure of. I mean, you can always ask the lecturers, but it would be good where you could get feedback from the Internet itself, instead of trying to track down the lecturers, going backwards and forwards. That's the sort of stuff we want to see on the Web, not lecture notes and that, but worked solutions and stuff that's going to help us do our revision.

In this way, the students felt a measure of welcome independence in their learning.

PROVISION OF HELP IN LEARNING AND STUDY SKILLS

McDowell's review suggests that students need to look objectively at how they learn and take control of it. The CAAs were designed to place considerable emphasis upon students, identifying that they themselves are primarily responsible for the success of their own knowledge construction. They also aimed to give them opportunities to exercise self-management in relation to the planning, conduct and evaluation of their learning activities.

Most valued the practice tests because they helped them, personally, to identify areas for improvement, thus helping them direct future effort in fruitful directions:

> I learned quite a lot about what I needed to improve on. Just general brushing up. This stuff on satellites, I thought I'd got it right and found

> out that I hadn't. And it made me think, well, I'd better check up on that, go back and have another look at it, work it out a bit better.

One explained how he found himself actively engaged in the business of making judgements about the extent of his understanding by trying the practice test, which then acted as a spur to find out, from the computer-assisted feedback, how to tackle the problem more effectively:

> [While performing the test] you tend to know yourself how you've done, by what you can't do so easily. When it tells you what you should have done, I tend to realize straight away then. It clicks. It needs to be there and then for you to realize.

Many stressed the value of being able to 'have a go' at actively applying their learning and then receiving feedback and guidance. Indeed, several recognized that computer-assisted practice tests replicated the ideals of traditional seminars, when they prepared seminar questions that were later discussed in small groups. Some explained, however, that the guidance they received from seminars was not as useful as the guidance from the practice tests because:

> They [staff] do give you the chance to have a go at some seminar problems and then take your answers along. But I tend to do it on a bit of a scrap of paper, and it's pretty messy and I can't read it when I get there, and anyway, by then I've forgotten what was going on in my mind when I was trying to work it out!

OPPORTUNITIES FOR COLLABORATIVE LEARNING

McDowell's review outlines the benefits students gain from discussion and from hearing about other students' approaches and conceptions. There was some evidence that, in a few cases, students had formed peer support groups to tackle the practice tests:

> I went along with Jim to do it [the formative test], actually. That's quite good, because you can discuss why and how you got your answers, why you were wrong or right. That can be good, explaining it.

When this had happened, students reported the results positively, to the extent that the project's next developmental steps are to formalize and encourage collaborative learning and group work in the practice test environment.

PROVISION OF CLEAR INFORMATION ABOUT GOALS, STRUCTURE AND EXPECTATIONS

McDowell underlines the importance of clarifying expectations and offering explicit information about learning objectives. Some students claimed that one of the main benefits of the practice tests was in helping them gain a fuller sense of the course in advance of lectures, thus enabling them to make more beneficial use of lecture time:

> The thing is, those formative tests, we tried them before we'd covered some of the stuff in class, and so it was handy that you'd already had a go at the questions before you'd got on to that subject.

In other words, it gave students an accurate sense of the targets they were aiming to achieve, the curriculum it was important to cover and the skills and qualities they needed to be able to achieve.

> It gets you the background knowledge before you go to the lecture, so you can make more sense of it. Especially with the feedback, you've already done a little bit of work on it, before you cover it properly.

Others claimed they used the practice tests to gain vital information about the standards that they were expected to achieve:

> In the previous practice tests, I personally went on about three times for each one, because it gave you the gist of what was going to be asked and the level they expected you to be at.

PROVISION OF FEEDBACK

Finally, McDowell emphasizes that students need to know how they are doing on a course. Lack of feedback can lead to ineffective learning, poor use of time, anxiety and lack of motivation.

Quality and timeliness

Students overwhelmingly appreciated the quality of the feedback made available by the practice tests, especially in comparison with end-point exams:

> [In exams] you just get a mark, ages later. You still don't know where you went wrong.

The practice tests, however, gave feedback in time to direct future action.

> Through testing myself on the mock test I understood where I'd gone wrong, in time to do something about it.

> I made a mistake about satellites on the practice test. When I came to the real test I knew what I was supposed to do. If I was preparing myself just with past papers, as I do normally, revising for normal exams, I would never have made it, because I would never have realized that I was wrong.

• 11

A mobile phone company is required to serve 100,000 customers over an urban area.

How many base stations (i.e. how many cells) must be set up if there are 40 duplex channels available per cell, and an average of useage 25 subscribers per channel ?

• 12

A mobile phone company uses a 7-cell repeat pattern, with 40 channels per cell and a channel separation of 25 kHz.

What bandwidth must be allocated to provide nationwide coverage for five million subscribers ?

- **7 MHz**
- **25 kHz**
- **900 MHz**
- **25 MHz**
- **1 GHz**

Please enter your name and password and press the SEND button.

SEND

Figure 19.1 *Example of test items students see on the screen*

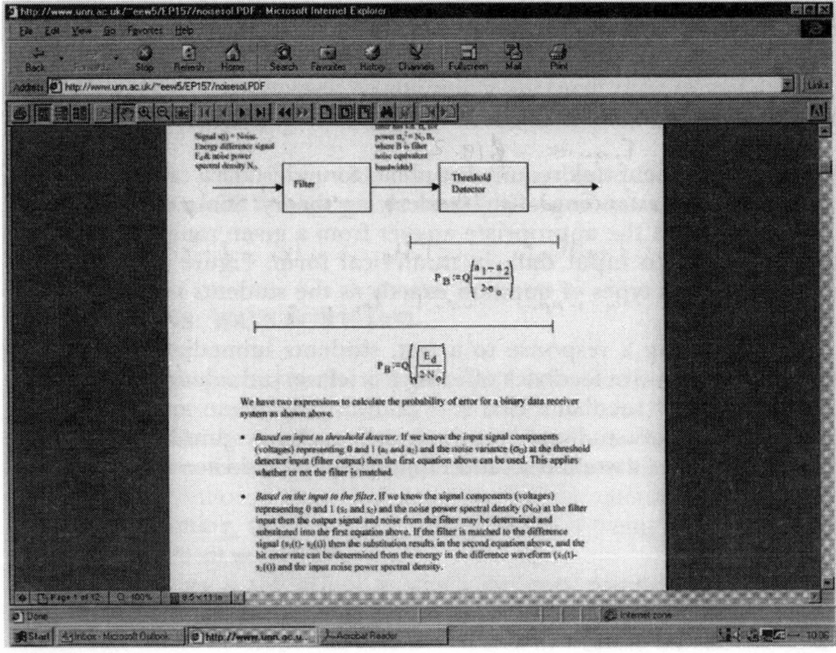

Figure 19.2 *Example of the detailed feedback students are offered*

REFERENCES

Barnard, J M (1998) 'Factors affecting the uptake of CAL in Further Education', paper presented at the Higher Education Close Up conference, 6–8 July, University of Central Lancashire, Preston

Berry, J and Whitworth, R (1989) Case study: access engineering through HITECC, *Education and Training Technology International*, **26**, 23–30

Birenbaum, M (1996) Assessment 2000: towards a pluralistic approach to assessment, in *Alternatives in assessment of achievements, learning processes and prior knowledge*, eds M Birenbaum and F Dochy, pp 3–30, Kluwer, Boston

Birenbaum, M and Dochy, F J R C (1996) *Alternatives in Assessment of Achievements, Learning Processes and Prior Knowledge*, Kluwer, Boston

Boud, D (1995) *Enhancing Learning Through Self-assessment*, Kogan Page, London

Brown, I (1991) To learn is to teach is to create the final exam, *College Teaching*, **39** (4), pp 150–153

Brown, S and Dove, P (1992) Self and peer assessment: a guide for enterprising students, *MARCET Red Guides*, Series 3, University of Northumbria at Newcastle

Brown, S and Knight, P (1994) *Assessing Learners in Higher Education*, Kogan Page, London

Dochy, F and McDowell, L, Assessment as a tool for learning, *Studies in Educational Evaluation*, **23** (4), pp 279–298

Dochy, F and Moerkerke, G (1997) Assessment as a major influence on learning instruction, *International Journal of Educational Research*, **27** (5), pp 415–432

Erstad, B, Armstrong, E, Callahan, P and Keller, P (1997) Evaluation of practice site learning experience for entry-level Doctor of Pharmacy students, *American Journal of Pharmaceutical Education*, **61**, 87–90

Klenowski, V (1995) Student self-evaluation processes in student-centred teaching and learning contexts of Australia and England, *Assessment in Education*, **2** (2), pp145–163

Knight, P (1996) 'Quality in higher education and the assessment of student learning', paper presented to the 3rd European Electronic Conference on Assessment and Evaluation, 4–8 March, EARLI-AE list European Academic and Research Network

Light, P, Colbourne, C and Light, V (1997) 'Computer mediated tutorial support for conventional university courses', *Journal of Computer Assisted Learning*, **13**, 228–235

Light, P and Light, V (1998) Analysing asynchronous learning interactions: computer-assisted communication in a conventional undergraduate setting, in *Learning with Computers: analysing productive interaction*, eds K Littleton and P Light, Routledge, London

McDowell, L (1995) Effective teaching and learning on foundation and access courses in engineering, science and technology, *European Journal of Engineering Education*, **20** (4), pp 417–425

Moerkerke, G (1996) *Assessment for Flexible Learning*, Lemma, Utrecht

Nitko, A (1995) Curriculum-based continuous assessment: a framework for concepts, procedures and policy, *Assessment in Education*, **2**, 321–337

Sambell, K and McDowell, L (1997) The value of self and peer assessment to the developing lifelong learner, in *Improving Students as Learners*, ed G Gibbs, pp 55–66, OSCD, Oxford

Sambell, K and McDowell, L (1998) The construction of the hidden curriculum: messages and meanings in the assessment of student learning, *Assessment and Evaluation in HE*, **23** (4), pp 391–402

Snyder, B R (1971) *The Hidden Curriculum*, Knopf, New York

Wolf, D P (1993) Assessment as an episode of learning, in *Construction versus choice in cognitive measurement*, eds R E Bennett and W C Ward, pp 213–240, Erlbaum Associates, Hillsdale, NJ

Conclusion: a glimpse of the future

INTRODUCTION

This book has explored the issues surrounding the use of CAA in higher education. It presents a picture of current activity and highlights not only the potential benefits but also the challenges and opportunities facing individual academics, departments and institutions. It is clear that a range of technologies, methodologies and pedagogies is being implemented to support CAA. There is a growing indication that CAA is increasingly being implemented with the primary purpose of motivating students and enhancing their learning. Chapters by Steven and Hesketh, Robinson and Sly and Rennie all demonstrate this. While emphasis is still placed on efficiency gains, it is evident that this is underpinned by the desire to provide valid and reliable assessments which motivate students to learn (see Sims Williams, *et al*). Furthermore, student views and anxieties are becoming increasingly important in the design and implementation of CAA (see Brosnan and Sambell *et al*).

This chapter discusses the direction in which CAA might seek to develop in the future. Developments must take on board a range of issues to be effective. The nature of CAA presents a unique challenge for all those involved. To achieve the efficiency gains which are often attributed, but rarely formally evaluated and yet to be proved, organizational structures and boundaries may need to be at the least examined and probably challenged. Technology progresses at a rapid rate and will impact the future of CAA substantially. It will not only aid the progress of CAA, but may also threaten its use as technologies are developed which can break test security (Colton, 1997). This chapter does not attempt to predict the evolution of technology but the issues discussed must be used to influence the developing technology in order to maximize the potential of CAA. There are four main issues which need to be considered and integrated, with each other and with existing structures and systems, in order to effectively utilize CAA.

PEDAGOGY

The pedagogy of CAA must evolve and advance supported by rigorous evaluation. The scope of computers to offer varied, adaptive, focused and unique assessments is still underdeveloped. This book has offered an insight into the potential of CAA, with examples of innovative practice in the UK and overseas. However, assessments are often simply converted from paper to screen and usually prove inadequate as examples of CAA. There is minimal utilization of multimedia, sound and animation. The true benefit to student learning often fails to be demonstrated, on anything other than a small scale. Methodologies for integrating CAA with other traditional and technology-based teaching and learning methods must be sought and evaluated. The development of CAA, which supports and motivates students to learn, collaborate and communicate, is critical if the true potential of CAA is to be realized.

MANAGING ASSESSMENT

The implementation of CAA raises issues about managing assessment, issues that appear to be rarely dealt with for traditional assessment (Yorke, 1998). It is a challenging and sometimes problematic activity because it forces institutions to manage the process, rather than adopt an *ad hoc* approach often experienced in the implementation of CAL (McDonough, *et al*, 1994). A cross-section of staff from a range of central support departments and faculties needs to be involved, particularly if summative assessment is developed. This often requires individuals and departments to find new ways of working, dealing with activities that do not fit easily into anyone's remit (Stephens *et al*, 1998). Implementation of CAA can raise issues and concerns which should be, but are rarely, planned and evaluated for all assessments.

The provision of support and training for all students, particularly those with special needs, should be addressed at an institutional level. Institutions need to take responsibility for supporting research and evaluation of CAA, which can be fed back into the design of assessments, the systems and the mechanisms which support them. The time-saving aspect of CAA can be elusive, and may merely represent a shift in workload from academic to support staff. This needs to be recognized and acknowledged in order for academic departments and faculties to work effectively with central support services.

QUALITY ASSURANCE AND STAFF DEVELOPMENT

Perkin (Chapter 6) discusses the role of CAA in evaluating student performance and the possible improvements in validity and reliability of assessment. CAA allows rapid detailed statistical analysis which can be used to ensure the quality of the assessment method. Quality assurance policies and procedures may well need to be developed or amended to take account of the type of assessment and delivery mechanism used. Policies and practical measures are needed to assist staff in the development and maintenance of question banks, which utilize the statistical analysis possible ensuring questions and tests are evaluated and amended. It may be that the improved quality assurance measures possible for CAA will promote greater analysis and monitoring of traditional assessments. Standards for the construction of questions and tests need to be developed to ensure the validity of both content and structure. The interoperability of questions and tests is currently being considered by the Instructional Management Systems project, supported in the UK by a JISC funded project (http://www.imsproject.org.uk). Definitions and classification of question types will lead to an object-oriented model which will assist in creating open standards and compatibility in both materials and support systems.

A key obstacle to the effective implementation of CAA is time for, and provision of, staff development. The merging of technology and pedagogy requires skills and abilities which until recently have not previously been practised to a great extent in higher education. A lack of expertise in many institutions can hinder the development of high quality materials or the implementation of systems requiring more than standard IT skills. The pressure on academic staff to teach, research and perform an administrative function often means there is little time to invest in learning new skills and evaluating their outcomes. The lack of recognition at an institutional and national level for innovation in teaching, learning and assessment means that even where appropriate staff development is provided, to encourage and support innovative assessment methods, it rarely achieves the priority it deserves.

ORGANIZATIONAL AND STRATEGIC INTEGRATION

CAA links the pedagogy and methods of teaching with the IT and administrative systems which underpin an institution. On a large scale, it requires the bringing together of IT support, individual academics, their departments, staff developers, quality assurance units and impacts on students and external agencies. It is truly an institutional concern, not simply the remit of individuals and there are strategic and long-term planning issues of importance to be considered. There is a need to focus on organizational and strategic benefits that such systems offer if properly implemented.

Systems need to be integrated and streamlined: implemented with an eye to the long-term enhancement of firstly, student learning and then, efficiency gains. They must be developed with reference to teaching and assessment methods and delivery mechanisms for administrative systems to enable faster, more efficient transfer of results and updating of record files.

But the nature of CAA can defy organizational structure, falling outside the remit of all but the recently emerging posts in the field of learning technology support and development. Such posts are frequently supported by temporary, short-term internal or external funding. This lack of stability hinders development and leads to the reinvention of wheels. A clearly identified need is for the involvement of a range of staff, including senior management, in the decision-making process and implementation of CAA systems. Effort to date has been focused on the pedagogical and technical development of CAA; in order to truly benefit from the potential, it is necessary for departments and institutions to consider the operational, organizational and strategic issues of implementing CAA. Otherwise, there will be the duplication of effort and output seen in CAL (Darby, 1996).

The cultural and political issues surrounding the implementation of CAA are deep-seated and present a serious barrier to the development of more efficient and effective assessment systems. Challenging the long-established pre-conceptions and expectations of traditional assessment is problematic. Introducing technology to the equation, which many fear will result in job losses, is adding fuel to the fire. Culturally, CAA may be seen as going against the established ethos of academic power over the assessment process. A shift is required in terms of the investment of time – from after the event to prior to it. This may well clash with other activities in the academic calendar and needs to be addressed at an organizational level.

The nature of funding (both internal and external) of teaching and learning technology research and development is fluid and short-term, impeding progress and leading to the loss of hard to find skills and expertise. Short-term investment is unlikely to provide the efficiency gains sought. Funding at a national level needs to be provided to assist institutions in adopting effective strategies for implementing CAA as part of evolving teaching and learning strategies.

Focus must be placed on the translation of strategy into operational practice, as Yorke (1998, p 111) states: 'Between strategy and operationalization lies fertile ground in which flaws may flourish'. Flaws may flourish to the point where strategy is lost. CAA currently lacks co-ordination within and between institutions, planning and research prior to adoption, and is often deficient of strategic support from senior managers. Investment, both financial and strategic, must be made if the advances that are possible with CAA are to be made.

There is a need not only for organizational and strategic support at an institutional level but also at a national level. The Computer Assisted Assessment Centre (http://caacentre.ac.uk) is a recently funded TLTP3 project (HEFCE, 1998) that aims to meet some of these needs. The project will pilot and disseminate models of implementation and evaluation, and develop good practice documentation and staff development materials to support CAA activity throughout the HE sector. The models and guidelines will support individuals and focus on the strategic implementation of CAA within departments, faculties and institutions. The project, which is led by the University of Luton, will also provide a national centre for higher education to advise and support individuals, departments and institutions in CAA activity.

THE FUTURE

Bennett (1998) identifies three generations of computer-delivered tests: the first combines developments in psychometrics with technology to deliver widespread adaptive tests; the second 'incorporates advances in technology, psychometrics and to a growing extent, cognitive science'; the third stage testing reinvents itself from traditional methods in several ways.

Bennett believes that the future of CAA lies in reinventing assessment, with the seamless integration of CAA with teaching methods driven by competitive global markets. While we are a long way from the first of Bennett's generations, what is apparent is that CAA challenges the conceptions of traditional assessment and will eventually lead to a slow, but radical, reconsideration of the way in which assessment *per se* is set, delivered and managed across departments and institutions.

The true potential of CAA has yet to be realized, in every sense. The capabilities of computers to deliver unique assessments should and will be exploited. The power of networks to transfer, upload and download data automatically should also be exploited. The benefits to student learning of receiving specific, timely and encouraging feedback are utilized by only a few. The advantages of detailed feedback on student and group performance, delivered rapidly enough to allow academics to deal with student misconceptions during a module and enhancing student learning, are yet to be achieved.

A vision of the future for CAA is that it shall provide innovative, reliable and valid assessments, freeing staff to engage with students, streamlining administrative functions, motivating students and enhancing learning by utilizing the potential of computers to enrich and diversify assessment. To achieve this we need high-level technology, which retains a human touch, and is implemented strategically at institutional and national levels.

REFERENCES

Colton, G D (1997) 'High-tech approaches to breaching examination security', Paper presented at the annual meeting of the National Council on Measurement Education, Chicago

Darby, J (1996) 'Eight years with the CTI: a personal reflection on learning technology in UK higher education'. Paper given at the *Association of Learning Technology Conference*, September, Glasgow

HEFCE (1998) *TLTP Phase 3: Funded Projects*, Higher Education Funding Council for England, May 98/20

McDonough, D, Strivens, J and Rada, R (1994) 'University Courseware Development: comparative views of computer-based teaching by users and non-users', *Computers in Education*, 23 (3), pp 211–220

Stephens, D, Bull, J and Wade, W (1998) 'Computer-assisted Assessment: suggested guidelines for an institutional strategy', *Assessment and Evaluation in Higher Education*, 23 (3), pp 283–294

Yorke, M (1998) The Management of Assessment in Higher Education, *Assessment and Evaluation in Higher Education*, 23 (2), pp101–116

Index